Corbridge

Risingham

R. T.

nd

R. Tweed

Cappuck

Traprain Law

Newstead

High

Bew

Netherby

Carlisle

Oxton

Inveresk

Firth of Forth

Cramond

Raeburnfoot

Burnswark

Birrens

Burgh-by-Sands

Bowness

Carriden

Lyne

Camelon

Castledykes

Milton

R. Annan

Solway Firth

Mollins

Bothwellhaugh

Crawford

Dalswinton

Carzield

R. Nith

Glenlochar

Loudoun Hill

R. Clyde

Bishopton

R. Dee

ROME'S
NORTH WEST
FRONTIER

ROME'S NORTH WEST FRONTIER

...

THE ANTONINE WALL

WILLIAM S. HANSON AND
GORDON S. MAXWELL

EDINBURGH UNIVERSITY PRESS

© Edinburgh University Press 1983
22 George Square, Edinburgh

Set in Monotype Ehrhardt
by Speedspools, Edinburgh, and
printed in Great Britain by
Alden Press, Oxford

British Library Cataloguing
   in Publication Data
Hanson, William
Rome's north-west frontier
1. Antonine Wall
1. Title   11. Maxwell, Gordon
936.1'3   D777.7
ISBN 0 85224 416 9

CONTENTS

ILLUSTRATIONS

ACKNOWLEDGEMENTS

The authors and publisher would like to thank the following individuals and institutions for permission to reproduce the following illustrations: The British Museum, pl.1.5; Cambridge University Committee for Aerial Photography, pl.3.4; Hunterian Museum, University of Glasgow, pls 3.2, 4.1, 6.3, 6.4, 7.2, 8.1, 9.4, 10.2; Professor G. D. B. Jones, pls 3.1, 3.3; National Museum of Antiquities of Scotland, pls 1.6, 1.10, 6.2, 6.7, 7.1, 8.2, 9.2, 9.3, 9.6; National Museum of Denmark, Copenhagen, pl.1.7; Royal Commission on the Ancient and Historical Monuments of Scotland, pls 1.1–4, 2.1, 2.2, 4.2, 5.1, 5.3, 6.5, 6.7, 9.5, 10.1 (Crown copyright reserved); Scottish Development Department (Ancient Monuments), pls 6.1, 6.6, 9.1 (Crown copyright reserved).

PREFACE

The monuments raised by Imperial Rome were many and various. Throughout half the countries of the ancient world their massive remains present striking testimony to the power and ambition which exalted a mere city-state to the mastery of an empire. Those we know best are situated, for the most part, in lands linked by a common sea, the Mediterranean, where they speak grandiloquently of ambition achieved and power attained; and rightly so, for as public monuments they were also the vehicles of state propaganda, proclaiming amid all the changes of imperial fortune a message of confidence and national stability.

History shows us, however, that this confidence was often inappropriate, that on many occasions the air of tranquillity was shattered by internal disorders and the threat of external assault. Paradoxically, the category of monuments most sensitive to these vicissitudes, and one which records most faithfully not only the aspirations and achievements but also the failures, lies not at the Empire's heart, but on its boundaries: it comprises the military works that guarded the frontiers of the Roman world. The outermost provinces, wherein they lay, contained the bulk of Rome's military power, and it was from this source that the emperor ultimately derived his authority, reserving the army under his direct control. The imperial fortunes were thus inextricably linked with the fate of the frontiers and *vice versa* – a fact which students of Roman history ignore at their peril.

In few countries have the monuments of the Roman frontier and their historical context been so vigorously studied as in Britain;

in none are the frontier's various elements better preserved. The authors' conception of this volume, on the nineteen hundredth anniversary of Rome's first penetration into Scotland, may thus be interpreted as an act of *pietas*; in presenting this up-to-date account of the military works on Rome's most northerly frontier, we are, in a sense, restating both our historical links with the centre of the Roman world and our academic dependence upon past generations of Romanists.

It was not our intention to provide a guide to the Wall as it survives today, nor to give a detailed description of its physical remains as understood from archaeological excavation. Rather, we were concerned to locate the frontier within its historical background, to try to explain why and how it was built, how it functioned, and to assess what effects it had upon the later history and development of the northern frontier.

For convenience of writing, the chapters were divided between us, W.S.H. taking Chapters 2, 5, 7 and 8 and Appendix 2, G.S.M. being responsible for Chapters 4, 6, 9 and 10 and Appendix 1. Chapters 1 and 3 were written jointly. We hope that the joins are not too much in evidence, for the text was then passed between us more than once for amendments, additions or deletions. The end-product is very much a co-operative effort.

Any work of this kind builds upon earlier scholarly endeavour. Even if the new edifice requires the demolition of the old, the foundations upon which it rises remain the same. It will be evident, therefore, to all who may read this book how indebted we are to numerous scholars and friends, both for their published opinions and for the benefit of their advice and criticism. We have tried to acknowledge these debts in the text by employing the Harvard system of references, but hope that we will be forgiven for any omissions. However, we would particularly like to thank Drs D.J.Breeze and L.J.F.Keppie, who have generously made available the unpublished results of their recent researches and provided a frequent source of stimulating debate. Additional thanks must go to Dr J.Close-Brooks, Miss L.Macinnes and Mr J.Cannell for allowing us to read unpublished papers or make use of unpublished plans; and to the officers of the Ordnance Survey (Archaeology Branch) for their advice on innumerable points. Not least, we owe a debt of gratitude to Mrs Myraid Dodds, who typed the bulk of the text.

We would particularly like to draw to the reader's attention that the illustrations of sites and structures have been designed *ab initio* as an integral part of the book. To give a hitherto unattained ease of visual comparability between Roman works of different types, on the one hand, and between Roman sites and all manner of native dwellings on the other, most of the drawings accompanying this work have been prepared at standard scales. Thus all site plans may be compared at 1:4000, with appropriate enlargements being made available where this was deemed necessary; similarly, smaller structures have been illustrated, for the most part, at 1:2000, although plans of the very smallest Wall installations are reproduced at 1:500, and the same scale is used to illustrate various types of building in the interior of the Wall forts. Larger works associated with the Wall, together with the military complexes at Castledykes and Dalswinton, are portrayed at 1:10,000. Furthermore, except where specifically indicated, in all drawings it is assumed that the text page is aligned on true North – the purpose being, in the case of the Wall sites, to emphasise that their positioning was governed by tactical considerations. It is obvious that such a system of illustration could not have been achieved without the skill and close co-operation of the draughtsmen involved, and we are happy to acknowledge our indebtedness in this respect to Ian Scott and Ian Parker, who were responsible for the planning and execution of all the line-drawings that illustrate the text.

The last word, however, must go to General Pitt Rivers, one of the pioneers of modern archaeological research. Writing in 1894, in his capacity as the first Inspector of Ancient Monuments, to the secretary of the Glasgow Archaeological Society on the subject of the Antonine Wall he stated:

> This work is not a mere Scotch Monument; it is more
> even than a National Monument. Being the most northerly
> boundary of the Roman Empire, it is of interest to the whole
> civilised world, and the nation that allows the last vestiges
> of such work to perish will stand badly by the side of
> others that take a more enlightened
> view of such matters.

Glasgow and Edinburgh
January 1982

ABBREVIATIONS

I. THE OPPOSING FORCES

The study of Roman military archaeology is pursued all too often with little or no reference to Rome's adversaries. But unlike many other Roman monuments, frontiers have much to say about the non-Roman world, for by their very nature they reflect the presence of a hostile native population as well as an occupying power. Thus, before turning to the nature and development of the Roman frontier in Scotland, it is important to examine the relative strengths and weaknesses of the opposing forces: the Roman army and the tribes of the Scottish Iron Age.

Roman society was literate. We may bewail the limited references to Britain in the classical sources augmented by only a few thousand brief inscriptions, but we should remember that no such records are available to express the native viewpoint. The nearest we can get are the Irish sources of much later date (Jackson 1963). Roman society was consumer oriented, with a money economy, mass production of goods and consequent archaeological benefits in the form of abundant artefactual remains on Roman sites. The contrast with native sites of the Scottish Iron Age could not be more marked. With rare exceptions, the material culture recovered is sparse.

In the summary of the structure, organisation and operation of the Roman army which follows, much of the evidence is of non-Scottish origin. It is tempting to fill out the sparse record of native society in the same way by reference to the broader framework of Celtic culture across Europe as a whole. But whereas the Roman army was organised and operated in much the same way whether it was in Britain or on the Danube frontier, it would be a gross over-simplification to assume that Celtic culture was uniform throughout Europe, and more especially towards the geographical limits of its distribution. Non-Scottish Iron Age evidence has been utilised, therefore, only to underpin

I

an interpretation by analogy.

The Roman army is one of the most famous and intensively studied military institutions of all time (Cheesman 1914; Parker 1928; Webster 1978; Holder 1980). For convenience the structure of the army can be considered in two parts: legionary troops and auxiliaries. The legions each comprised a little more than 5000 Roman citizens, who by the mid-second century were drawn mainly from the long established provinces of the empire. They were the backbone of the army, providing both heavy infantry, with only a minimal cavalry element, and all the building and engineering skill which any efficient fighting force requires. Every legion was subdivided into ten cohorts and each cohort, except the first, further divided into six centuries of eighty men. In the first century AD, for reasons which remain unclear, the first cohort was larger than the rest and contained five double centuries, or 800 men (Frere 1980). The legionary commander, the legate (*legatus legionis*), would have been a senator in his early thirties but would have had prior military experience only as the senior tribune (*tribunus laticlavius*), or second-in-command of a legion, some ten years previously. The junior tribunes (*tribuni angusticlavii*), members of the equestrian class, would have had previous military experience only as the commander of one of the minor auxiliary cohorts. The third in command of the legion was the prefect of the camp (*praefectus castrorum*), an ex-centurion of many years' service, who was largely responsible for the smooth running of the administration. The legions did not always operate in full force and it was quite common for a detachment or vexillation under the command of one of the senior officers to be engaged in some activity away from the rest of the legion. The centurions who commanded the individual centuries were usually men who had risen through the ranks, thus ensuring that each legion possessed a constantly replenished core of experienced officers. Legionary centurions are sometimes even found in command of auxiliary units, as on the Antonine Wall at Rough Castle (RIB 2144) and Westerwood (Wright 1968), though these would only be temporary appointments brought about by the incapacity or death of the original commander, or the absence of a suitable candidate from the normal sources.

The auxiliary troops, for the most part, were not citizens. They tended to be recruited from the borders of the empire, their ethnic origin evident in the unit name, with the reward of citizenship at the end of their 25 years' service. However, once a unit was stationed in a particular province away from its place of origin, further recruitment and replacements would come from the local area. Thus a soldier in a Thracian cohort stationed at Mumrills on the Antonine Wall was a Brigantian from northern England (RIB 2142). The auxiliaries provided additional second-class infantry, sometimes with special expertise such as the archers from Syria stationed at Bar Hill, but more importantly they supplemented the legions by the provision of the essential mobile cavalry arm. Some auxiliary units, the most prestigious, consisted solely of cavalry (*alae*), while others were made up entirely of infantry (*cohortes peditatae*). The most common units, however, contained a mixture of infantry and second-string cavalry (*cohortes equitatae*). The nominal strength of the units was either 500 (*quingenaria*) or 1000 (*milliaria*) men. The smaller unit is represented most frequently, while one of the larger units, the *ala milliaria*, occurs only once in Britain. Like the legions, the infantry cohorts were divided into centuries probably 80 strong, while the cavalry were organised in troops (*turmae*) of approximately 32. The commander (*praefectus*) of a quingenary cohort need have had no previous military experience whatsoever, though he would normally have had administrative experience as a town magistrate. His lack of military expertise would have been compensated for by his professional junior officers, the centurions in charge of the centuries and the decurions in charge of the mounted troops. Should the senior officer prove himself an able commander, he could continue to follow a military career, possibly gaining promotion to the praefecture of a cavalry unit via a junior staff position in a legion (Birley 1953, 138–9). Those not suited to a military career would, however, be returned rapidly to civilian life, having inflicted the minimum of damage on the system.

The total number of troops known to have been in Britain in the mid-second century is about 52,000, though clearly not all would have been available for deployment in Scotland. Large vexillations from all three legions then stationed in Britain (*II Augusta*, *VI Victrix* and *XX Valeria Victrix*) would have provided the core of the campaign force used during the Antonine reconquest of southern Scotland, together with an accompaniment of at least 25 auxiliary units, the latter figure being an estimate based upon the size and number of forts built to house the garrison of occupation.

In order to ascertain something of the organisation of the native forces, on the other hand, it is necessary to look at the structure of their society. Both archaeological and literary sources confirm that it was tribal. Ptolemy's *Geography*, composed between AD 140 and 150, lists some fifteen or sixteen tribes occupying what is now Scotland and northern England. The forms of the tribal names suggest strongly that most of the peoples encountered by the Romans shared a common tongue, British, which was one of the Brittonic group of Celtic speeches; and the close similarity of the names themselves – the Cornavii of Caithness and the Cornovii of Shropshire and Cheshire, the Dumnonii of south-west England and the Dumnonii of Central Scotland – underlines the closeness of the relationship, at least on the linguistic side. However, to the north of the Forth-Clyde isthmus – the area known to the Romans as Caledonia – it is probable that on the eve of the invasion the inhabitants were only partly Celtic, the Brittonic-speaking element in the

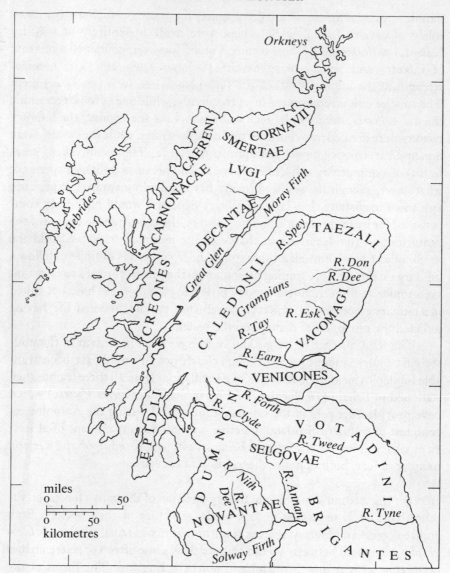

FIGURE 1.1 *North Britain in the Iron Age.*

population having been quite recently superimposed upon peoples using a non-Indo-European language. Tacitus specifically refers to their physical traits – long limbs and red hair – as indications of a different ethnic origin from other Britons (*Agricola* 11), and his other references to Caledonia (*Agricola* 23) confirm that the Romans saw it as forming a distinct cultural province. On the other hand, in AD 83, when the final stand was made against Agricola, the Caledonian tribes ranged themselves under the banner of a chieftain with a Celtic title, 'Calgacus', the swordsman, although the site they chose – Mons Graupius according to Tacitus – may have been known to the locals by a non-Indo-European name (Rivet and Smith 1979, 370–1).

Fortunately for the invading army, the linguistic unity of the British tribes contrasted sharply with their usual political relationships, as indicated by the abundance of defensive habitation sites. Although the tribal boundaries are difficult to identify on the ground, prehistorians have tended to divide northern Britain into four geographical provinces with apparent cultural significance: Tyne-Forth, Solway-Clyde, North-Eastern and Atlantic. Few today would accept the original more detailed concept (Piggott 1966), but in the absence of more precise information, the 'provinces' serve as a useful framework within which to order the data.

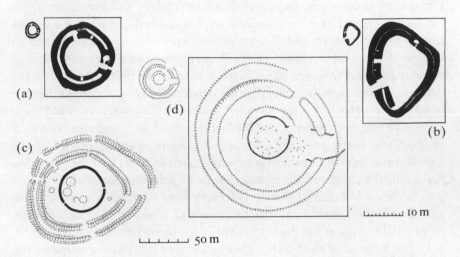

FIGURE 1.2   *Typical native settlement types: a) broch, Dùn Mòr Vaul; b) dun, Kildonan; c) hillfort, Arbory Hill; d) homestead, West Plean.*

The Atlantic province presents a more uniform appearance than other regions of north Britain. These northern and western parts of Scotland – an area containing the most rugged and broken terrain anywhere in Britain – provide evidence throughout the Iron Age of a highly fragmented society, typified by the multiplicity of small defensive 'homesteads' called brochs or duns (MacKie 1975; Maxwell 1969) (fig.1.2). Although at some time during the Roman period builders of such habitations began to migrate southwards and eastwards into lowland districts, they remain essentially peripheral to the question of interaction between Roman and native.

The range of Iron Age habitation sites to be found between the Tyne-Solway line and, say, the Moray Firth, is extensive. At present most are systematised according to their superficial remains as determined by field survey, since excavation has been employed to examine only a tiny fraction. Nevertheless, there are sufficient regional variations of form and structure to permit the tentative identification of areas of shared characteristics, which may in turn indicate a common social or political identity. In the Tyne-Forth province, for example, the most visually impressive surviving monument is the hillfort (pl.1.1). To the best of our knowledge, this province is largely coextensive with the tribal territories of the Votadini and Selgovae, and, although hillforts are found elsewhere in north Britain, in no part are they so densely distributed; there are literally hundreds of examples. Excavation has demonstrated that many of these sites have a long and complex history (Hill 1979). The obsession with security in that area has been taken to indicate that the two peoples were implacably hostile to each other – a situation which the Romans would have been happy to exploit. Indeed, the relative distribution of Roman military installations in the two tribal areas would seem to indicate differential treatment by the Roman authorities, with the Votadini possibly awarded 'favoured-nation' status. Most of the hillforts are small, the defences seldom enclosing more than one acre (0·4 ha) (fig.1.2), but a number of larger forts (fig.1.3) – the so-called minor *oppida* (Feachem 1966) – are known. In fact, over 70 per cent of the forts over 6 acres in area are to be found in the Tyne-Forth province. This concentration in the territories of the Votadini and Selgovae has been reasonably taken to imply that the two tribes had attained a comparatively advanced state of political coherence.

Enclosed but less obviously defensive sites of varying sizes are also abundant in the area, and it is tempting to erect a hierarchical model of settlement relationships as has been proposed in southern Britain (Cunliffe 1971, 59f), but for most of the Scottish sites as for their English counterparts, the basic question of contemporaneity remains unanswered. However, recent aerial reconnaissance has suggested that a number of the hillforts in the east are physically related to systems of land-boundaries taking the form of interrupted ditches and pit-alignments (pl.1.1); such boundaries have not yet been identified in precisely the same form elsewhere in Scotland. In these cases it may eventually be possible to establish the nature of the relationship between unitary monuments and the surrounding landscape, thus providing a more extensive frame of reference against which to set the variety of smaller settlements.

Recent fieldwork in Lanarkshire has suggested that upper Clydesdale too, fell within the territory of the Selgovae (RCAHMS 1978, 32), the large Roman forts at Castledykes near Carstairs and Newstead near Melrose marking the approximate boundaries with the Dumnonii and Votadini respectively. The dense clustering of unenclosed platform settlements in the upper tributaries of the Clyde mirrors that in upper Tweeddale, an indication that

6

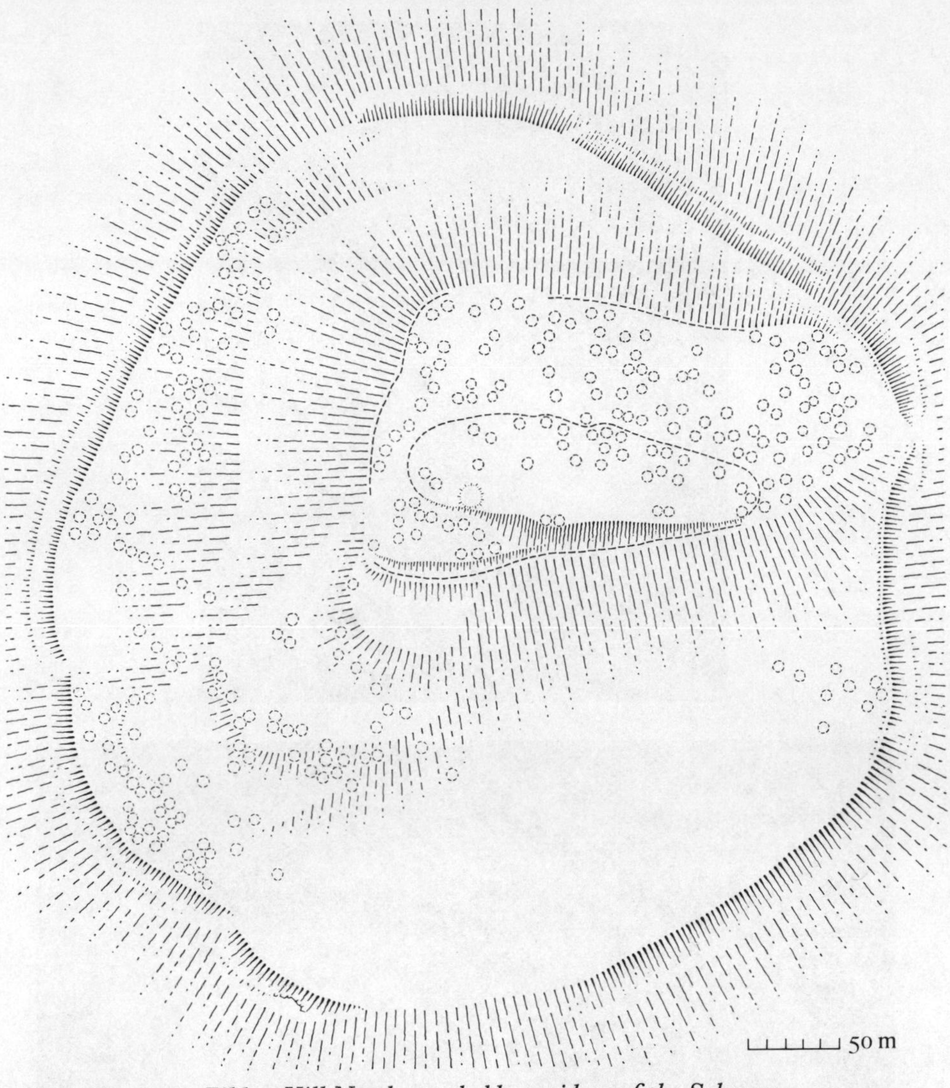

FIGURE 1.3 *Eildon Hill North: probable oppidum of the Selgovae.*

the cultural identity of the Selgovae may go back at least as far as the early 1st millennium BC. There are, however, certain types of site which are absent from these areas but common in other parts of Selgovan territory – palisaded enclosures and scooped types of habitation (fig.1.4) for example – which would perhaps suggest that the tribal groups cited by Ptolemy may have been of a confederate nature, incorporating a number of once-distinct cultural entities. For this reason it is uncertain where we should draw, for example, the southern boundary of the Selgovae. The hillforts and settlements of Eskdale and Annandale represent an admixture of types. Though differing in detail,

a

b

c

PLATE 1.1   *Iron age hillforts from the air : a) ploughed out traces at*
Riddell, Roxburghshire ; b) upstanding remains at Cow Castle,
Lanarkshire ; c) upstanding remains at Chesters, East Lothian,
with adjacent pit-defined land divisions showing as cropmarks.

they are clearly in the same 'enclosed' tradition as those already discussed.
Indeed, some of the local varieties of form, the 'birrens', for example, are
partly explicable in terms of differing geological context. Nevertheless, the
absence of unenclosed platform settlements, which are common in both
Clydesdale and Tweeddale, makes a link with the Selgovae unlikely and
suggests that the area may rather have been part of Brigantia, possibly representing the territory of an originally independent tribe, swallowed up by the
Brigantes in pre-Roman times.

9

We know even less about native society in areas to the west of the Rivers Clyde and Annan, the area generally referred to as the Solway-Clyde province. Such information as we have, however, suggests that there was a real cultural difference between the peoples living there, respectively the Dumnonii and Novantae, and the groups to the immediate south and east. For example, large fortified enclosures are rare; and the habitations on lower ground, as revealed by aerial photography, include a much higher proportion of unenclosed houses, homesteads and simple enclosures (Jones 1979). Nor is it simply that traces of 'developed' society are absent from the record in the west, for the cultural division appears to persist into the Roman period. There is, moreover, at least one type of settlement which points to the presence of different traditions: the crannog, or lake-dwelling (fig.1.4). Several examples have been excavated, revealing that they were structures of some architectural sophistication – basically a large timber building of circular plan set on an artificial island of stone or an elaborate foundation of wooden piles, and often equipped with harbours, landing stages, and causeways providing access to the land. They were certainly occupied in the Roman period and survived as a type into early Christian times. At least one example, Milton Loch, is believed to have been constructed in the middle of the 1st millennium BC (Guido 1974). There are good reasons, therefore, to identify them with common elements in the ancestry of the Novantae and Dumnonii, over whose territories they are so widely spread.

The Dumnonii may have extended as far north as eastern Perthshire, according to Ptolemy (Rivet and Smith 1979, 140), and it is interesting that such an extension would also embrace another group of crannogs whose members may also have originated in the 5th century BC (DES 1981, 40). Although assigned to what has been designated the north-eastern province, it is possible that the area from, say, the Campsie Fells to the upper Tay valley represented the homeland of a distinct sub-group of the Dumnonii, standing in relation to the main tribal territory as, it appeared, Eskdale and Annandale might have stood to Brigantia. Some additional confirmation of this may be provided by the distribution of distinctive oval or circular palisaded structures (pl.1.2), probably homesteads, which survive as cropmarkings in the upper valleys of the Rivers Forth and Teith, but also extend some way south of Stirling (Maxwell 1982a), thus complementing the curiously restricted pattern composed by the larger fortified sites of Stirlingshire; the same factors may also lie behind the similarly compact grouping of the Stirlingshire duns (RCAHMS 1963, 29). It is impossible to determine the precise location of the boundary between the Dumnonii and Votadini. The most westerly example of the 'Votadinian' type of pit-alignment so far discovered lies a little to the southeast of Linlithgow; the valley of the River Avon, the historical boundary of Lothian, would not have been an inappropriate line.

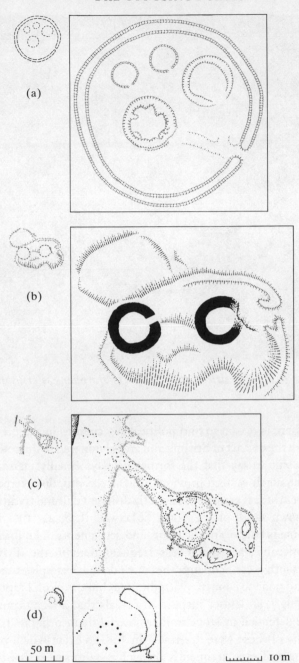

FIGURE 1.4 *Typical native settlement types: a) palisaded site, High Knowes, Alnham; b) scooped settlement, Kirkton Burn; c) crannog, Milton Loch; d) souterrain and associated round house, Newmill.*

11

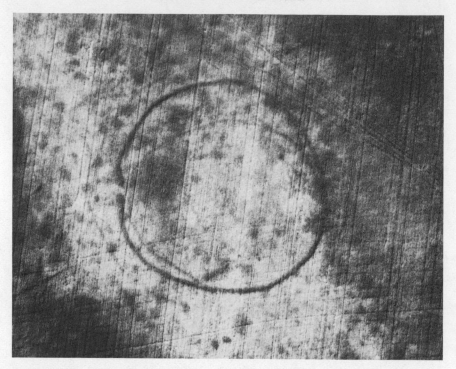

PLATE 1.2   *The palisaded settlement at Mains of Burnbank, Perthshire, from the air.*

However, if there is reason to find political associations in the pre-Roman Iron Age between the district of Stirling and areas lying well to the south of the Forth, it is also true to say that the former displays equally many cultural affinities with the north-eastern province. In the recently discovered square barrow cemeteries there is evidence of a vastly different cultural tradition from anything yet known south of the Forth (Maxwell 1978, 44; DES 1977, 5) (pl.1.3). The same is true of fortifications and settlements. The former, it is immediately noticeable, are much less frequent than in the Tyne-Forth Province; as in south-west Scotland, they include few examples of any considerable size, and none to compare with the great hill towns of Traprain Law or Eildon Hill (fig.1.3). Closer inspection reveals that a significantly large proportion were defended by stone walls whose fabric incorporated a timber framework; many of these were destroyed by fire, an event which produced vitrifaction of the wall-core, frequently on such a scale as to ensure the complete abandonment of the site and the virtually indestructible preservation of the remains. Timber-lacing appears to have been imported into north Britain as a technological innovation between the 8th and 6th centuries BC. Excavation at a few sites in south-east Scotland, Broxmouth and Castle Law for example,

PLATE 1.3   *The square barrow cemetery at Invergighty Cottages, Angus, from the air.*

suggests that its rarity in Eastern Scotland south of the Forth may be only apparent, i.e. that it was in fact employed at many sites but that evidence of its use has been concealed by later re-shaping of the defences. The converse of this is the case in the north-eastern province, where, after the initial phases of fortification, many hillforts which must have been key points in the landscape, such as Finavon and Greencairn, Balbegno, in Strathmore, and Cullykhan and Craig Phadrig, to the north of the Mounth, were for some as yet unknown reason abandoned and either never re-occupied or else only brought back into use some time after the Roman army had effectively ceased to operate north of the Forth-Clyde isthmus (cf. MacKie 1976).

What event caused the disappearance or waning of the hillfort in these parts, or when it happened, is not yet known, but it must be seen against another distinctive feature of north-eastern archaeology, the ubiquity of the 'ring-ditch' and its variants. The interpretation of these structures, which, for the most part, take the form of cropmarkings, is hedged around with difficulties (Maxwell 1982b); nevertheless, allowing the possibility that a certain proportion are the traces of funerary sites – itself interesting evidence of differentiation between the Tyne-Forth and north-eastern provinces, a large number must be presumed to represent the remains of round timber houses, few of which were located within defensive perimeters. We are thus

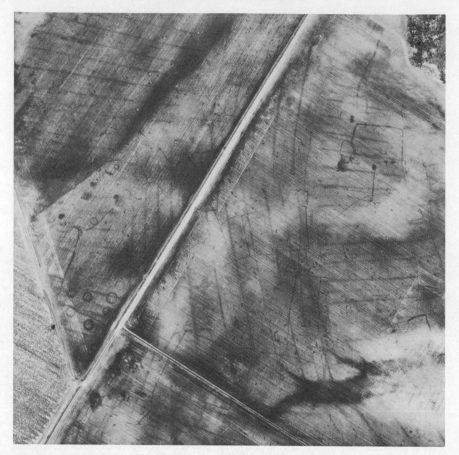

PLATE I.4 *The open settlement at Leuchars, Fife from the air.*

left with the clear indication that enclosed settlement north of the Forth was apparently far less common than it appears to have been to the south. Prolific cropmark-producing areas like those centred on Leuchars, Fife, as well as the extensive fluvio-glacial deposits in northern Angus, furnish splendid instances of open settlements comprising widely spaced groups of round timber-houses (pl.1.4). Here and there they were situated in intriguing proximity to field-systems and other more extensive land-boundaries, occasionally in the form of paired-pit alignments quite distinct from the small and generally more regular alignments of south-eastern Scotland. Only one such complex, at Douglasmuir in the Lunan valley, has been excavated so far (Kendrick 1982); the date of this group, *c.*600 BC, is roughly contemporary with the earlier timber-laced hillforts, but comparable types of unenclosed settlement have been identified in association with various types of souterrain, underground stone-walled structures of the 1st and 2nd centuries BC/AD

PLATE 1.5   *Bronze armlets from Castle Newe, Aberdeenshire.*

(Wainwright 1963; Watkins 1980a and b) (fig.1.4).

Another interesting feature of such settlements is that so many appear to be un-nucleated: individual houses of various kinds, occasional homesteads, and fields apparently scattered across the landscape. The contrast with the more 'orderly' landscapes of Lothian is total. Does it point to a different tradition of land-tenure, or a less hierarchical form of social organisation? Dio (LXXVI, 12.1) in the 3rd century AD claimed that the natives of Caledonia possessed 'no cities or walled settlements'. Given what we can now see of their habitations, it is easy to understand why he might have written thus, and easier to appreciate the reasons which led the Roman army on two separate occasions to draw their frontier across the narrowest neck of land south of Caledonia.

Thus, although there are evident variations, settlement archaeology alone would suggest that Iron Age society in Scotland was tribal and probably mainly hierarchical, particularly in the south-east. The building of well-defended habitation sites represents a considerable investment of time and manpower. Such public works could be organised on a communal basis, but seem more likely, in the light of other evidence, to reflect the coercive power of a few. Study of various items of metalwork suggests that there was an appreciative market for the more exotic pieces. Skilled craftsmen were on hand to undertake work in glass, enamel, bone and wood, and there was an evident potential for the development of schools or traditions in crafts that later produced such handsome objects as, for example, the Castle Newe armlets (pl.1.5). Such objects imply the existence of a wealthy element within society. What we know of Celtic society from classical writers, notably Caesar, and the later Irish

PLATE 1.6   *The carnyx (war-trumpet) from Deskford, Banffshire.*

tradition indicates a highly stratified society, the latter source emphasising that fighting and feasting were the main pastimes of the upper classes. The concept of a Celtic warrior aristocracy is widespread throughout Europe and finds archaeological support in the distribution of Iron Age burials with weaponry which spread as far as northern England (Collis 1973). It is generally assumed in deference to the classical sources (Diodorus Siculus v.29), that Celtic warfare was a highly ritualised affair involving only the aristocracy and employing a system of champions in the Homeric fashion (Powell 1980, 127). While this may have been the case during the normal process of intertribal rivalry, it is hard to believe that faced with the threat of an external aggressor with the power of Rome the lower echelons of society would not have been involved in the fighting. Although tribal differences have so far been emphasised, the presence of an external threat could unite otherwise inimical groups, as in the case of the force which was assembled to meet Agricola at Mons Graupius (*Agricola* 29). Nor need one assume that native groups were totally disorganised in battle. What have been interpreted as Celtic war standards are represented on certain continental monuments (Pauli 1973) which would imply some form of organisation within their forces, probably by kinship grouping. While no such standards have been found in Scotland the remains of a boar's head carnyx or war trumpet similar to those represented on the

16

PLATE 1.7   *A detail from the Gundestrup Cauldron, Denmark, showing Celtic warriors with war-trumpets.*

Gundestrup cauldron was discovered at Deskford in Banffshire (pls 1.6 and 7) (Piggott 1959).

Tacitus' account of Agricola's famous battle in Scotland provides us with our only clue as to the number of men likely to have been ranged against the Romans (more than 30,000; *Agricola* 29), though, as with all such accounts, the figures should be viewed with caution. It is extremely difficult to assess the number of people present in a large throng – witness the differing figures

17

quoted as the attendance at large open-air rallies – and there is the possibility of deliberate over-estimation for effect. The figure does not, however, appear to be grossly inflated. Any attempt to proceed beyond this and assess the probable population of north Britain at the time of the Roman arrival is doomed to failure, for there are too many unknown factors. Settlement density suggests some considerable concentrations of population in certain areas, notably the eastern lowlands, with, for example at least 300 house sites visible within the large hillfort at Eildon Hill (fig.1.3). Despite the account of classical writers, there is no need to think in terms of vast areas of impenetrable forest interspersed with small pockets of human habitation (Hanson and Macinnes 1980), although it would be rash to say more at present.

Not surprisingly, in time of war habitation sites had a significant role to play, and many were provided with defensive circuits. Consequently, this is one aspect of native warfare about which we are comparatively well-informed, for such defended settlements are particularly susceptible to archaeological examination, and the hillfort, representing the ultimate stage in this defensive tradition, is often regarded as the archetypal Iron Age monument, though its variable distribution in Scotland has already been noted (Feachem 1966). Few Scottish hillforts show the complexity or magnitude of defences noted in sites elsewhere in Britain (Cunliffe 1978, 43–55), but the general siting of the forts, taking advantage of strong topographical positions combined with as many as four or five lines of rampart and ditch, emphasises their preoccupation with defence. While the largest examples, Traprain Law and Eildon Hill (fig.1.3), might extend to as much as 40 acres (16 ha) in area, and several in the south-east of Scotland exceed 6 acres (2·4 ha), the vast majority are much smaller, their defences enclosing on average little more than 0·4 acre (0·16 ha). Too few examples have been extensively excavated to allow more than a rudimentary sketch of their development to be made, and even that cannot yet be applied to all regions where defensive settlements have been recorded. Nevertheless, it would appear that simple stockades or palisades, occasionally revetting, or set within, earthen banks and rubble ramparts were an early feature of the evolutionary sequence, while defence in depth, with multiple stone-faced walls, or banks and ditches, may have been the culmination reached on the eve of the Roman invasion. Whether this last was a reaction to new methods of assault or merely represented another means of disposing of the community's wealth cannot be determined. Whatever the explanation, the emphasis on strength would seem to betoken a widespread feeling of insecurity.

In like manner, the broch – a round drystone-walled tower, averaging 25 feet (7·5 m) in internal diameter – is a pre-eminently defensive structure both in terms of its architecture and topographic siting. The examples which are found within the Roman sphere of penetration are situated in naturally defended positions, as at Leckie in Stirlingshire and Torwoodlee in Selkirk-shire, the latter placed within the confines of an earlier hillfort. In fact, the broch demonstrates an almost snail-like defensive mentality whereby the inhabitants locked themselves into their massive stone-walled towers until the danger had passed, in complete contrast with the literary accounts of Celtic warfare. We may deduce from this two things: that it was probably the non-combatants who were resident in these positions of safety and that the local tribesmen lacked the offensive skill of siege warfare, otherwise such struc-tures would rapidly have become obsolescent. It may be significant that the only example of such a site thought to have been taken by direct assault, the broch at Leckie, may have been under attack from Roman forces (MacKie 1979, 54).

The location and structure of native fortifications contrasts sharply with those built by the Romans. Rather than seeking the added protection of hill-tops or natural promontories, Roman forts in the early Empire are normally to be found near the valley bottom. The most common siting would be on slightly raised ground by a river, thus controlling movement down the valley both by land and water; their defences were usually neither elaborate nor particularly strong. No Roman fort was ever provided with more than one rampart. In the first century and for much of the second, this was built of turf measuring some 20 feet (6·1 m) wide at the base, and was surmounted by a timber breastwork, giving an overall height of c.15 ft (4·6 m) (Jones 1975, 68f). Stone-walled forts did not become the norm until late in the second century. The only two known on the Antonine frontier had walls between 6 and 7 ft (1·85–2·15 m) thick. Forts were normally surrounded by at least one and up to 3 or 4 ditches usually 8–20 ft (2·4–6·1 m) wide and 4–9 ft (1·2–2·7 m) deep (Jones 1975, 106f). The end result was to produce an effective but not extravagant defence.

When on campaign in hostile territory, the Roman army constructed a fortified camp, usually referred to in the archaeological literature as a tem-porary or marching camp. These camps were defined by a single ditch rarely more than 10 ft (3 m) wide and 4 ft (1·2 m) deep, but usually rather less. The material from the ditch was thrown up inwards to create a small earthen bank surmounted by wooden stakes (*pila muralia*), two of which were carried by each legionary precisely for that purpose. A considerable expenditure of effort would have been necessary each day for the production of even a minimal defensive circuit, but the psychological advantage it gave to the men encamped within doubtless far outweighed its real defensive value (Adcock 1940, 13f). The area so enclosed varied according to the size of the army on campaign. Quite often they are found to cluster around fort sites (fig.1.5), as one might expect if the latter were also normally situated a day's march apart, though some of such camps will undoubtedly have housed the party responsible for the construction of the fort. Similar camps were also erected by the builders of the Antonine Wall itself (see below pp.117–21).

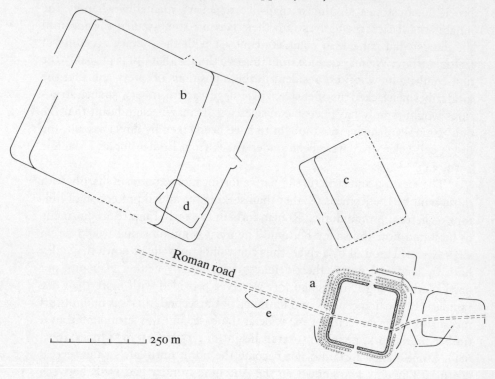

FIGURE 1.5   *The clustering of temporary camps (b–e) around the fort (a) at Castledykes.*

Our information on the arrangements within temporary camps derives mainly from literary evidence and the representations on Trajan's Column, for short-term accommodation in tents is rarely likely to reveal much to the spade. Our knowledge of the internal arrangements of the more permanent works is, however, considerably better. The type and number of buildings within each fort varied according to the unit that it held. Clearly, barrack accommodation for the garrison was essential and is generally readily identified. The main body of the barrack block was divided into two-room units (*contubernia*) intended to house 8 men, the equivalent of a tent group in a temporary camp. In the case of cavalry units a high proportion of stabling would also have been necessary, although archaeologically such buildings have not been so easily recognised (Wells 1978). Some sort of central administrative building (*principia*) was the norm, with a private residence for the commanding officer (*praetorium*) nearby. Storerooms with raised floors usually referred to as granaries (*horrea*), are found in most forts, while some

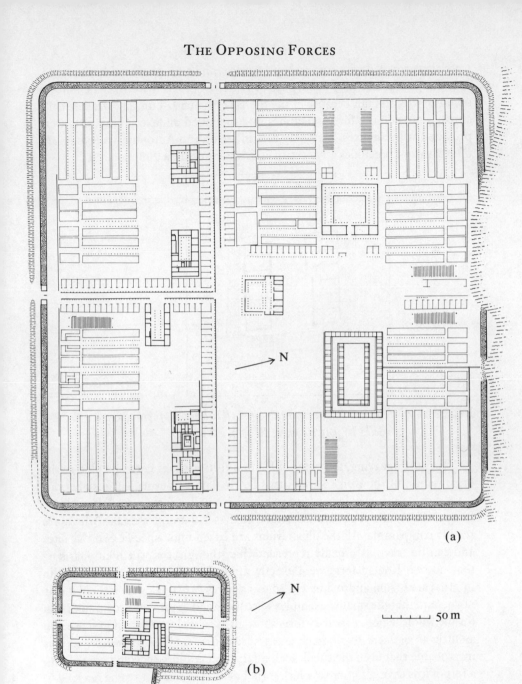

(a)

(b)

FIGURE 1.6 *Typical Roman military installations: a) legionary fortress, Inchtuthil; b) auxiliary fort, Fendoch.*

were also provided with a workshop (*fabrica*) and a hospital (*valetudinarium*). A bathing establishment was always provided not merely for hygiene but as a social centre, though because of the fire risk, the bath-building was normally situated outside the fort, sometimes in a defended anncxc. Many forts wcrc provided with annexes, including a number on the Antonine Wall, but lack of excavation precludes any certain assessment of their function.

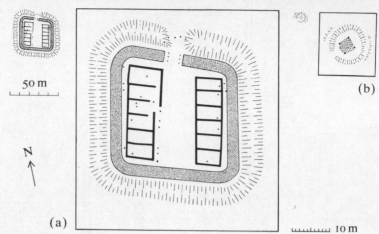

50 m

(b)

N

(a)

10 m

FIGURE 1.7   *Typical Roman military installations: a) fortlet, Barburgh Mill; b) watch tower, Beattock Summit.*

Broadly speaking, the types of Roman fortifications corresponded to the organisation of the Roman army, that is, the largest permanent installations were meant to house legionaries, while the smaller forts were for auxiliary troops. The basic types are illustrated in figs 1.6 and 7 at scales which are readily comparable. All the illustrations are based upon specific Scottish sites and can be taken as broadly representative, though it is worth emphasising that no two Roman forts were exactly alike. Legionary fortresses range in internal area from approximately 40 to 55 acres (16·2–22·3 ha), though it is not certain that the smaller examples were intended to provide accommodation for the whole legion. Auxiliary forts show an even wider variation in size, from as little as 0·5 acre to as much as 15 acres (0·2–6·1 ha). However, as it is improbable that even the smallest auxiliary unit could be accommodated into a fort of less than *c*.2·5 acres (1 ha), forts below that size tend to be referred to as small forts and may be presumed to have housed some fraction of a unit. At the other end of the scale, the largest auxiliary unit, the *ala milliaria*, is unlikely to have required more than 8 or 9 acres, which implies that forts above that size must have contained more than one unit, though others of smaller size may also have done so (see below pp.159–61).

Permanent sites of less than half an acre (0·2 ha) in area are also common (fig.1.7). They fall into two main categories: fortlets and watch or signal posts. The former are, as their name suggests, miniature forts, though they rarely contain more than barrack accommodation. They are usually surrounded by a single ditch unless attached to a linear barrier, although fortlets on the Antonine Wall also have ditches. The watch or signal posts are the smallest permanent Roman installations known. They are normally circular or subrectangular, defined by a single ditch and sometimes a small bank or rampart, and contained a tower for observation or signalling purposes. All the certain free-standing towers known in Scotland are timber built, though the turrets on Hadrian's Wall indicate that stone was also utilised. The provision of such towers emphasises the Roman concern for early warning of hostile activity so that any attack could be met on grounds of Roman choosing.

As a fighting force the Roman army was supreme. It has even been stated recently that 'Roman history is the essentially unique story of a nation trying to catch up with the situation produced by the incredible success of its army' (Mann 1974a, 509). But the Celts, too, were renowned for their fighting ability. Strabo, writing in the early first century AD called the whole nation 'war-mad' (IV, 4.2). There seems no reason to doubt that both the Romans and the native forces came from warlike backgrounds and were imbued with the appropriate martial spirit, but an examination of the evidence makes it clear that the Romans had the advantage in every other respect: technically, tactically and in terms of organisation, training and discipline.

The basic offensive equipment of the legionary infantryman in the second century AD was his short sword (*gladius*) and javelin (*pilum*). For protection he wore a simple iron helmet (*galea*), chest armour (*lorica*) with little or no cover for the lower limbs, and carried a large curved rectangular shield (*scutum*) (pl.1.8). The auxiliary troops were similarly equipped, though their swords tended to be longer and their spears designed for thrusting rather than throwing. Some were provided with slings or bow and arrows. Like the legionaries they, too, wore helmets, though of somewhat lesser quality, but their body armour was chain-mail and their shields flat and oval (pl.1.8). The Celts, on the other hand, were famous for eschewing the use of body armour, preferring to go into battle naked (Polybius II, 29-9). Such a practice seems to have applied in Scotland also, according to the literary evidence (Herodian III, 14.6) and the portrayals on monumental sculpture (Keppie 1979, 9f) (pl.6.3). There is archaeological evidence of Celtic chain-mail from England and the Continent, both from graves (Laver 1927, 248; Rusu 1969, 276) and on monumental sculpture (Pauli 1973), and Varro attributes its invention to the Celts (*de Ling. Lat.*, v.24.116), but the iron links discovered in a scrap metal hoard from Carlingwark Loch in Kirkcudbrightshire are probably of Roman military origin (Manning 1972, 242 *contra* Piggott 1953, 38-40). If

PLATE 1.8 *Legionary and auxiliary troops on Trajan's Column.*

armour was worn, it is likely to have been restricted to the very wealthy. Similar observations can be made about helmets, which are known on the continent (Schaaf 1974) but rare in S England and unknown in Scotland. The only defensive equipment which is clearly attested is the shield, though the only actual example known from Scotland is a fragment of a shield-boss from Traprain Law which may, in fact, be Roman in origin (Ritchie 1969).

The only offensive weapons that we know to have been used by the Scottish tribes were the sword and spear. Both are referred to in the literary sources (Dio LXXVI, 12.3; Herodian III, 14.6) and represented on the distance slabs of the Antonine Wall in association with fallen warriors (pl.6.3). Tacitus makes much of the superiority of the short Roman thrusting sword over the long and unwieldy sword of the Caledonian warriors at Mons Graupius (*Agricola* 36), and a similar contrast had been noted in accounts of clashes between Romans and Celts elsewhere, some three centuries earlier (Polybius II, 33). In general this comparison is substantiated by archaeological finds, although there is an observable tendency for later Celtic swords to be shorter and more pointed (S. Piggott 1950, 17–21). In fact, there can be difficulties in distinguishing between Roman auxiliary and native Celtic weaponry because many auxiliaries were themselves of Celtic stock and may have been using some of their own weapons, while the native Celts were quick to copy Roman types (Breeze *et al.* 1976, 81–7). However, even if the effect of this process was to negate Roman technical superiority in auxiliary weaponry, a more plentiful supply of raw materials would have ensured that Roman armouries were better stocked.

There is no doubt of the importance and strength of cavalry in the Roman army. Whether this wing also played a major part in native warfare is uncertain. At the very least, it can be said that the horse occupied an important position in everyday life in Scotland. One tribe in Kintyre were even known as the Epidii, 'the horsefolk', and there is no shortage of metalwork associated with the use of horses. Indeed, one of the most famous finds of wealthy Celtic metalwork in Scotland is the decorative pony-cap from Torrs, Kirkcudbright-shire, while a number of horse-bits are known from the same general area (Ward-Perkins 1939, 183–5). Celtic cavalry are attested on the continent on monumental sculpture and on the Gundestrup cauldron (pl.1.7), but their use in Scotland is unsubstantiated. What did impress the Romans, however, was the use of war-chariots. This Celtic device had gone out of fashion on the continent probably by as early as the second century BC, so that Caesar was surprised to be faced with it in southern Britain (*B.G.* IV, 33–4). However, in Britain the chariot seems to have remained in use throughout most of the Roman occupation, for both Tacitus (*Agricola* 36) and Dio (LXXVI, 12.3) describe its use against Roman armies in the first and third centuries. Items of metalwork such as terrets, linch-pins and even iron tyres are not frequent discoveries on Scottish Iron Age sites, but are attested at Traprain Law (Burley 1956, 194–8), though whether these derive from war-chariots or more utilitarian forms of transport remains uncertain. It is tempting to speculate on the possible association between chariot-burials and the recently discovered square-barrow cemeteries in eastern Scotland north of the Forth, as in the well-known examples from eastern Yorkshire. However, none of the latter were associated with weaponry and the presence there of such vehicles is now seen merely as part of a continuing funerary tradition without any martial significance (Stead 1979, 20).

A major technical advantage possessed by the Roman legions was the use of artillery and siege engines. Roman artillery came in two types: stone-throwing (*ballistae*) and arrow-shooting (*catapultae*) machines, both of which resembled a cross-bow in design. The single-armed stone-thrower (*onager*) did not come into general use until the later Empire (Marsden 1969, 189). The large *ballistae* were designed for sieges, but the *catapultae* could also be used during open battle mounted in carts, as seen on Trajan's Column (pl.1.9). Such artillery was certainly available in Scotland, for catapult bolts are quite common finds on Roman sites, and the hillfort at Burnswark in Dumfriesshire seems to have been used as a practice area for *ballistae* (see below). There is, however, no evidence of siege operations being mounted against any occupied native settlement in Scotland, with the possible exception, as noted above, of the broch at Leckie.

PLATE 1.9 *Mobile artillery on Trajan's Column.*

The most striking aspect of Roman superiority was in terms of training, discipline and organisation. As one would expect with a professional army, recruits were put through a rigorous training programme before they entered the ranks. This probably varied according to the branch of the army they were entering, the legionaries undoubtedly experiencing the most intensive training, although our main literary source on this subject, Vegetius, does not appear to draw any distinction. Recruits were taught to march, ride, swim and use all manner of weapons from swords and spears to slings and bows (Davies 1969, 219–21). Nor did the training cease on entering active service (Seneca *Ep.* 19.6; Tertullian *ad Mart.* 3; Josephus *Bell. Jud.* III, 72–5). There are several examples of training areas in Britain, which indicates that the troops were kept up to scratch with exercises when not actively campaigning. In Wales, on Llandrindod Common, there is a series of very small square enclosures with a disproportionately large and elaborate entrance in each side. Clearly, these were built to provide practice in the construction of temporary camps, concentrating as they do upon the difficult portions, the gateways and corners (Daniels and Jones 1969). The native hillfort at Burnswark, Dumfriesshire, is, as it were, gripped between two Roman encampments, one of which seems to have been a semi-permanent enclosure with internal roads, evidently the base of a legionary detachment bombarding the hillfort defences with *ballistae*. Recent excavation has demonstrated, however, that the hillfort was not occupied at the time when artillery fire was directed against it (Jobey

26

1978b), the operation being presumably a training exercise. The nature of the earthworks at Woden Law, Roxburghshire, which have long been identified as the product of Roman field-exercises (RCAHMS 1956, 169–72), require fresh consideration before it can be determined beyond doubt that they are not, in part at least, related to non-Roman dykes or land-boundaries of superficially similar character. Such manoeuvres as the above would have necessitated a relatively lengthy absence from barracks; day-to-day training must have been carried out nearer home. A number of forts in Wales and the N of Britain, for example, were provided with parade-grounds, which have been associated with cavalry training (Davies 1968). From N Africa comes further evidence in the form of an inscription which records a speech made by Hadrian commending both legionary and auxiliary troops for their efforts during military exercises (CIL VIII, 18042). Sometimes exercises were organised as formal games particularly for the cavalry (Arrian *Tactica*, 34–5), and there are examples in Britain of items of sports equipment such as the ornate cavalry helmets with moulded face-covers from Ribchester and Newstead (Robinson 1975, 113–15) (pl.1.10).

The advantages of careful training and discipline were reflected in the field of battle. The Romans did not rely upon brilliant generals: they were not renowned tacticians. They could and did rely, however, upon the discipline and training of their troops, so that even an incompetent general could win a battle. The soldiers were trained to fight not only as individuals but as part of a unit. This is exemplified most clearly in the most famous siege tactic, the tortoise (*testudo*) (Dio XLIX, 30), in which an assault group protected itself by a shell of overlapping shields, as seen in operation on Trajan's Column (pl.1.11). The tight formation, achieved only after careful practice and demanding strict discipline, ensured a safe approach towards an enemy position while under fire. The basic Roman battle tactic was to break through the centre of the enemy. The legionaries would advance in the centre, protected by auxiliary troops on the flanks, until within range, when they would throw their *pila*. If the javelins failed to find a human target they would become embedded in enemy shields rendering them too cumbersome for effective use. Thus the opposition lay exposed to the relentless advance of the legionaries, each man pushing with his shield and thrusting with his sword (Tacitus *Annals* XIV, 36.4). Once the main body of the enemy had been broken, the auxiliary cavalry could pursue those in retreat. This tactic was developed during the Republic and remained in use with little change throughout the early Empire. It was generally highly successful against other organised armies, though disasters could occur when faced with a general of the ability of Hannibal, so the effect on massed Celtic warriors is not hard to imagine. As the auxiliary troops became better trained and more reliable, they were employed to a greater extent and the legionaries kept in reserve, as at Mons

27

PLATE 1.10   *The cavalry parade helmet from Newstead, Roxburghshire.*

Graupius (Tacitus *Agricola* 35). Cavalry were also employed as a shock weapon, especially against infantry or other cavalry, as they had been since the days of the Republic (Polybius 11, 34).

Literary accounts of Celtic methods of warfare place great emphasis upon the convention of single combat between champions (Diodorus Siculus V.29), but it seems unlikely that such methods would have been employed against the Romans. In the brief accounts by Caesar, Tacitus and Dio Cassius, of battles which took place in Britain, the impression gained is of frantic but disorganised activity, with the deliberate creation of much noise and confusion, particularly by the chariots. Caesar is quite specific that the chariots were used merely to get warriors to or away from the battle (*B.G.* IV, 33), though the employment of cavalry against chariots at Mons Graupius may imply that they were fighting on equal terms (Tacitus, *Agricola* 36).

Our knowledge both of the Roman army's training procedures and of its battle-tactics make the near-total concentration upon set-piece manoeuvres more comprehensible. The Romans were well aware that they were at their most vulnerable while on the march. In hostile territory they employed a particular order of march, the hollow square formation (*agmen quadratum*), designed to allow speedy transformation into battle order (Tacitus *Annals* 11, 16 and XII, 40), but if the enemy chose to employ hit-and-run tactics there was little that the Romans could do to counter them. Thus the aim of any Roman commander was to force a battle by ravaging an area until the local inhabitants could stand it no longer. Once the enemy forces were committed, the outcome was rarely in doubt.

The same offensive approach can be seen to underlie Roman frontier policy from the Republic to the third century AD. The expansion of Roman horizons during the Republic proceeded on an *ad hoc* basis determined as much by the ambition of individual generals as by any state policy. Perceived threats to security were met by offensive action, almost as if it were intended to teach the enemy a lesson, while territorial expansion came about almost by accident.

With the establishment of the principate, power came into the hands of one man. Augustus maintained his Republican heritage but rationalised the territorial gains by further expansion into less hospitable areas such as Dalmatia and Pannonia. Yet territorial aggrandisement was not undertaken for its own sake. Wherever Roman power could be extended by treaty, by the political control of an efficient client state, such arrangements were preferred, and they remained a vital element of Roman policy in the eastern Mediterranean especially. This policy did not represent any abrogation of the expansion of the Empire, however; rather it facilitated further expansion by maximising control with the minimum of force (Luttwak 1976, 198–200). Although, traditionally, Augustus' policy has been seen as fundamentally

PLATE 1.11   *Legionaries in* testudo (*tortoise*) *formation on Trajan's Column.*

defensive (Meyer 1961), his own epitaph belies any such interpretation (*Res Gestae* 26–30). Indeed, *imperium sine finibus* seems to have been his aim until the combined effects of the Illyrian revolt in AD 6 and the loss of three legions under Varus in AD 9 (Wells 1972, 3–13). By that time Augustus had been in power for 40 years and was nearing the end of his life. Geographical appreciation of the real extent of the world had expanded with the Empire and recognition of the enormity of the task that he had set himself must have begun to weigh heavily on Augustus' shoulders. It is in this light that the famous admonition to his successor – to restrict the Empire within its present frontiers – should be seen (Tacitus *Annals* I, 11).

This is not to suggest that Roman frontier policy changed overnight from one which had concentrated primarily upon offence to one of defence. Rather it serves to emphasise how much any policy during the principate depended upon the whim of one man, the emperor. The reign of Claudius saw a return to expansion with almost Republican motivation. Lacking both military and political credibility, Claudius used the invasion of Britain as propaganda to bolster his position with the army and the people of Rome.

It was not until the arrival of the Flavian dynasty in AD 69 that more fundamental changes began to occur, although these were probably forced upon Vespasian and his sons by circumstances, rather than being indicative of a rational change in the philosophy of Empire. Until the late first century, troops in Germany had been concentrated at strategic points ready for offensive action, with some fortresses containing two legions. This arrangement was brought to an end (Suetonius *Domitian* 7) mainly through fear of mutiny, and thereafter the troops were spread out more evenly along the frontier. It was a time of considerable movement, significant advances being made in Britain and in Germany, while campaigns of punishment were also mounted, particularly across the Danube. But it was also a period which saw the beginning of a move towards the concept of defined limits of control. It is no coincidence that it is at this time that the term *limes* first appears with the meaning of a lateral frontier (Frontinus *Strat.* 1, 3.10; Tacitus *Germania* 29 and *Agricola* 41), rather than as a line of penetration, its original meaning in a military context (Velleius Paterculus 2.120). Thus, under the Flavians we see the first clear examples of linear demarcation of a frontier: across the Forth-Clyde isthmus and along the Gask Ridge in Britain (see below pp.39, 44–5) or in the Taunus and Wetterau in Germany (Schönberger 1969, 159).

The accession of Trajan saw a return to aggressive expansionism in the Republican mould. The soldier emperor was responsible for the Empire reaching its widest extent, with the conquest and annexation of Dacia and Parthia, the former exploit so magnificently depicted on Trajan's Column. Trajan's motivation was largely one of personal glory and his campaigns suggest an optimistic return to the old principle of world conquest. It is worth stressing, however, that to facilitate major advance on these two fronts, retrenchment was necessary elsewhere, notably in Britain with a withdrawal to the Stanegate frontier (see below pp.45–51).

A new emperor saw a total reversal of frontier policy again. Despite, or possibly because of his extensive military experience, Hadrian was determined to rationalise the extent of Roman suzerainty. Of all the emperors since Augustus, Hadrian was the only one to display a concern for the frontiers which was both clear and consistent. He instigated no further conquests, even giving up some territory in the east that Trajan had won, and he attempted to make the administration of the Empire more efficient by defining clearly and precisely the limits of Roman responsibility. The construction of linear barriers may have been an innovation, but it also represented the logical conclusion of a process which had begun under the Flavian emperors. Moreover, Hadrian recognised what effect his policy would have upon the army and was careful to ensure that the troops were kept up to maximum efficiency by training exercises. Thus, the emphasis remained upon offence as the best form of defence. Nevertheless, although Hadrian's reign marked the beginning of the end of an era of frontier development, the processes which he set in motion took a considerable time to develop; the period of the Antonine emperors who succeeded him is still seen as the 'golden age' of the Empire.

II. CONQUEST, CONSOLIDATION
AND WITHDRAWAL

Precisely when the Romans first ventured north of the Tyne-Solway line is a matter of debate. Since the days of Claudius, the security of northern England had been founded on a treaty between Rome and the Brigantian queen, Cartimandua. The use of client-kings to maintain the security of the borders of the Empire was quite common in the first century AD and enabled Roman power to be extended with the minimum expenditure of physical resources (Luttwak 1976, 195–200). But such political arrangements were notoriously insecure, relying upon the predominance of the pro-Roman factions within the client state, and could never be regarded as a permanent solution to frontier problems. Thus in AD 69, when Cartimandua was ousted by her husband Venutius, taking advantage of civil war within the Empire, friendly relations between Rome and the Brigantes came to an abrupt end and, in the words of Tacitus, 'the kingdom was left to Venutius, the war to us' (*Histories* III, 45). At a time of political turmoil within the Empire, the governor, Vettius Bolanus, was able to do little more than rescue the queen. There are hints of rather more military activity during his period of office than Tacitus allows, but it seems highly improbable that Bolanus operated in Caledonia as the poet Statius implies (*Silvae*, 142–9).

The arrival in AD 71 of the new governor, Q. Petillius Cerialis, who was related to the newly established Flavian dynasty, saw renewed activity in Brigantia. Tacitus refers to Cerialis winning not altogether bloodless battles against the Brigantes after campaigning widely in their territory (*Agricola* 17), but it is unclear how far north he penetrated. A series of *c.*20 acre (8 ha) temporary camps extending across the Stainmore pass on a route towards

33

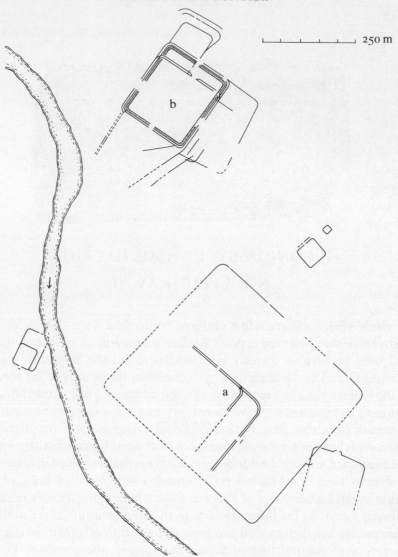

FIGURE 2.1 *Roman forts at Dalswinton: a) Bankfoot; b) Bankhead.*

Carlisle is normally attributed to Cerialis, but without definite evidence of their date. A pre-Agricolan origin for a fort at Carlisle has been postulated on the basis of the quantity of early Flavian samian ware from the city (Hartley 1971, 58) – a theory which derives some support from the numismatic evidence (Shotter 1978, 203), although the most recent excavations have produced nothing which would necessarily indicate such an early foundation (Charlesworth 1980, 210). The position of the recently excavated s-facing gateway, however, indicates that the fort to which it belonged must have lain to the

34

north of the presumed site beneath the centre of the city, where characteristic-ally military structures have been recorded in the past (Ferguson 1893). Consequently, there still remains the possibility of a second fort adjacent to, and, thence unlikely to be contemporary with, the Agricolan one. Furthermore, three sites in south-west Scotland display a structural complexity which is difficult to fit into the known pattern of first-century occupation: at Dalswinton, aerial photography has recently revealed the presence of a second two-period double-ditched enclosure – possibly a semi-permanent fort – in an inferior position to, and therefore, probably earlier than, the known two-period Flavian fort (fig.2.1); at Milton a double ditch ran below the defences of the Flavian fort and appeared to have preceded it by some time if the depth of silting is of any guide (Clarke 1950, 205); while at Loudoun Hill, four Flavian phases are reported, the first two somewhat reminiscent of the situa-tion at Milton (Taylor 1949, 98). Unfortunately, none of the sites has pro-duced detailed evidence for the dating of these primary phases. Nevertheless, the possibility that some are associated with an early Flavian penetration into Scotland must be borne in mind, although at present no certainly pre-Agricolan fort is attested north of Malton in Yorkshire.

Credit for the subjugation of Scotland, however, is rightly given to Gnaeus Julius Agricola. Our knowledge of this period is greatly enhanced by the writings of the eminent historian Tacitus, who, by some happy circum-stance, married Agricola's daughter and wrote a brief biography of his father-in-law, although some care must be taken when using this particular source since it was a laudatory biography written as an act of *pietas*. Agricola's first full season of campaigning was in north Britain. Tacitus refers to the conquest of 'many states' without being more specific (*Agricola* 20), but presumably meaning the several septs of the Brigantes, although it might imply a campaign against unnamed tribes in Lowland Scotland. The permanent occupation of northern England does, however, seem to have been undertaken by Agricola, although this does not mean, as has too often been assumed, that all forts in the region were established by him. Some, as yet unrecognised, may have been earlier, and some were certainly later, notably in the Lake District (Potter 1979, 356–8). On the other hand, an Agricolan foundation for forts such as Ribchester, Lancaster and Brough under Stainmore seems assured (Shotter 1979, 9).

In a *blitzkrieg* operation, Agricola then pushed rapidly northwards into Lowland Scotland, penetrating as far as the Tay (fig.2.2). He even had time to establish some forts (*Agricola* 22), a process normally reserved until the following season, which would appear to indicate a lack of resistance on the part of the local tribesmen. The Votadini in the eastern Lowlands are generally seen as pro-Roman, for, despite intensive aerial survey of the Lothians and Berwickshire, there is a distinct lack of Roman forts to the east of Dere Street.

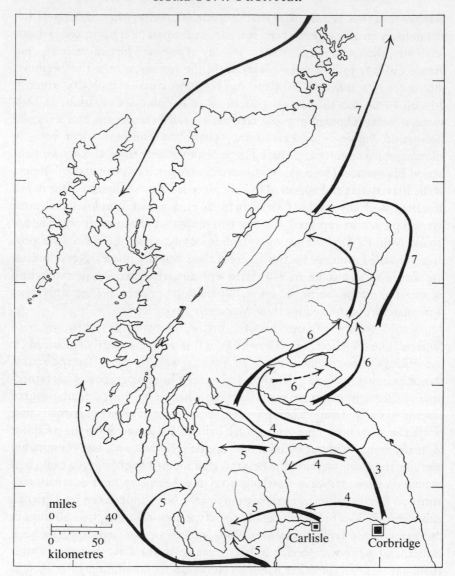

FIGURE 2.2   *The location of Agricola's campaigns in North Britain.*

Furthermore, their capital, the hillfort at Traprain Law, seems to have continued to be held throughout the Roman occupation, an unlikely occurrence if there was any chance that it might have become a centre of disaffection. Contrast the fate of Eildon Hill North, the probable capital of the Selgovae; a Roman watch tower was constructed at its very centre and a large Roman fort built only a stone's throw away at Newstead on the bank of the Tweed. This in turn, would imply that the Selgovae were not deemed friendly and nor, if one may judge by later dispositions, were the Novantae. Why, then, did these tribes fail to resist the conquest with anything like the success achieved by the Welsh tribes over several seasons? It may simply have been the speed and force of Roman arms, or the brilliance of Agricola's generalship, but it is equally possible that the tribes had been softened up on earlier campaigning by Cerialis, or Frontinus his successor, or even Agricola himself in the previous season. Furthermore, contrary to generally accepted opinion, the lightning drive to the Tay may well have been a concentrated push up the eastern side of the country with the right flank secured by the friendly Votadini (Hanson 1980a, 17). We now have evidence for a base camp or supply depot for such a push at Red House, Corbridge (fig.2.2), where a number of open-ended barn-like structures, arguably stores buildings, and a workshop were revealed in the 30 m wide swathe cut across the site by road building in 1974 (Hanson *et al.* 1979). No similar supply depot is yet known for the postulated complementary advance on the west side of the country; the recently-discovered Agricolan fort at Carlisle is too small, while the fort at Kirkbride should now be seen as part of the later 'Stanegate' frontier (see below p.48ff). On the other hand, the lack of sufficiently large temporary camps along the line of Dere Street does imply the division of the total forces at Agricola's disposal for the march north (Maxwell 1980).

The following season, Agricola's fourth in Britain, was spent in the consolidation of the Lowlands, although if the above interpretation is correct this would have been preceded by some campaigning in the west. The method of containing an area of rugged country was to construct a network of roads with forts at strategic intervals, normally approximately one day's march (c.16 Roman miles) (fig.2.3) apart. The intention seems to have been not so much to coincide with concentrations of native population, but rather to control movement and thus localise any disaffection. Such a pattern had already been employed in Wales by Agricola's predecessor, Frontinus, a noted strategist, and was adopted by Agricola in northern England and Lowland Scotland. The two main north-south routes, marked by Dere Street on the east and the road through Annandale to Clydesdale on the west, were linked by two east-west roads across the less hospitable central massif. Surprisingly little is known of the forts disposed along these routes, despite many years of research. The reasons for this are threefold: very little of the excavation which has taken place has been more than small-scale sampling of the sites; much of that excavation was undertaken some years ago when recognition of the ephemeral traces of timber buildings was not so readily achieved as today; and many of the sites were re-occupied in the second century, further complicating the internal stratigraphy and discouraging the destruction of the upper levels to reach the earlier. It is, therefore, difficult to make a reasoned assessment of the nature of the Agricolan occupation. Three points, however, do stand out. By virtue

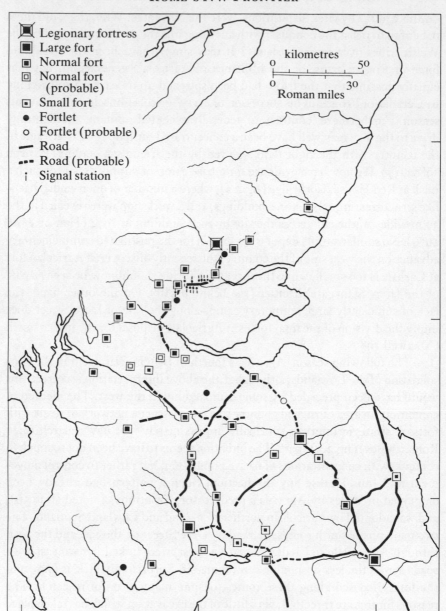

FIGURE 2.3 *Flavian permanent installations in North Britain*
c. AD 80–90.

of its size, and strategic situation, the *c*.10·5 acre (4·2 ha) fort at Newstead must have been a key site, though the nature of its garrison is uncertain. The use of fortlets or small forts such as Cappuck, Chew Green, Crawford, Mollins and possibly Birrens and Castle Greg may indicate a shortage of manpower. This should hardly occasion surprise, since, in the space of three years, which saw the construction of some fifty new forts, the limits of Roman-occupied territory had advanced from north Wales to the Forth-Clyde isthmus. Finally, a number of the forts demonstrate varying degrees of apparent experimentation in their defensive layout, notably Newstead and Milton, though this need not have anything to do with Agricola himself (Breeze 1980a), despite Tacitus' praise for his abilities in the selection of fort sites (*Agricola* 22).

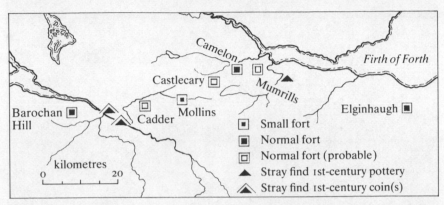

FIGURE 2.4 *Agricolan 'praesidia' on the Forth-Clyde isthmus.*

It was during this consolidation of Lowland Scotland that the value of the Forth-Clyde isthmus as a boundary was first recognised. For once Tacitus' narrative is geographically precise:

> ... a good place for halting the advance was found in Britain itself. The Clyde and Forth, carried inland to a great depth on the tides of opposite seas, are separated by only a narrow neck of land. This isthmus was now firmly held by garrisons (*praesidia*), and the whole expanse of country to the south was safely in our hands. (*Agricola* 23)

Unfortunately, few sites can positively be attributed to Agricola. Since so many forts in Lowland Scotland have both Flavian and Antonine occupation, many scholars have assumed that these first-century isthmus garrisons must lie beneath the later Antonine Wall forts. In no case, however, has this been proved by the discovery of any structural remains, though it seems a strong possibility at three sites, Cadder, Castlecary and Mumrills, on the basis of the number and variety of first-century artefacts recovered there. The only forts on the isthmus whose Flavian origin is known for certain are Mollins (pl.2.1) and Camelon, both situated away from the line of the Wall, but probably combining with the three above-mentioned sites beneath or in the vicinity of Wall-forts to form a line of *praesidia* stretching across the isthmus. The presence of Agricolan forts at Barochan Hill and Elginhaugh suggests that the system may have continued some way along the southern shores of both

Clyde and Forth (fig.2.4), and doubtless more sites remain to be discovered (Hanson 1980b). It seems likely that the decision to halt on the isthmus was deliberate imperial policy on the part of Titus in recognition of the fact that resources were stretched, but the decision was reversed on his death, or shortly thereafter, by his brother Domitian.

PLATE 2.1 *The small Agricolan fort at Mollins, Lanarkshire, from the air.*

The area affected by Agricola's fifth campaign has been the subject of considerable debate, for in the account of this phase of operations Tacitus reverts to his normal geographical imprecision:

> Agricola started his fifth campaign with a sea passage, and in a series of successful actions subdued nations hitherto unknown. The side of Britain that faces Ireland was lined with his forces. (*Agricola* 24)

Since the Clyde and the Forth were the last stretches of water referred to (*Agricola* 23), the requirements of Latin grammar, the reference to Ireland and, indeed, the general sense of the earlier passage all point to action north of the Clyde (Reed 1971). Unfortunately, at present, these arguments falter for want of archaeological evidence of Roman interest in the western Highlands. A less unlikely area of Roman activity in AD 82 is Galloway, where local topography would have made penetration by sea from across the Solway the easier option, and permanent establishments of Flavian date are known at Dalswinton (fig.2.1), Glenlochar and Gatehouse of Fleet. To the north, the as yet isolated fort at Loudoun Hill points to additional undiscovered sites farther west in Ayrshire. If this interpretation is correct, Tacitus must be accused of considerable imprecision, not to say obfuscation of his account. The apparently long line of communication left open to attack from the west prior to this consolidation need occasion no surprise. Precisely the same principle had been employed in Cumbria, where much of the Lake District was left ungarrisoned for nearly a decade (Potter 1979, 356–8). On the other hand, as has been argued already, earlier campaigns on the fringes of the area may have served to discourage serious opposition. Given the lack of evidence for contemporary Roman occupation of sites on the south coast of the Solway Firth, the embarkation point for this naval foray must have been somewhat further south, possibly as far away as Chester (Hanson 1980a, 23).

The following year, Agricola's sixth campaign, saw a resumption of the northward advance (fig.2.2), stimulated to some extent by threats of enemy action including an attack on certain Roman forts (*Agricola* 25–6). Where these sites lay is not clear, but somewhere north of the Forth-Clyde isthmus is implied, if not stated. Now, any operations north of the isthmus would have been dependent on good supply lines. This was achieved, in part at least, by a co-ordinated land and naval attack (*Agricola* 25), but one would expect the land route to have been particularly well protected, and an early foundation of forts such as Ardoch and Strageath, which guard the road into Strathmore, must therefore be assumed. The road and its forts would also have served to protect the tribes of the Fife peninsula who appear to have had as much in common with the apparently pro-Roman Votadini as with the tribes north of the Tay. The series of timber watch-towers disposed along this road from Ardoch to Bertha, best known from well-preserved examples on the Gask Ridge, may just possibly fit into this context, although a slightly later date would be more probable (see below p.44).

The halting-places of Agricola's army during the last two campaigns will have been marked by the customary temporary camps. The limited number of periods when campaigning is known to have taken place north of the Forth-Clyde isthmus has tempted archaeologists to try to relate particular camps to Agricola's operations (St Joseph 1969, 113–14; 1977, 143–4). But such attempts rely largely upon circumstantial evidence, the dating of temporary structures by archaeological means being notoriously difficult. Only two of the groups identified can be assigned to the Flavian period with any confidence (Hanson 1978b; Maxwell 1980): the so-called 'Stracathro' camps, named after the site of the first example which was identified from the air, at Stracathro, near Edzell, in Angus, are unlikely to be later in date than the beginning of the second century since they feature a *clavicula* as part of their distinctive gateway design (Lenoir 1977); the *clavicula*, which takes the form of an extension of both ditch and rampart in a quarter-circle on the outside and, occasionally, the inside of a camp gateway, was intended to provide additional defence against direct assault. In 'Stracathro' camps it is accompanied by a straight external traverse which sprang obliquely from the defences on the opposite side of the entrance. Such a combination is unknown in Britain outside the Flavian period, and it is wholly unrecorded elsewhere in the Roman Empire. At six sites in Scotland camps of this type are closely associated with known Flavian forts (pl.2.2), although only the two most northerly camps, Ythan Wells and Auchinhove, are sufficiently similar in size to represent part of the route of an army on the march. The second group, of which only two examples have so far been identified, at Dunning and Abernethy, both covering some 115 acres (46·5 ha), is dated by a fragment of late-Flavian samian recovered from within the ditch at the latter (St Joseph 1973, 220). Nevertheless, there seems little doubt that Agricola penetrated deeply into north-eastern Scotland, probably reaching the shores of the Moray Firth (Rivet 1977). A policy of deliberate frightfulness eventually succeeded in drawing the Caledonii into a pitched battle at Mons Graupius, whose result was a foregone conclusion, the Romans being supreme in open conflict; victory was achieved with the minimum loss of Roman blood (*Agricola* 37). The location of Mons Graupius remains something of a mystery, for although St Joseph has recently outlined a strong circumstantial case for Durno, some 17 miles north-west of Aberdeen (1978), until some concrete evidence of a major battle comes to light, the site must remain unconfirmed; the discovery of war burials and caches of weaponry at Krefeld in Germany, marking the site of the main battle of the Batavian revolt (Ruger 1980), demonstrates that such proof is possible. Once the battle was won, Agricola sent his fleet on to circumnavigate the island and marched back to winter quarters (cf. Keppie 1980c).

Shortly thereafter, presumably in late AD 83/84, Agricola was recalled to Rome and once again the absence of literary record casts its shadow over the northern frontier. Presumably the process of consolidating the gains of the previous two years' campaigning was put in hand by Agricola before his departure, but it is hard to believe that all the first century forts in the northernmost area were founded by him. He may well have completed the chain of forts protecting his line of supply as far as Stracathro on the North Esk, possibly with the intention of holding the whole island, but further expansion was not to be.

A glance at a map of Flavian dispositions north of the Forth-Clyde isthmus reveals a considerable concentration of forts in Strathearn and at the

PLATE 2.2   *The Flavian fort and Stracathro-type temporary camp at Dalginross, Perthshire, from the air.*

southern end of Strathmore (fig.2.3): the fort at Dalginross (pl.2.2) at the mouth of Glen Earn lies *c*.8 miles (12.8 km) from both of the forts on the supply road at Ardoch and Strageath; Fendoch at the mouth of the Sma Glen is only 6·5 miles (10·5 km) north of Strageath; while the newly confirmed Flavian fort at Cargill is situated less than 3 miles (4·8 km) from the legionary fortress at Inchtuthil. Such a density of military occupation is unprecedented in Flavian Scotland and suggests that more than one phase is represented. An early date for the forts guarding the supply line has already been put forward; the logical corollary is, therefore, that the so-called glen-blocking forts, at least from Drumquhassle to Inchtuthil, belong to later activity. This is supported by the dating evidence from Inchtuthil where coins indicated occupation continuing till at least AD 86, some 2 or 3 years after Agricola's recall, yet the site was incomplete when abandoned. While it is possible that the construction in timber of a 53-acre legionary fortress would take over 2 years, such leisurely progress seems unlikely, and thus any direct association with Agricola improbable. The construction of the legionary fortress must then be attributed to Agricola's successor, and with it, possibly, the intention of further campaigns and consolidation (Breeze and Dobson 1976b, 128–9). But no such campaigns took place. Inchtuthil was demolished even before its construction was complete; and such superfluous items as the 11 tonnes of unused nails, too heavy to carry south, were buried to prevent them falling a valuable prize to enemy hands. The auxiliary forts at the mouths of the glens, too, were abandoned, a *terminus post quem* for the withdrawal being provided by unworn bronze coins of AD 86 from Inchtuthil and Stracathro. Yet, the context for this change of policy should be sought not in Britain itself but on

43

the continent. Throughout the last campaigns of Agricola, troops had been withdrawn from Britain for service in Domitian's other wars, notably against the Germans (ILS 1025; 9200), while further troubles on the Danube resulted in the withdrawal from Britain of *legio II Adiutrix* stationed at Chester and the pulling back of *legio XXV.V.* to fill the gap. However, since the presence of *II Adiutrix* in Moesia is not attested before AD 92, its withdrawal may have been a consequence of, rather than the cause of the evacuation of the northern frontier (Frere 1978, 139–40). Nonetheless, it would have been the shortage of manpower – auxiliaries as much as legionaries – which finally prevented the consolidation of the conquest of Scotland.

The hold on Scotland north of the Forth-Clyde isthmus does not seem to have been relinquished totally, for it is possible that the forts on the road from Camelon to Bertha were now re-occupied: both Ardoch and Strageath have recently produced hints of possible semi-permanent occupation which preceded the better attested Flavian forts, which themselves probably relate to this phase of activity (Frere 1979, 40–1; St Joseph pers. comm.). A period when the road from Ardoch to Bertha served as the northern limit of permanent occupation would seem to provide the best context for the series of fifteen timber towers known along its length. Such towers are hardly relevant to the fluid situation which prevailed during Agricola's campaigns, and could be considered superfluous while Inchtuthil and the forts to the north were maintained. Despite their usual appellation as signal-towers (Robertson 1974a), the close spacing of these posts, none of which in the best preserved sector along the Gask Ridge are more than one mile (1·6 km) apart, suggests that lateral communications were not their primary function. Their purpose was to control movement along and across the road, thus providing a kind of frontier, presumably intended once again to protect or demarcate the tribes of the Fife peninsula, who may have been pro-Roman or at least neutral, from more hostile elements to the north. The importance of these towers in the development of Roman frontiers in Britain cannot be overstressed. They represent the first sure signs of a new approach to frontier defence, the establishment of a visible limit to the Roman province, which was to culminate in the massive linear barriers of the two Walls.

Very shortly, however, the towers were dismantled and this frontier line abandoned (St Joseph 1973, 218). The isthmus itself might well be expected to proffer an alternative halting place, but on present evidence cannot be shown to have done so. The dating evidence from Camelon is similar to that from all the excavated forts north of the isthmus: none provide any evidence of occupation later than AD 90 (Hartley 1972, 13–14). It could be argued, however, that Camelon at the southern end of the road through Strathmore, like Corbridge at the southern end of Dere Street, reflects the history of the forts to the north rather than those on the isthmus. No other isthmus site has yet

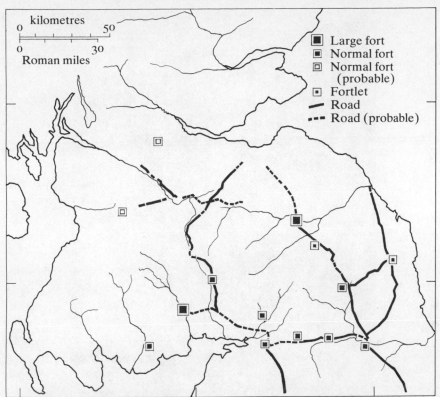

FIGURE 2.5   *Flavian permanent installations in North Britain*
c. *AD 90–105.*

been extensively excavated, but at Mollins trial trenching revealed strong
indications of deliberate demolition (Hanson and Maxwell 1980). Apart from
a fragment of samian pottery from Castlecary of Flavian-Trajanic date and
the apparently long but undated sequence of occupation at Loudoun Hill, we
must return to Newstead before we find evidence of occupation continuing
beyond AD 90. All the sites whose occupation extended into the last decade of
the first century lie south of a line between Newstead and Dalswinton (fig.2.5),
both of which were increased in size and seem to have served as strategic
centres; such large forts may imply the presence of cavalry, which would have
facilitated long-range patrolling. A *terminus post quem* for this re-organisation
is supplied by mint coins of AD 86 in the backfilled ditch of the first fort at
Newstead. Some of the troops which were withdrawn were probably transferred to Cumbria, which seems to have been permanently garrisoned about
this time (Potter 1979, 358).

   The re-structuring of the frontier outlined above seems to have survived
for a decade or so before the Romans temporarily abandoned all the territory

45

PLATE 2.3   *Severed heads displayed outside a Roman fort or camp on Trajan's Column.*

north of the Tyne-Solway line. While the earlier stages of withdrawal seem to have been matters of deliberate policy brought about by shortages of man-power, and are reflected in the archaeological record by the evidence of deliberate abandonment and demolition of forts and watch-towers, it has been suggested that this final withdrawal was the result of enemy action because of the evidence of burning and destruction from a number of fort sites (Daniels 1970, 93–4; Gillam 1977, 56). But other interpretations of the archaeological evidence are possible. Accidental destruction of timber buildings cannot be discounted, and there is increasing evidence that the Romans deliberately demolished their forts on abandonment, even going to the trouble of collecting together unwanted timbers and burning them (Hanson 1978a, 302–4; Charlesworth 1980, 201). The broken military equipment and even human heads found in the pits at Newstead might be taken as grisly evidence of an orgy of destruction by hostile natives. On the other hand, a recent study of the metalwork concluded that the equipment was surplus or damaged material

46

buried, like the nails at Inchtuthil, to prevent re-use of the iron by the natives (Manning 1972, 244–6). The heads could well have been discarded trophies such as are represented on Trajan's Column (pl.2.3), for many of the auxiliary troops were Celtic in origin with a traditional veneration for the human head. If the fort had been sacked by native Celtic tribesmen, it would have been the headless bodies of its defenders that were left to tell the tale.

At Corbridge, however, the story is rather different. The large base at Red House had been abandoned and demolished around AD 90 in favour of an auxiliary fort only just over half a mile (1 km) away. Excavations over many years at the latter has revealed extensive burning of structural timbers *in situ* (Gillam 1977, 55), whereas burning by the Romans as part of the demolition process generally seems to occur after the buildings had been dismantled. Furthermore, the Corbridge fort was almost immediately rebuilt, so that one might have expected to find signs of careful demolition rather than of a widespread conflagration. Whether the fort was fired by the enemy or by the Romans, it tells a tale of hasty evacuation in the face of hostile action such as occurred during the Batavian revolt in Germany (Tacitus *Histories* IV, 15).

There is no clear-cut solution to the question of the causation of the Roman withdrawal, but localised hostility may have encouraged the Roman high command in their decision. This is not to say that the Romans were forcibly expelled from Scotland, but rather that they chose to concentrate their resources in other parts of the Empire. Trouble on the northern frontier in Britain should be seen against the background of the Empire as a whole, for the strategic importance of an insular province cannot be compared with that of either the Danube or the eastern frontier. Seen in this light, it is less ironic that Trajan, the greatest expansionist emperor since Augustus, should have been responsible for a withdrawal in Britain and the establishment of the frontier on the Tyne-Solway line which was to become the most enduring in the history of the province.

III. THE TYNE-SOLWAY FRONTIER

Shortly after the beginning of the second century AD the Roman frontier in Britain seems to have rested on the Tyne-Solway isthmus, the most convenient east-west route south of the Forth-Clyde line. The precise nature of the northern defences of the empire at this time is poorly understood, partly because of an over-emphasis on theory at the expense of archaeological data (Daniels 1970, 94–5 *contra* Birley 1961, 132–50). However, recent fieldwork and excavation, particularly in Cumbria, are beginning to bring the picture into sharper focus.

The primary elements of the Trajanic frontier were the Flavian forts at Carlisle and Corbridge, situated astride the two main routes into Scotland, together with the east-west road which connects them, known to us as the Stanegate. Around AD 90, the Roman occupation of the north had undergone considerable modification, with a withdrawal into the central lowlands of Scotland (see above pp.45–7). At the same time, it is evident that consolidation of the established position took place in the immediate hinterland. Along the Stanegate the campaign base at Red House was demolished and replaced by a more normal auxiliary fort at Corbridge just over half a mile (1 km) away, probably intended to house a cavalry regiment, the *ala Petriana* (Gillam 1977, 53), while new forts may have been constructed at Chesterholm and Nether Denton, so that the distance between the four forts approximated to the norm in occupied areas, i.e. a day's march (Table 3.1). It is in the 90s also that we first get evidence of Roman occupation of the Lake District, probably including the fort at Kirkbride on Morecambe Bay, which appears at some stage to have been linked by road directly with Carlisle, some 10·4 miles (16·7 km) to the east (Potter 1979, 356–8).

TABLE 3.1   *The spacing of forts on the Stanegate in Roman miles*

Carlisle				
		8·4		
	14·5		Old Church (Brampton)	
		6·2		
Nether Denton				
		4·9		2·4
				Throp
				2·5
	11·9		Carvoran*	
		7·1		3·4
				Haltwhistle Burn
				3·8
Chesterholm				
		6·7		
	14·4		Newbrough*	
		8·0		
Corbridge				

* Occupation at this period uncertain.

The conversion of an ordinary military road into a frontier line is usually marked by a reduction in the spacing between forts disposed along it by at least a half, thus doubling the troop concentration. It is generally agreed that this process took place along the Stanegate at some time in Trajan's reign, probably coinciding with the final withdrawal from Lowland Scotland c.AD 105 (fig.3.1). Intermediate forts between the main four have long been postulated at Old Church (Brampton), Carvoran and Newbrough, but only the former can be attributed to this period with any degree of certainty (Simpson and Richmond 1936, 176). The gap between Nether Denton and Chesterholm was, however, split by two smaller works of less than 1 acre (0·4 ha) in internal area: Haltwhistle Burn and Throp; their date, on the basis of the pottery, seems to fall within the first two decades of the second century (Hartley 1966a, 14). The nature of the garrison at these two sites is uncertain. The stone internal buildings at Haltwhistle, the more extensively excavated of the two, are of little help; one is possibly to be identified as a barrack, while a second may have been a granary. Whether this multiplication of sites extended all along the road is as yet unproven. It was formerly assumed that larger and smaller installations alternated (Birley 1961, 132–50), but this can no longer be substantiated. Nor, until recently, has there been much evidence of an extension of the system beyond the original limits of the Stanegate road. A

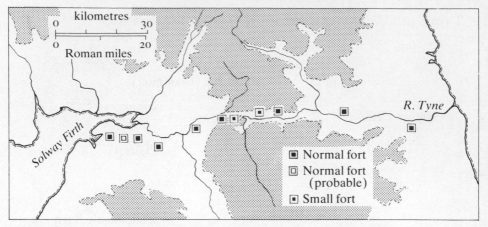

FIGURE 3.1   *The Trajanic frontier on the Tyne–Solway isthmus.*

timber-built fort discovered from the air at Whickham on the south bank of the Tyne (McCord and Jobey 1971, 120) may date to this period, for it conveniently bisects the distance between Corbridge and the coast. On the other hand, recent aerial survey and excavation by Professor G.D.B. Jones in Cumbria have begun to confirm that similar arrangements were made in the west. Approximately mid-way between the sites at Kirkbride and Carlisle a new fort has been discovered at Burgh-by-Sands (pl.3.1) only two-thirds of a mile (1 km) south of the Hadrianic fort of the same name. Excavation indicated occupation in the earlier part of the second century (Goodburn 1979, 281–3), although an early Hadrianic rather than a Trajanic context would seem more likely on present dating evidence. Since then another possible fort has been discovered at Fingland, which would further reduce the distance between installations.

A number of putative watch-towers are often assumed to have been associated with the Stanegate (Birley 1961, 136–50). The Hadrian's Wall turrets at Pike Hill and Walltown Crags seem to pre-date the construction of the curtain, but neither has produced any dating evidence to indicate occupation before the reign of Hadrian himself (Charlesworth 1977, 14). The other possible sites which are quoted, Mains Rigg, Barcombe and Birdoswald, are all of dubious relevance: no evidence of towers was recorded at either of the latter, while two excavations at Mains Rigg have failed to produce any artefacts of a Roman date. However, a timber-built tower which was found beneath the fort at Burgh-by-Sands was probably part of the Trajanic system. Clearly much more research is necessary before we have anything approaching a complete picture, but the apparent growth in the number of installations in the first decades of the second century indicates an intensification of the garrison across the isthmus at this time and an increase in the facilities for

PLATE 3.1   *The fort and earlier watch-tower at Burgh-by-Sands,*
Cumberland, from the air.

surveillance and control of movement – in other words the hallmarks of a
frontier line.

There is no way of ascertaining the immediate effectiveness of Trajan's
frontier, but by the end of his reign in AD 117 there was evidently trouble in the
north, and Hadrian on his accession found that the 'Britons could not be kept
under control' (SHA Hadrian, 5.2). The first requirement being to restore
stability, Q. Pompeius Falco was despatched as governor, presumably with
orders to do no more than remove the cause of the trouble. Yet, the indications
are that even such a task may have cost the Roman army dearly. A letter
written by Cornelius Fronto to the adoptive grandson of Hadrian, Marcus
Aurelius, compares Roman army losses in Britain during the Hadrianic period
with those sustained in the Jewish rebellion of AD 132–5, and it is generally
reckoned that the casualties referred to were those of the opening years of the
reign, although it is no longer possible to ascribe to the British troubles the
ignominious defeat and disappearance of *legio IX Hispana*.

The source of unrest is still far from certain. The phrase 'could not be
kept under Roman control' seems to indicate that the trouble had flared up
within the province, and it is therefore tempting to think of the Brigantes as
the instigators of the uprising. On the other hand, the Roman army, however
static its troop dispositions, would surely have sought to exercise at least some
degree of supervisory control over native tribes lying immediately beyond the
border of the province. Any unrest among such groups would have been

51

considered in the same light, and from what we can infer of pro-Roman and anti-Roman tendencies manifested by the tribes in this area, it seems not unlikely that any outbreak of rebellion among, say, the Selgovae of Greater Tweeddale, would have spread swiftly to the neighbouring Brigantes; and before long the whole northern *limes* could have been engulfed in war. As yet, however, a serious border upheaval is not reflected in the archaeological record. The end of the second period of occupation of the fort at Corbridge at about this time seems to have been peaceful, in sharp contrast to the fate of its immediate predecessor (Gillam 1977, 60–2), while limited excavation of the relevant period at Chesterholm revealed signs of deliberate demolition rather than wanton destruction (Birley 1977, 108–10).

PLATE 3.2   *Britannia issue of Hadrian AD 119–38.*

In all probability, whatever its cause and location, the fighting had been brought to a successful conclusion for the Romans in or slightly before AD 119, when the earliest of a series of coins bearing the type of Britannia was first issued (RIC Hadrian 577a) (pl.3.2). By AD 121 or possibly 122, the emperor Hadrian himself, having completed a tour of inspection in Gaul and Germany, arrived in Britain to supervise personally the shaping of the new frontier. The visit, which probably coincided roughly with the arrival of a new governor, Aulus Platorius Nepos, and the replacement of the Ninth Legion at York by the Sixth, was but one part of a wider programme devised by Hadrian to bring lasting peace to the frontiers of his newly acquired empire. The innovation which the emperor brought with him was, if not actually his own brainchild, at least a project with which he identified very closely; it was the apotheosis of the fixed defence-line, the supplementing of an open frontier-zone comprising tactically dispersed garrisons with a continuous barrier. The same policy manifested itself elsewhere on the Imperial frontiers: in Upper Germany, for example, the outermost line of watch-towers, which resembled the Flavian surveillance-system on the Gask Ridge, was now strengthened by the addition of a stoutly-built wooden palisade, behind which the occupants of the watch-posts might be sheltered from small-scale hostile incursions. In Britain more ambitious measures were evidently called for, and the length of the Tyne-Solway frontier, only 80 Roman miles, made it feasible to build most of it in stone, as opposed to the more usual turf, with an original width of 10 feet (3 m). Nevertheless, the concept was apparently still very much the same: the new frontier was designed to discourage rather than positively prevent enemy penetration of the province. The actual number of troops stationed on the frontier was to be comparatively low, sufficient for surveillance, but not for defence, that task being left in the hands of regiments stationed some distance to the rear, along the Stanegate. A major point of departure from the German frontier, however, was the decision to dispose the watch-posts in a regular series, separated from each other by a third of a Roman mile, the installations to be integrated with the actual fabric of the barrier. Moreover, every third post was to take the form of a fortlet or mile-castle capable of accommodating one or two *contubernia* of troops, and thus able to serve as the permanent base of the men required to operate the watch-posts or turrets on either side, each fortlet being thus responsible for surveillance of a mile of Wall; structural and functional parallels have been identified among the fortlets of the Trajanic *limes* in Germany, for example Degerfeld in the Wetterau (Jorns and Meier-Arendt 1967). Some way behind the barrier, separated from it in some instances by as much as two miles (3·2 km), lay the forts of the regiments providing the frontier's main defensive and offensive striking force. Many, if not all of these, had been in existence since the time of Trajan, as we have seen, but their re-use in the first phase of Hadrian's Wall does not necessarily signify that their role was unaltered. At Corbridge and possibly Chesterholm this new phase coincided with extensive remodelling of the forts. The writer of the Augustan History indicates that the construction of the new frontier was preceded by a period in which Hadrian 'set many things to rights' (Hadrian 11, 2) operations which might have included a re-structuring of the control-system of the northern frontier, if this had failed in the late uprising. In view of the new situation, with access to the north restricted to the number of milecastle entrances locally accessible, the control of troop movements in the Wall zone would have assumed a new importance, even without the need to remedy past defects; improved communications must have played a significant part in this organisation, which the towered milecastle-gateways and intermediate turrets would naturally have facilitated.

The channels of movement open to the military were, of course, also applicable to the control of civilian traffic, and we must remember that the close supervision of this was probably the main day-to-day function of the running barrier (see below p.163ff). Passage across Hadrian's Wall was possible for all persons going peaceably about their lawful business, but only with the permission of the troops occupying the milecastles. In origin, Hadrian's Wall served as a physical demarcation of the Roman province – a political as well as military dividing-line – and the scale of its construction was doubtless

PLATE 3.3   *The milefortlet at Biglands, Cumberland, and connecting Hadrianic coastal palisade.*

intended to impress the northern barbarians as much as it was hoped it would discourage. That this primary idea of defining Roman territory was implicit in the re-furbished Upper German *limes* is suggested by the similar phraseology used in the Augustan History's account of either frontier (Hadrian, 11.2; 12.6). The significance of this early political apartheid would not have been lost on the local tribesmen, particularly in the western half of the Wall-zone, where the newly-built barrier seems to have cut across tribal territory belonging to the Brigantes, isolating a considerable portion of the tribe's lands lying in the lower dales of the Rivers Esk and Annan (Birley 1953, 36). Effectively, such artificial boundaries restricted and distorted the traditional currents of trade and social intercourse, not to mention the movements of beasts in long-established patterns of local transhumance. It is possible, therefore, that even in the earliest phase of the Hadrianic re-organisation there were already outpost forts at Netherby, Bewcastle and Birrens, but whether this showed a desire on the part of the Romans to guard against possible disaffection amongst such Brigantian outliers, or a political acknowledgement of the Roman army's duty to protect these tribesmen as part of a subject people, cannot be determined. However, the sensitivity of the western sector of the Wall is emphasised by the fact that the series of milecastles and turrets was continued from the end

54

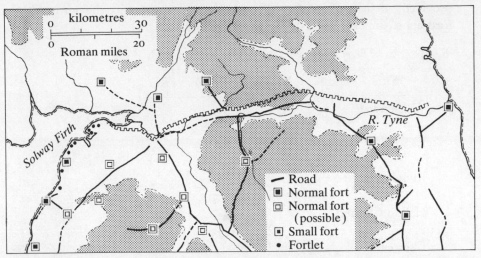

FIGURE 3.2   *The Hadrianic frontier system.*

of the mural barrier down the Cumberland coast probably as far as St Bees'
Head, being reinforced by the construction of a fort at Maryport. Recent
aerial survey by Professor G. D. B. Jones (1976) has revealed that the smaller
installations were originally enclosed by a pair of parallel ditches 100 to 150 ft
(30–45 m) apart (pl. 3.3). Evidently, the native peoples of south-west Scotland
also represented a source of anxiety to the frontier garrison. Significantly,
there were initially no outlying forts to the north of the eastern half of the Wall,
where the Roman frontier gave on to the territory of the Votadini.

The new Wall had been under construction for about two seasons when
decisions were taken which led to the complete transformation of the frontier:
the garrisons occupying the Stanegate forts were moved up to occupy a new
series of forts situated on the Wall itself, in several cases occupying the sites of
milecastles or turrets (fig. 3.2). Initially, it seems to have been intended that
all these additional structures should project to the north of the curtain, thus
making it possible to have three gates in each site giving access to the terrain
beyond the Wall, as if in reaction to the problems experienced when all the
troops had been obliged to make their way through the gates in an adjacent
milecastle. Before all of these forts had been constructed, it was probably
realised that such an exposed position was neither necessary nor desirable, and
the later forts, such as Greatchesters, were therefore added behind the Wall.
Excluding the two new forts constructed on the Solway coast, one of which,
Moresby, might have been a slightly later addition (RIB 801), there were thus
twelve garrisons provided to defend the frontier from the line of the barrier
itself. These new posts, all large enough to accommodate a full unit and
relatively evenly disposed along the 80 Roman miles of the Hadrianic frontier,

55

provided a density of manning that was almost exactly twice the norm, with forts approximately half a day's march apart (Table 3.2).

Table 3.2 *The spacing of primary forts on Hadrian's Wall*

Site	Wall miles	Miles	Km
Wallsend			
	6·3	5·25	8·4
Benwell			
	7	6·6	10·6
Rudchester			
	8	7·2	11·6
Halton Chesters			
	6	5·4	8·7
Chesters			
	9·3	7·6	12·2
Housesteads			
	6·3	5·5	8·8
Greatchesters			
	6·3	5·5	8·8
Birdoswald			
	7·3	6·6	10·6
Castlesteads			
	9	8	12·9
Stanwix			
	6	4·7	7·6
Burgh by Sands			
	8·3	6·9	11·1
Bowness on Solway			

Contemporary with the decision to relocate the permanent garrisons on the Wall was a realisation that, for whatever reason, the new mural frontier required some form of protection on its southern side. In consequence, a flat-bottomed ditch 20 ft (6 m) wide and 10 ft (3 m) deep was provided all the way from Newcastle to the Solway; it was cut with exceptional care, its steep sides being revetted with stone or built of turf where the nature of the ground made normal digging impossible (Collingwood Bruce 1978, 30–1). Set back 30 ft (9 m) from the lip of the ditch on either side was a mound 20 ft (6 m) wide, composed of the upcast material retained by laid turves. A strip of ground 120 ft (36 m), or one Roman *actus* wide, was thus defined immediately to the south of the Wall, across which it would have been difficult to pass unobserved (pl.3.4). The purpose of this demarcation ditch (incorrectly, but traditionally

PLATE 3.4   *Hadrian's Wall and the* Vallum *in the central sector at Cawfields.*

known as the *Vallum*) is plain: it was to deny or restrict unauthorised access to the rear of the Wall and its associated installations – serving the same purpose as the barbed-wire entanglement of more modern times. Nor can there by any doubt about the relationship of the *Vallum* to the primary forts; wherever it comes into close proximity to a fort, the *Vallum* deviates from the established alignment, a clear indication that the fort already existed or was already planned. Similarly, original causeways in the *Vallum* ditch, with massive gateways on the southern side, occur opposite the primary forts and possibly also at points where existing roads led northwards through the Wall. It may be asked what new factor had arisen to make the Roman High Command apparently so sensitive about the vulnerability of the new frontier. Some have ventured to suggest that it was a fresh upsurge of unrest among the native peoples north of the Wall, serious enough to bring about a dislocation of ongoing construction work and a drastic revision of the defensive requirements of the frontier (Stevens 1966, 50–66). If this was so, the evidence of the re-positioning of the forts and the elaborate precautions inherent in the *Vallum*

57

suggest that the Brigantes to the south of the Wall were among the disaffected elements. On the other hand, the relocation of the forts could be explained on purely logistical grounds, for the inconvenience of having to file through a milecastle in order to gain access to the north must have become rapidly apparent; after all the presence of barbed-wire around modern military installations does not imply local hostility, merely a concern for security.

Such changes naturally resulted in delays to the Wall-building programme, and one major effect was a decision to reduce the gauge of the stone curtain from 10 ft (3 m) to 8 ft (2·4 m) or even less, doubtless with the aim of saving expense and materials, as well as speeding up a task which may have begun to appear never-ending. Governors came and went. Platorius Nepos departed in *c*.AD 126, possibly under a cloud, and still the work of building and modifying continued. The last of the primary forts was built behind the curtain; additional forts were inserted at Carrawburgh, overlying the infilled *Vallum*, at Carvoran, and probably at Drumburgh (RIB 1550 and 1778); the curtain itself was extended roughly four miles eastwards to Wallsend, the presence of the River Tyne to the rear doubtless being reckoned a sufficiently strong substitute for the *Vallum*, which is lacking in this sector; and finally, near the end of Hadrian's reign, the stretch of turf Wall from the River Irthing to just west of milecastle 54 was rebuilt in stone, the opportunity being taken to lead the new stone curtain up to the northern angles of Birdoswald fort, so that it no longer projected beyond the line of the Wall as it had originally when added to the turf Wall (Breeze and Dobson 1976a, 76). It is very possible, therefore, that construction or modification never stopped on Hadrian's Wall from its beginning in AD 122 until the death of Hadrian himself in AD 138. The experience which inspired these alterations was a vital factor in the design and development of the more northerly frontier that was destined, however briefly, to replace it – the Antonine Wall.

IV. THE ANTONINE CONQUEST

c.AD 139–145

The decision to abandon Hadrian's Wall and to advance the frontier of the
province more than 70 miles represented something of a *volte face* for the
Roman high command. As we have seen in the preceding chapter, for almost
four decades the military strategists had been accustoming themselves to a
policy of holding the southern isthmus between Tyne and Solway with a
frontier of increasing complexity and with a garrison that was growing continually more static, ever more densely concentrated and, in consequence, less
able, or willing, to commit itself to offensive operations.

   The decision to take the offensive once more coincided with the accession
of a new emperor, Antoninus Pius, as well as the arrival in Britain of a new
governor, Q. Lollius Urbicus. Born in Numidia, Urbicus seems to have come
to the attention of Hadrian, serving on the emperor's staff during the Jewish
rebellion. He had already served as governor of *Germania Inferior* when he was
appointed to the same post of responsibility in Britain in AD 139 (Birley 1981,
112–14). Indeed, Hadrian may have been grooming Urbicus for this task, for
quite a number of governors of Britain in the second and early third centuries
seem to have gained previous experience in Germany (Birley 1979, 38),
although there is no reason to believe that the new policy reflected the ideas
of that emperor. On the contrary, it is most unlikely that Hadrian would have
contemplated abandoning or even 'mothballing' the frontier installations that
were such a magnificent monument to himself and upon which so much time
and effort had been expended. Even when, in AD 136, he had nominated
L. Aelius as his heir, it is improbable that his selection of someone with experience of commanding a frontier province (Pannonia) signified that he expected

59

offensive policies to be pursued immediately by his successor. Indeed, when L. Aelius died on 1st January 138, Hadrian's choice fell on Antoninus Pius, who apparently possessed no military distinctions, but had, instead, won golden opinions in the administrative field, having been appointed to the proconsulship of Asia. This choice is surely a significant one, implying that in Hadrian's eyes the Empire now appeared secure enough for the appointment of a leader who could approach the problems of its administration in the same practical and re-appraising spirit that he himself had displayed in re-organising the frontiers. Thus, the speed with which Urbicus set to work preparing for the advance (see p.69 below) suggests that he had arrived with specific instructions from the new emperor himself.

The reasons for this dramatic change of policy, however, are not so obvious, and alternative explanations have been put forward, either political or military. There has been a suggestion, for example, that Antoninus engineered the new aggressive policy in north Britain as a *douceur* to the marshals of the emperor Trajan, who had experienced twenty years of inactivity under Hadrian, and whose support he now needed (Birley 1974, 17–18); alternatively, the move has been interpreted as an attempt by Antoninus to win military prestige for himself and thus justify his selection for imperial honours by personal association with a successful campaign of territorial expansion. On the other hand, local strategic or tactical reasons have been advanced, suggesting that the move north was a direct response to unrest on the frontier at this time (Frere 1978, 173–4).

Indeed, it could be argued that Antoninus' political position in Rome was not entirely secure; he could be seen as a stop-gap choice of successor, adopted on the death of L. Aelius to hold the fort until the young M. Annius, the future Marcus Aurelius, came of age (Birley 1974, 17). Yet Antoninus was sufficiently popular with the Senate to persuade them to grant the deification of the dead emperor much against their wishes; indeed, he himself was granted the honorific title Pius. To suggest that he deliberately engineered a war in order to ingratiate himself with the ageing 'hawks' in the Roman high command not only flies in the face of Pausanias' testimony that he never voluntarily involved the Romans in warfare (*Descr. Graeciae* VIII, 43, 3), but simply does not make sense; the honours of a single campaign could hardly be shared among a large group, and indeed the leading role fell to Urbicus, who had already received his fair share of whatever military patronage Hadrian had been willing, however reluctantly, to dispense.

The suggested parallel with the position of the emperor Claudius on his accession is, however, more convincing. The important role of the army in the establishment and maintenance of the emperor had been openly affirmed often enough; to suggest that Antoninus was unaware of this would be to accuse him of political naivety, which is not justified by the later history of his reign. With no direct personal military experience – nor, in all probability, the desire to obtain any – Antoninus needed to establish his credibility with the body of the army and gain military prestige. Claudius, too, had lacked military experience and went as far as personally participating in the later stages of the invasion of Britain in AD 43 with the sole purpose of acquiring military laurels to bolster his political position with the populace and the army. Although Antoninus does not seem to have made the same political capital out of his conquests in Britain, it was the only occasion of his reign, despite frontier advances in Germany and probably Africa, that he accepted the imperial acclamation for a victory (CIL X, 515) which was then celebrated on a series of coin issues (RIC Antoninus Pius, 743–5) (pl.4.1), and in contemporary speeches (*Pan. Lat. Vet.* VIII (V) 14). That the emperor was not personally involved seemed to matter little, for all conquests were achieved in his name and redounded to his greater glory.

PLATE 4.1   *Victory issue of Antoninus Pius AD 142–44.*

But it would be perverse, and still contrary to the explicit statement of Pausanias noted above, to suggest that this was the only motivation for the new policy in north Britain; rather it provided the political background against which unrest on the frontier might be seen as an opportunity to be grasped. Certainly it would be wrong to assert that the British frontier was totally pacified, although the evidence in support of a major upheaval is distinctly limited and the precise location of unrest uncertain. Little real information can be derived from the terse account of these events in the Augustan History: '(Antoninus) through his legate Lollius Urbicus, also conquered the Britons, driving off the barbarians and building another wall, this time of turf' (Antoninus Pius, V, 4). Much has been made of the words '*summotis barbaris*' which recall, perhaps intentionally, the phrase '*summotis hostibus*' in Tacitus' account of Agricola's fourth campaign (*Agricola* 23). It has even been suggested that the reference here is to wholesale deportation of fractious natives from southern Scotland to other frontiers of the Empire, notably Upper Germany where *numeri Brittonum* are first attested at this time

(Macdonald 1934, 49; Collingwood and Myres 1937, 146). However, although such an enforced exodus is not so impracticable as some scholars have implied – a *deportatio iuvenum* being one of the means advocated by King James VI to pacify the Borders in more recent times (Mackie 1978, 189) – the archaeological evidence is against it: excavations at Hesselbach in the Odenwald in Upper Germany have shown that the *numeri* garrisoning that site probably originated several decades earlier (Baatz 1973, 71), while extensive fieldwork in south-eastern Scotland has failed to produce evidence of any large-scale depopulation, rather the reverse (Gillam 1958, 66; Jobey 1974). It is, of course, possible that the words were not intended to have a specific application, being merely a stock phrase or verbal padding (cf. Aurelius Victor *de Caesaribus* XX, 4). Nevertheless, it is tempting to see in the echoes of Tacitus a parallel with the situation which faced the Roman army in AD 80–81 when the establishment of the Agricolan chain of *praesidia* effectively insulated the province from the risk of barbarian inroads from the north (see above pp.39–40).

Matters are further complicated by the contemporary reference in Pausanias to trouble amongst the Brigantes at some time in the reign of Antoninus Pius: 'Also he (Antoninus) deprived the Brigantes in Britain of most of their territory because they had taken up arms and invaded the Genounian district, of which the people are subject to the Romans' (*Descr. Graeciae* VIII, 43, 4). Until recently this was identified as the occasion for the abandonment of the Antonine conquests in the late 150s (see below p.143ff), but Pausanias' comment appears as part of a description of all the wars fought in Pius' reign; it seems hardly credible that the reconquest of Scotland, for which Antoninus took the only imperial acclamation of his reign, should have been overlooked in favour of a minor revolt. If this refers to events in Britain at all, and some scholars have argued strongly that it does not, it ought to be to the campaigns of Lollius Urbicus and thus should provide a clue to the nature of the trouble which stimulated that campaign. The naming of the Brigantes and the location of the Genounian district thus assumes considerable importance in our attempt to locate the source of that unrest. Unfortunately, no one has ever located a Genounian district in Britain, although numerous ingenious emendations of the text have been suggested in an attempt to do so (e.g. Maxwell 1977, 30). It is furthermore pointed out that in Raetia on the Danube frontier there is a tribe with an almost identical name, the Genauni, whose immediate neighbours were the Brigantii (Hind 1977; Rivet and Smith 1979, 47). It is hard, therefore, to resist the conclusion that some confusion has arisen in the text of Pausanias. However, one cannot dismiss the reference entirely as irrelevant to Britain (*pace* Todd 1980, 165) as this would still leave Antoninus' major conquest unmentioned in Pausanias' list. The Brigantes must surely have been involved, for they provide the link which precipitated the textual error, but neither the locality nor the nature of their actions in

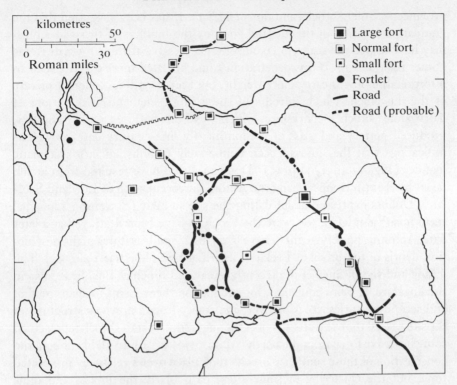

FIGURE 4.1   *Permanent installations in North Britain during the first*
                Antonine occupation.

Britain is recoverable from Pausanias' text. Since Brigantian territory seems
to have extended north of Hadrian's Wall (Birley 1953, 33–6), an attack on
Roman-held territory from without is not impossible, but Pausanias can no
longer be quoted in support of such a view. Nor should it be surprising that the
Brigantes, who had apparently given grounds for some uneasiness during the
building of Hadrian's Wall (if the present interpretation of the function of the
Vallum is correct), took the opportunity of a possible hiatus in frontier policy
to trouble the province on the accession of Antoninus. Moreover, the disposition of garrisons in south-western Scotland in the first Antonine period,
concentrating in the valleys of the Annan and Nith (fig.4.1), in and immediately adjacent to the area of probable Brigantian settlement north of the Wall,
is of considerable significance. At the very least this must indicate a perceived
threat, even if the reduced level of occupation in the area later on implies that
the threat had been overestimated or successfully contained.

On the native side, the only archaeological trace of events which might
have led to unrest on the northern frontier is represented by the distribution in
southern Scotland of two types of fortified dwelling originating in the Atlantic

63

province – namely brochs and duns (fig.8.1). It has been suggested that the gradual penetration of the lowland zone by the builders of these structures may have tipped the scales in favour of an aggressive attitude towards Rome (Steer 1964, 20–1). If this penetration could be dated more exactly, such an interpretation might carry more weight, but there is still no coherent picture of the movement which introduced these exotic elements. Excavations at Torwoodlee broch, Selkirkshire, which was built within an earlier hillfort, produced pottery and glass of predominantly first-century date, as well as indications that the site had been deliberately demolished in a systematic manner (Piggott 1951, 113–15). This could well have resulted from action taken by Roman troops during the Antonine reoccupation of Lowland Scotland. Doubts expressed about dating the site so early (Stevenson 1966, 35) seem unsubstantiated, for, were the broch to have been destroyed at a later date, Antonine pottery ought to have been discovered, as it was in the destruction debris of the broch at Leckie in Stirlingshire (MacKie 1979, 54). The dating and significance of the recently excavated broch at Buchlyvie, also in Stirlingshire, is more equivocal, for occupation there seems to span the first and second centuries AD. Moreover, continuity from a previous structure on the site has led the excavator to reject the suggestion that the broch represented some intrusive force from the north (Main 1979, 50–1). In all likelihood, the construction of these southerly brochs took place over a relatively protracted time, but the clustering of some sites, particularly the brochs and duns situated in the Stirling district, suggests that there might have been at least one major influx and that it occurred after the Flavian withdrawal from central Scotland. Whether or not it was part of a gradual process, and regardless of its political or military purpose, a movement of population, if that is what it betokens, would clearly have been a matter of concern to the Roman authorities, for it would have brought pressure to bear on the native tribesmen rather closer to the Tyne-Solway frontier.

If we could trace the line of march taken by Urbicus in his northward advance we might gain further insight into the anticipated trouble-spots, but no Antonine temporary camps have been identified with any certainty away from the line of the Antonine Wall itself. Indeed, it is only really in the area north of the Forth-Clyde isthmus that any detailed analysis of temporary works has been undertaken, and that has attributed all camps to the campaigns of either Agricola or Severus (St Joseph 1969, 113–19; 1973, 228–33). Nearly all the dating criteria, however, are circumstantial, and some of the camps – notably those of the so-called 30-acre (12 ha) group with their tertiate plan – may eventually prove to be Antonine (Hanson 1978b, 144–5). The 45 acre (18 ha) camp at Lochlands some way to the north-west of the fort at Camelon, overlooking a convenient crossing-point of the River Carron, may also be Antonine; although provisionally assigned to the earliest Roman advance northwards (Feachem 1956a, 336–9), the recent identification of two smaller camps with Stracathro gates occupying more advantageous ground immediately to the west may indicate that this larger camp is somewhat later.

Large numbers of temporary camps have been discovered in the area south of the Forth-Clyde isthmus during the past thirty years, but relatively few have been securely dated, and only four, all assigned to the Severan period, are so spaced in relation to each other as to indicate a line of march. It is remarkable, too, that few of the camps greatly exceed 50 acres (20 ha), and those that do appear to be associated with either the Severan or the Agricolan campaigns, when we know that a large force was operating in Scotland. There are, however, a considerable number of camps between about 42 and 54 acres (17–22 ha) in area, all capable of accommodating at least one legion and the appropriate complement of auxiliary troops, and possibly a good deal more – certainly a field army of not inconsiderable strength. Is it possible to distinguish Antonine sites among these, and, if so, how might one recognise them? Flavian camps tend to be square in plan (Maxwell 1980), but this is of limited use in reducing the possible candidates for, although perhaps 60–70 per cent of presumed Agricolan camps in Scotland fall into this category, the existence of perfect tertiate examples in Wales and the Welsh Marches indicates that it is by no means an infallible criterion, most temporary camps in these areas being Flavian or earlier. A more positive guide is the spatial relationship between the camps and forts or roads. There is a tendency for camps to cluster around forts (see above p.19f), and this can be helpful when the latter were occupied during only one period of the Roman presence. Unfortunately, most of the forts in Lowland Scotland served in both the Flavian and Antonine occupations. If, however, a camp appears to respect a road, it is likely to be later in date than the Flavian period, for the first campaigns were undertaken before any roads had been constructed.

The criteria for identifying groups of Antonine temporary camps might therefore be a tendency to tertiate plan and a relationship to adjacent roads which suggested a need to avoid impinging upon them. Such features are, of course, manifest in the presumed Severan categories of camp, notably those at Newstead, Channelkirk and further north at Ardoch and Innerpeffray, the long axis in each case running parallel to the adjacent road. The same is probably true of the largest camp at Pathhead, for although the precise course of Dere Street is not known at this point, the configuration of the ground and the alignment of the sector of the road immediately to the north make it likely that the road passed down the eastern side of the camp. Yet the latter intersects and, almost indubitably therefore, overlies the southern end of a much smaller camp, also tertiate and similarly aligned, which is approximately 50 acres (20 ha) in area. Camps of closely comparable size and proportions are known elsewhere on or near Dere Street at Pennymuir, Millside Wood, St Boswells

PLATE 4.2   *Temporary camps at Millside Wood, Roxburghshire, situated
on either side of Dere Street, which survives as a tree-lined
field-boundary.*

and Blainslie, while another of similar size may be indicated by the traces of a
partially-known site at Inveresk, some way to the south of the Antonine fort.
Whether such camps are in fact Antonine cannot yet be demonstrated beyond
doubt; nor indeed can their association with the same phase of campaigning,
regardless of date. Nevertheless, the situation at Millside Wood and Pennymuir, where the camps relate significantly to the Roman road, suggests that a
second-century date is more likely than not. Moreover, as the Millside Wood
camp faces another tertiate camp of 20 acres (8 ha) apparently aligned on the
opposite side of Dere Street, either it or its companion must surely fall to be
considered as post-Flavian sites. Other c.42-acre (17 ha) camps approaching
tertiate proportions that are known in southern Scotland include: Feather-
wood West, further south on Dere Street; Bankhead, and possibly Castlecraig,

66

on the main east-west arterial route between Tweeddale and Clydesdale. Cornhill on the Clyde near Biggar is of the same dimensions, but its distance from the Roman road would seem rather to favour a Flavian origin. It is interesting that examples of the larger category (*c.*50 acres, 20 ha) are also found on the east-west route at Lyne, a little to the north of the road and nearer to the Antonine fort than the smaller camp, and at Cleghorn in the Clyde valley.

TABLE 4.1   *Possible Antonine temporary camps south of the Forth*

Site	NGR	Approx. dimensions in metres	Area acres	Area hectares
Bankhead 1	NS 982450	460 × 365	41·5	16·8
Bankhead 2	NS 982450	380 × 335	31·4	12·7
Beattock	NT 084026	265 × 320	28·8	11·6
Blainslie	NT 552442	518 × 365	46·8	18·9
Castlecraig	NT 124444	533 × 325	42·9	17·3
Cleghorn	NS 910459	500 × 335	46·7	18·9
Featherwood West	NT 813058	472 × 345	40·4	16·4
Glenlochar	NX 735645	440 × 305	33·3	13·5
Inveresk	NT 348710	500 × 450	55·6	22·5
Little Clyde	NS 994159	440 × 290	31·4	12·7
Lochlands	NS 856817	475 × 380	44·7	18·1
Lyne 1	NT 200410	518 × 393	49·0	19·8
Lyne 2	NT 205405	340 × 310	27·0	10·9
Millside Wood	NT 690220	503 × 380	47·3	19·2
Pathhead	NT 396636	530 × 385	50·6	20·5
Pennymuir	NT 755140	518 × 335	42·9	17·4
St Boswells	NT 604316	550 × 395	53·5	21·7
Torwood	NY 120818	455 × 305	34·4	13·9
Ulston Moor	NT 687216	340 × 230	19·2	7·7

The distribution of the postulated Antonine temporary camps (Table 4.1) (fig.4.2) would then point to operations extending northwards along Dere Street, presumably starting out from Corbridge, then diverging westwards into the main valleys of the Tweed and penetrating as far as middle Clydesdale. The position in Upper Clydesdale and Annandale, indeed in the south-west generally, is more obscure. The identification of smaller camps, some 30 acres (13 ha) in size and tertiate in shape, at Glenlochar and Little Clyde, as well as Bankhead and probably Torwood and Beattock, may well be representative of Antonine activity in that area. However, some operations north of the Forth do seem to be indicated, although their precise limit and strength remain uncertain. But that Caledonia rather than lowland Scotland was deemed the major long-term threat is implied by the very strength of the Antonine Wall itself.

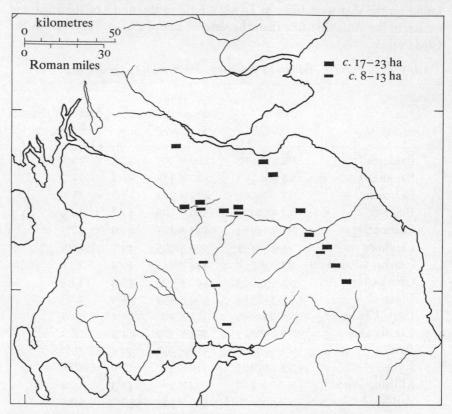

FIGURE 4.2   *Temporary camps of probable Antonine date in North Britain.*

Whether or not economic considerations came into play in the frontier policy decisions taken in Rome – and one should not dismiss the possibility, since emperors were all too conscious of the state of imperial finances and the possible economic returns from conquest (Strabo 2, 5, 8; Appian *Praefatio* 5) – the re-occupation of Lowland Scotland brought within the province once again the lands of the Votadini. Not only would this have made it easier to ensure the safety of a tribe which appears to have been amicably disposed to the occupying power, but it would also have secured for Roman enjoyment, if not exploitation, the fruits of perhaps the most fertile and productive area of land in north Britain. In particular, the free-draining soils in the broad coastal plain extending along the south side of the Forth from the Avon to beyond Dunbar, would have provided, in conjunction with a drier climate, the best conditions for mixed and arable farming on a generous scale, thereby facilitating the local production of the supplies that would have been required by the frontier garrison. It is even possible that the political stability guaranteed by the occupation would have served to invigorate the native economy to such a stage that a marketable surplus was available. Similar motives may have inspired the eastward advancement of the Upper Rhine frontier somewhat later in the Antonine period, and certainly the dense distribution and variety of ancient settlements and land-boundaries in Lothian and Berwickshire indicate that the area was capable of supporting a considerable native population.

Accordingly, one might suggest that on his accession Antoninus was well disposed towards a short war of conquest because of his relatively insecure position with the army. At the time there may have been some minor unrest on the northern frontier in Britain which would have brought that area to his attention. Where better than the remoteness of Rome's most northerly province for a war of conquest to fire the imaginations and national fervour of the populace – the province first brought into the Roman realm by the very first of the Caesars. The area was well charted, some of the tribes were friendly, and the economic prospects quite promising. There were even sound strategic reasons for an advance: the new frontier could take advantage of a much shorter line and bring the Roman army closer to its main enemy, the tribes to the north of the Forth-Clyde isthmus. It is such a combination of factors which Antoninus, advised by his experienced generals, will have weighed before reaching the decision which was to result once more in a Roman occupation of Scotland.

Preparations for the advance were rapidly set in train. Inscriptions from Corbridge, whose history of occupation reflects that of Lowland Scotland, record construction work undertaken by *legio II Augusta* under the governor Q. Lollius Urbicus in Antoninus' second and third consulship, indicating a start on the new programme as early as AD 139 (RIB 1147–8). At one time it was even thought that the Ingliston milestone (RIB 2313) referred to contemporary work on the Roman road system between Trimontium (Newstead) and the Forth, which would have indicated such rapid progress in the occupation of southern Scotland as almost to suggest that the northward move had been contemplated in the closing months of Hadrian's reign. However, it now seems reasonably certain that the milestone records road-building completed in Antoninus' third consulship, probably under Urbicus' successor (Maxwell 1982c). The only other epigraphic record of Urbicus' activities consists of a commemorative slab recording building work at High Rochester on Dere Street, Northumberland (RIB 1276), together with the two inscriptions from the stone-walled fort of Balmuildy, overlooking the crossing of the River Kelvin on the line of the Antonine Wall itself (RIB 2191–2).

Even before the campaign began, part of the advance planning would have been to consider in general terms the best position for the new barrier. Although Ptolemy's *Geography* was probably not yet available for consultation, clearly the sources that he used, notably Marinus of Tyre, could have provided a general map of Scotland. The selection of the isthmus as the proposed frontier line would then have been an obvious choice, even allowing for the ancient cartographers' misplacing of Scotland in relation to the rest of the British Isles (Rivet and Smith 1979, 107), and would have been reinforced both by Tacitus' striking reference to it (*Agricola* 23) and its utilisation as a *terminus* by Agricola in AD 80–81 (see above pp.39–40). Indeed, we may be sure that some kind of official records existed, detailing the Flavian dispositions across the isthmus, but the sort of information required before detailed planning of the new frontier could begin would not have been available until the south of Scotland had been overrun.

Such matters as the strength and disposition of garrisons other than those on the new Wall would have been decided, probably in some detail, before the legions moved north, being much influenced by the records of Flavian activity. It is instructive to note, therefore, in what respects the first Antonine occupation pattern differed from the various stages of the Flavian (figs.4.1 and 2.3). All the road system south of the Tay was put back into working order and garrisoned in strength. North of the isthmus a chain of forts extended for more than 30 miles (50 km), arching across the base of the Fife peninsula from Camelon to Bertha, thus isolating that area from the rest of Caledonia and hindering its use as a springboard for hostile operations against the right flank of the Antonine Wall. Apart from the two forts just mentioned there were intermediate garrisons at Ardoch in Strathallan and Strageath at the crossing of the River Earn, while a third has probably yet to be discovered at or near the crossing of the Forth to the north-west of Stirling (see below pp.102–3). These dispositions seem to mirror quite closely one stage of the fluctuating Flavian commitment in that area.

Concern for the hinterland of the Antonine Wall is shown by the weight and density of troop dispositions on the flanks (see below p.100f) and to the rear of the barrier itself. The Roman grip was assured by the densest and most comprehensive network of forts and smaller installations ever constructed in the military zone of the British province. Central to this system was the 14-acre (5·6 ha) fort at Newstead, which straddled Dere Street at the crossing of the River Tweed near Melrose. Its garrison of two cohorts of *legio XX Valeria Victrix*, brigaded together with a quingenary auxiliary cavalry regiment, formed the hub of military control, economically and efficiently taking the place of a full legionary base (Richmond 1950, 15–23) (fig.4.3). From this point the road system provided communications radiating out in all directions: westwards into Upper Tweeddale past the new milliary garrison at Lyne, and thence into Clydesdale, where Castledykes, although roughly half the size of Newstead, provided enough space to house at least a milliary regiment of auxiliary troops, if not a compound garrison of some sort. Further west still, the fort at Loudoun Hill guarded anew the road leading to the Ayrshire coast, while to the north-west a route, possibly now constructed for the first time, gave access to the western end of the Antonine Wall, a new fort capable of holding a quingenary regiment being built at Bothwellhaugh to guard its course through lower Clydesdale (Maxwell 1975a). Between Newstead and Corbridge the road was protected by full quingenary garrisons at Risingham and High Rochester, with a minor *castellum* at Cappuck, capable of holding only a part of a regiment, with a still smaller road-post at Chew Green at the head of Redesdale (Richmond 1940, 73–6). A similar minor installation occupied a roughly intermediate position at Oxton between Newstead and Inveresk to the north, and other examples may await discovery elsewhere on this northern sector of Dere Street; one may be situated in the vicinity of Crichton, where Roman masonry was discovered in the fabric of a native souterrain (RCAHMS 1929, 53–4). The majority of these sites were built over or immediately adjacent to Flavian installations, indicating that the methods of holding down the area and the general intentions of the two occupations were similar. Only Oxton and Bothwellhaugh do not fit into this category, but the possibility of undiscovered Flavian sites in the vicinity of each should not be discounted.

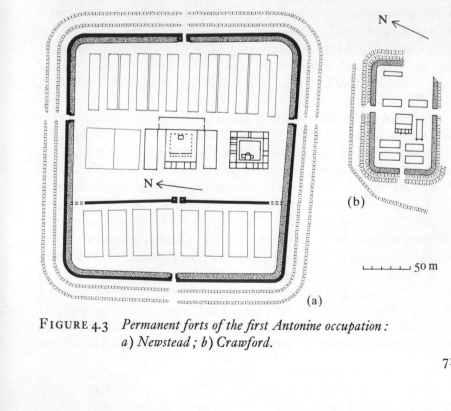

FIGURE 4.3 *Permanent forts of the first Antonine occupation:*
a) Newstead; b) Crawford.

TABLE 4.2   *Antonine fortlets in Tweeddale, Clydesdale,*
Nithsdale and Annandale

Site	NGR	Dimensions in metres	Area in m²
Barburgh Mill	NX 903884	29·5 × 28·5	840
Burnswark	NY 189786	c.32·0 × 22·8	c.730
Durisdeer	NS 903048	32·0 × 18·3	585
Lamington	NS 977307	uncertain	
Lyne	NT 187408	27·4 × 27·4	750
Milton	NT 092014	39·6 × 22·9	907
Redshaw Burn	NT 030139	19·8 × 17·4	345
Shieldhill	NY 031854	c.27·0 × 26·5	c.715
Wandel	NS 944268	c.19·0 × 18·0	c.340

However, much more complex arrangements were made to ensure the stability of the south-west of Scotland (fig.4.1) which, as the disposition of Hadrianic outpost forts shows (fig.3.2), had long given reason for anxiety on the part of the Roman high command. Of the former Hadrianic outposts, Birrens and possibly Netherby were prepared for their new role, the former being rebuilt to accommodate most of a part-mounted milliary regiment, *cohors I Nervana Germanorum* (Robertson 1975b, 78–88). Further west, however, the situation appears to have changed quite drastically. The large first-century nodal stronghold of Dalswinton on the Nith was replaced by a quingenary cavalry regiment at Carzield, some 3 miles (5 km) further downstream (Birley and Richmond 1939). At the head of the Clyde the small fort at Crawford was rebuilt (fig.4.3), but in Annandale the Flavian fort at Milton (Tassiesholm) was replaced by a fortlet of distinctive elongated plan, only 0·22 acres (0·09 ha) in internal area (fig.4.4). This type of small installation typifies the Nithsdale-Annandale-Clydesdale area in this period (Table 4.2). Fortlets very similar in plan to that at Milton were now built at Burnswark, below the abandoned hillfort, and at Durisdeer at the head of the Nith valley (fig.4.4), both securely dated to the Antonine period. Excavation at the first and last named sites produced traces of rectangular post-built structures indicative of permanent occupation (Clarke 1952a and b). The closest parallel to such tiny works is the unusual milefortlet of Cardurnock 1 on the Solway coast, one of a chain of Hadrianic shore defences (Simpson and Hodgson 1947, 85–9). Less elongated examples are known varying in size from tiny Redshaw Burn (fig.4.4) which approximates to the fortlets on the Antonine Wall, to Barburgh Mill in the Nith valley, which has an internal area of 0·21 acres (0·08 ha). Few of these fortlets have been positively dated, but excavation at the latter confirmed its Antonine occupation and indicated that it had

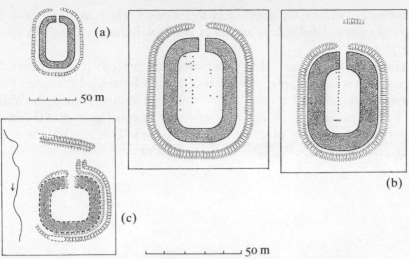

FIGURE 4.4   *Fortlets of the first Antonine occupation: a) Milton;*
b) Durisdeer; c) Redshaw Burn (not aligned to North).

contained sufficient accommodation for a full century of eighty men (Breeze
1974, 144) (fig.1.7), which we may surmise to have been the intended
garrison of most of the larger posts. The troops were probably provided from
the units stationed at Birrens, which appears to have held less than the full
complement of a milliary unit, and at Crawford in upper Clydesdale (Maxwell
1977, 29). The latter fort was capable of holding only half the strength of a
quingenary regiment – a similar situation had existed there in the Flavian
period – but the presence of a full-scale headquarters building in the Antonine
period suggests that it then served as the headquarters of the unit, possibly a
part-mounted regiment (fig.4.3) (Maxwell 1972, 178). Excavation of the
small fort at Raeburnfoot, which guarded the road leading through the uplands
from Newstead direct to Annandale, failed to identify the nature of the garrison
of that site (Robertson 1962), but consideration of the irregular layout, small
size and the character of the buildings would lead one to believe that here, too,
was stationed a vexillation of an auxiliary unit charged with some kind of
surveillance. However, further west at Glenlochar on the River Dee, although
the identity of the garrison is also unknown, the large size of the fort (8·3 acres:
3·4 ha) is adequate to contain at least a milliary regiment or even a dual
contingent. In general, however, the south-west is characterised by a pre-
ponderance of smaller installations whose dispositions, sizes and relationship
to the larger forts, both physically and in terms of presumed organisation,
betray a special preoccupation with controlling the movement of native popula-
tions in the area. The efficiency of this comprehensive system of watch and
ward was no doubt materially improved by its combination with a series of

watch-towers, occasionally doubling as signal-posts, which may have been a feature of such isolated upland sectors as Beattock Summit (Maxwell 1976) (fig.1.7).

However, if adequate advance warning and protection from external foes, together with stringent supervision of occupied rearward areas, was the firm foundation on which the new Antonine edifice was to be raised, the Wall itself was the *raison d'être*; it would be strange if an equal amount of thought had not been given to its planning and construction. That this was the case will become apparent in the following two chapters.

V. THE ANATOMY OF THE WALL

In classical literature (SHA Antoninus Pius v) the Antonine frontier is referred to as a *'murus caespiticius'* – a turf wall; the Distance Slabs, which record the completion of sections of the construction (see below p.113ff), refer to it as the *opus valli* or 'work of the wall'. But for the average visitor the term 'wall' is misleading, for it leads to the expectation of a stone edifice like Hadrian's Wall, whereas the turf rampart of the Antonine Wall rarely survives in a form readily recognisable as a mural barrier.

Visually, the most impressive structural element of the Antonine frontier at the present time is the ditch. In places such as Watling Lodge or Easter Dullatur it still presents an imposing obstacle some 40 ft (12·2 m) wide and 12 ft (3·66 m) deep. The ditch was, like most Roman military ditches, V-shaped in profile, the scarp and counter-scarp sloping up at an angle of approximately 30° to the vertical (Glasgow Archaeological Society 1899, 136) (fig.5.1). In places along its length there are indications of a square cleaning-channel at the bottom (Macdonald 1934, 90), but too few complete sections have been cut through the infilled ditch to be certain that this was a consistent feature. Also occasionally noted are stones demarcating the top edge of the scarp and/or counterscarp (Glasgow Archaeological Society 1899, 104 and 112). The precise function and frequency of these stones is uncertain, but if they served to consolidate the ditch edge, they might only be present where the subsoil was less stable; more probably they served as an occasional revetment to the inner edge of the upcast mound.

Although often taken as the norm (Robertson 1973, 13), the dimensions of the ditch noted above were by no means always adhered to. The recorded width varies from as little as 14 ft (4·3 m) on Croy Hill to over 48 ft (14·6 m) on Bar Hill, and as much as 68 ft (20·7 m) in Callendar Park, with corres-

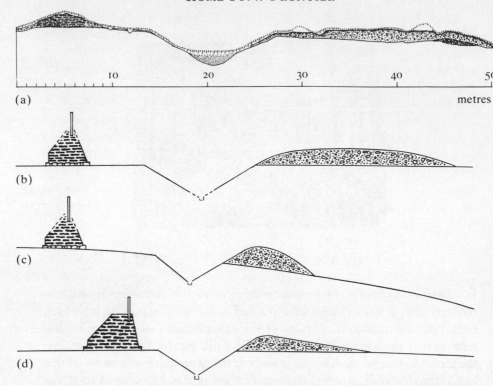

10   20   30   40   50

(a)   metres

(b)

(c)

(d)

FIGURE 5.1   *Sections through turf-built frontier: a) the Antonine Wall at Tentfield as excavated; b) and c) hypothetical reconstructions of the Antonine Wall where the upcast mound is either spread or heaped; d) hypothetical reconstruction of Hadrian's Turf Wall.*

ponding variations in depth. With the exception of Croy Hill, where the narrowness of the ditch can be accounted for by the particular hardness of the rock and the strong naturally defensive position, the central sector of the Wall from Falkirk to Kirkintilloch exhibits ditch dimensions approximating to the accepted norm (Keppie 1974, 156–8). To the west of that sector a number of sections averaging 20–25 ft (6·1–7·6 m) are recorded, while to the east the evidence is both more limited and less consistent. A localised reduction in ditch width could be explained in various ways; thus geological factors might be cited on Croy Hill, where basalt outcrops are quite numerous, or tactical ones at Balmuildy, where the combination of the river and the siting of a primary fort might be thought quite adequate defences in themselves. On the other hand, the presence of a second ditch to the north of the Antonine ditch at Duntocher implies the need for additional defensive capability in front of the fort there. Again the factors may be of a con-

76

structional nature, appearing, for example, as discontinuities between the stints of different work-gangs. The consistently slighter dimensions at the western end of the Wall may well be the result of the need to expedite building operations which had been delayed by laborious ditch-cutting through the solid basalt on Croy Hill and further disrupted by both changes in the original plan and the building of additional forts (see chapter 6).

The material dug from the ditch was not, for the most part, used to construct the rampart behind it, for this would have produced a relatively unstable structure, unless, that is, elaborate precautions had been taken to revet it. Instead, the soil was thrown up on the northern lip to form what is known as the outer or upcast mound. Early investigation suggested that the mound took two main forms: where there was only a slight fall of ground from north to south across the ditch, the upcast was spread out to form a broad bank with a relatively flat top, but where there was an appreciable fall, it was piled up in a crest to add considerable height to the counterscarp (Glasgow Archaeological Society 1899, 139). The former case is more common (fig.5.1), but impressive examples of the latter may still be seen at Watling Lodge or in places on Croy Hill (pl.5.1). In the latter sector the outer mound has survived better than the Antonine Rampart itself. The explanation for this phenomenon is straightforward enough: the Wall was built of turf which has long since become compacted or been eroded away, while the upcast from the ditch is largely made up of rock rubble. It was evidently this situation which allowed the eighteenth-century antiquary Alexander Gordon to walk half way along the Wall before he realised that the curtain was in fact represented by the slight bank on the south of the ditch. Even today, after a further 250 years of denudation by man and nature, the outer mound still bulks significantly larger to the eye, occasionally eclipsing the ditch itself as the most conspicuous surviving trace of the Antonine frontier. Nonetheless, whether on Croy Hill or on other stretches, the height of the outer mound does raise the question of its effect on the function of the Wall as a military barrier (see below pp.162–3).

To the south of the ditch stood the rampart or turf wall. The open space between the two, called the *berm*, was seldom less than 20 ft (6·1 m) and quite often 25–30 ft (7·6–9·1 m) or even more. On the summit of Croy Hill, for example, the rampart climbs to the crest of the precipitous uppermost slope while the ditch follows the contour round its base, with the result that the berm in these parts reaches a maximum width of 116 ft (35·4 m). The width of the berm provided between the rampart and inner ditch of most turf and timber forts is less than 10 ft (3·0 m), often much less, so that some explanation of its magnitude on the Antonine Wall seems necessary. Keppie has recently suggested that, since the 20 ft (6·1 m) berm appears to be closely

a

b

PLATE 5.1   *The Antonine Wall across Croy Hill, from the air:*
a) following line of cliffs to the West of the fort; b) on the lower
eastern slopes, showing different forms of outer mound.

Please note that parts a and b of Plate 5.1 have been transposed.

associated with the wide (40 ft, 12·2 m) ditch, the broader berm could have been the direct result of the decrease in ditch width, since the central line of the latter may have already been surveyed, and hence fixed at a standard interval from the centre of the rampart (1974, 162). The available data provides broad support for this thesis, but, even allowing that the situation on Croy Hill is exceptional, there are still too many variations in berm width, even when associated with the full-size ditch, to make it likely that this is the explanation in every case. The compilers of the Antonine Wall Report considered it possible that the berm width allowed a sentry on top of the Wall a direct line of sight to the bottom of the ditch, although they recognised that there were objections to this theory (Glasgow Archaeological Society 1899, 132–4). A similar argument has been applied to the stone-built sector of Hadrian's Wall, where the berm width is similar but the ditch scarp steeper, to predict the original height of the curtain (Brewis 1927). Certainly, if one takes the average or normal measurements from the Antonine Wall, assuming the angle of the ditch scarp to have been 30° and the berm width about 20 ft (6·1 m), the resulting estimate of wall height, 10 ft (3 m), appears perfectly reasonable. However, the variations in berm width mentioned above are such as to cast doubt on this interpretation, and the calculations are not applicable to the turf sector of Hadrian's Wall, where the berm was normally only 6 ft (1·8 m) wide. Furthermore, it is doubtful whether either Wall ever functioned in such a way as to require this capability (see below p.83). Questions of structural stability may be more apposite. For example, on Hadrian's turf Wall the north wall of turret 54A collapsed into the ditch and had to be rebuilt further back (Simpson *et al.* 1934), and although the rampart of the Antonine Wall was not significantly more massive than that of a normal fort, the disturbance of the subsoil for the ditch was considerably greater. However, as it is generally accepted that a broad berm constitutes a weakness in a defensive system, its presence on the Antonine frontier must affect our interpretation of the function of the *limes* as a whole (see below pp.162–3).

The Wall itself was built mainly of cut turf blocks as was customary in the construction of fort ramparts in Britain during the first century, as well as in the Antonine period (fig.5.1). It should certainly not be assumed, on the basis of a comparison with Hadrian's Wall, that a turf rampart was necessarily intended as a temporary measure. It was the construction of Hadrian's Wall in stone which was the 'exception' (Breeze and Dobson 1976a, 85), and indeed a considerable portion of even that frontier was originally built in turf. After all, turf was a speedier rampart-building material than stone, both in terms of handling and availability, and it was probably this factor, rather than the question of permanence, which determined the materials employed in each case. Furthermore, it is just possible that the original intention may have been to build the Antonine Wall in stone, for the primary fort at Balmuildy was enclosed by a curtain of masonry, with stone wing-walls projecting from the northern angles as if in anticipation of their eventual junction with a stone barrier.

Sections cut through the Wall at various points along its length have shown some variation in its fabric and structure. A local shortage of suitable turf probably accounts for those instances where the interior of the rampart is composed of earth, and turf or clay is used for revetments at the front and rear, although attempts have been made to correlate the variations with the activities of different legionary work parties (see below p.131). This type of construction has been noted in a number of sections to the east of Watling Lodge (Keppie 1974, 156–7 and 1976, 77–8). Such a method of rampart construction is paralleled elsewhere, although the width of the cheeks normally represents a greater percentage of the rampart thickness than the 18 inches to just over 3 ft (c.0·5–1 m) recorded on the Antonine Wall (Jones 1975, 78–81). Compared with other turf- or clay-built ramparts, the Antonine Wall is rather narrow, being only 14–16 ft (4·3–4·9 m) wide at the base as opposed to the norm of 18–20 ft (5·5–6·1 m) (Jones 1975, 70–1). This may well indicate a deliberate attempt to reduce the volume of material utilised, possibly a result of experience gained in the building of the turf sector of Hadrian's Wall, whose width falls within the norm. Now, a reduction in width ought logically to have led to a decrease in height, but this may have been avoided by the provision of a regular stone base – a structural innovation which imparted additional stability to the fabric. Quite often, the stone foundation is all that survives to indicate the line of the Wall; it was made of large irregularly-shaped cobbles with a kerb of roughly-faced or hammer-dressed stones to front and rear (pl.6.7). Less elaborate forms of foundation, either cobbles or timber strapping, are encountered with some frequency beneath fort ramparts, though they do not always run the whole width (Jones 1975, 74). The stone base of the Antonine Wall served a further important function: it facilitated the regular provision of culverts which were constructed of roughly-squared stones, floored and covered with larger slabs. These may have occurred at regular intervals, perhaps every 50–60 ft (15–18·5 m), as at Bantaskin (Keppie 1976, 74–5), although shorter intervals are recorded, as at Wilderness West (Hanson and Maxwell 1982) (fig.5.6). Since the Wall would have acted as a barrier to natural surface drainage, such culverts served to prevent a build-up of water which might at best have been inconvenient, or at worst structurally dangerous. Indeed, at some points there is evidence of probable repairs to the Wall and although the reason for it is uncertain, it is possible that in many cases the rear face of the Wall had collapsed because of the presence of standing water (Keppie 1976, 75–6; Hanson and Maxwell 1982). It is noteworthy that when the turf sector of Hadrian's Wall was replaced in stone in the later Hadrianic period, the opportunity was taken to insert culverts at 20 ft (6.1 m) intervals.

Structural stability could also be affected by sharp changes in ground contour; thus where the Wall was required to negotiate an appreciable slope, as in Bearsden cemetery, the stone base was stepped like a massive staircase, so as to counter any tendency to subsidence, though whether there was a corresponding step in the superstructure is unknown. Similarly, at the north-east corner of the plateau at Cadder, where the brow traversed by the Wall sloped steeply down from south to north, the base was laid on an artificial terrace and in places even raised to a height of five courses (Clarke 1933, 10); less elaborate terracing is recorded at sundry other places.

Obviously a turf wall cannot rise vertically to the heights attained by a stone one, for its faces need to be battered to maintain stability, though less so than those of a rampart of loose earth. Unfortunately, nowhere along its length does the Wall survive to a height greater than 5 or 6 ft (1·5–1·8 m), and usually it is considerably less. Moreover, the effects of compaction and slumping are likely to have distorted the original profile in most cases. Consequently there are few sections recorded where the angle of batter can be reliably estimated, and none of these provides evidence for the front face. Three sections cut through the Wall across Croy Hill and Bar Hill by the Glasgow Archaeological Society (1899, 76, 84 and 86) indicated angles of between 58° and 83·5° for the south face of the rampart, but only at the first of these did it survive much above 3 ft (0·9 m) in height. The batter of the inner face of ramparts in Wall forts has been recovered at only two sites, Bar Hill and Rough Castle, where an angle of 76–8° is indicated (Macdonald and Park 1906, 424; MacIvor *et al.* 1980, 234). These disparate figures can be reconciled to some extent by a closer examination of the best surviving recorded example on Croy Hill: although the average angle of slope in the 5 ft (1·5 m) of rampart still standing was 63·5°, it is clear from the published photograph that the first 3 ft or so (*c.*1 m) rose almost vertically, beyond which the slope became more gentle. Moreover, the effects of slumping are likely to have been minimal, since the rear face had been rapidly incorporated within an expansion. Thus, since the very steep angles recorded seem to relate only to the first few feet above the base, it seems reasonable to assume that the profile at Croy Hill accurately reflects the original angle.

Examples of fort ramparts with a vertical lower portion in the rear face have been recorded at Inveresk, Strageath, Fendoch and Chester, though there is always the possibility that this is the result of the insertion of an oven or of some other feature cut into the back of the rampart, as at Caerleon. Hadrian's turf Wall provides a safer analogy, for it, too, shows a short almost vertical rear face immediately above a basal offset (Simpson *et al.* 1935, 222 and fig.3). Above that it is generally assumed that the slope was more gentle, and such profiles have actually been recorded at Chester and Tomen-y-mur. Evidence for the angle of the front face is even less common. An angle of 67° was observed in the Flavian rampart at Strageath, where the addition of a new face in the Antonine period seems to have protected the original profile (Frere 1979, 37), though 75° is assumed at Fendoch, Chester and on Hadrian's Turf Wall. With the data then available, assuming the need for a walkway 6 ft (1·8 m) wide on top of the rampart and a maximum slope of 1:2·5 for the front batter, the compilers of the Antonine Wall Report suggested a rampart height of 10 ft (3 m) (GAS 1899, 130). On the basis of the wider evidence set out above, such a conclusion still appears to be acceptable.

An alternative method of calculating the height of the rampart is to count the maximum number of turf lines recorded in sections cut through well-preserved portions of the Wall (fig.5.1) and multiply by their estimated original thickness. This gives a figure which must be decreased to allow for compaction during construction but increased to allow for later destruction and wear. Some 19 turf lines were recorded in each of three sections cut by the Glasgow Archaeological Society (1899, 76, 89 and 119), while up to 22 have been noted more recently (Steer 1957 fig.3). The regulation thickness for turf was, according to Vegetius (11, 8), 6 inches (0·15 m). The writers of the Antonine Wall Report considered this unattainable with Scottish turf and compromised at 5 inches (0·13 m), although it is clear from some sections that, even after compaction over many years, the vertical distance between decayed turf-lines allows acceptance of the regulation figure in principle. Thus the maximum number of layers recorded would indicate a minimum height of 11 ft (3·4 m). While some settlement would have occurred during the construction process, it is highly unlikely that it would have been of the order of 30–40 per cent implied by Keppie (1976, 77). Even after three years the reconstructed rampart at the Lunt near Coventry had settled only marginally (Hobley 1974, 79). At the fort of Crawford, on the other hand, where it was possible to observe the effect of gradual compaction on the ten layers of turf that underpinned the Antonine 11 rampart, the turf blocks appeared to have been reduced by as much as 37 per cent in thickness, but this, of course, was the result of more than 1800 years of pressure and decay (Maxwell 1972, 153 and fig.5). The original height of the turf stack being about 5 ft (1·5 m), the thickness of each sod could be seen to have approximated to the Vegetian norm. Given that the material in question had been subjected, as a foundation, to more pressure than would the actual fabric of a rampart, and allowing for the fact that it was a rather peaty turf, different in character to that used on the Antonine Wall, the correspondence between the thickness of each turf and that of the average layer in a Wall section – 3·8 inches as against 3 inches (9·5:7·6 cm) – is such as to inspire confidence that the rampart was at least 10 ft (3 m) in height. Indeed, the fact that there is evidence of a wide disparity in the recorded thickness of turf layers within the Antonine rampart suggests that in some cases the sods may have been laid grass-to-grass or earth-to-earth,

82

thus leading to an underestimate of the number of laminae, and hence of the original height. Furthermore, there is, of course, no way of ascertaining whether the uppermost surviving layer of turves was ever the actual summit of the curtain.

This uncertainty leads on to a further consideration. All previous writers have assumed that the rampart was 6 ft (1·8 m) wide at the top to allow for a walkway, but no positive archaeological evidence exists for any timber super-structure, which would have been a necessary element in such a feature. If it existed, we must assume either that archaeologists have failed to recognise the evidence of post-holes in the sections dug, or that such post-holes did not penetrate to the level at which the Wall now survives. If the latter is the case, then the top of the Wall must have been appreciably higher than the estimates given above to allow for the post-settings to have disappeared through wear. Thus an original height to the rampart walk of as much as 13 ft (4 m) may have to be postulated, which is more or less in accord with that estimated for the turf wall of Hadrian. Such a height, however, is simply not compatible with the calculations based on rampart batter. We are thus faced with a serious dilemma, one that might compel us to question the validity of the data upon which our assumptions have hitherto been based, were it not that there is yet another possibility to be explored: that the Wall top was never intended to be patrolled or used as a fighting platform (see below pp.162–3). The Hadrianic German 'wall' cannot have been so used, for it consisted merely of a timber palisade, while doubts have been expressed recently about the presence of such patrols even on Hadrian's Wall (Breeze and Dobson 1976a, 39). If one assumes that a broad rampart walk was not in fact required, it is possible that, given the presumed batter, the curtain rose to a height of 13 ft (4 m), but was still sufficiently wide at the top for the emplacement of whatever form of timber superstructure was deemed necessary to make the Wall an effective barrier (fig.5.1). Further progress in this matter is unlikely to occur without extensive and minute examination of the uppermost levels of the best preserved sectors of the rampart.

The third linear element in the frontier was the Military Way, the road which ran roughly parallel to the Wall, generally between 50 and 150 ft (15–45 m) to the south of it, all along its length. Such roads had always been an integral part of any frontier system and served to provide a swift and easy means of communication or transport along the frontier; it is noteworthy that on the eventual abandonment of the Antonine Wall a lateral link-road was one of the first structural additions to the refurbished Hadrian's Wall. Sections through the Military Way indicate that it was of standard construction, some 16–18 ft (4·9–5·5 m) wide with a pronounced camber and drainage ditches on either side. Traces of its camber can still be seen in sectors to the west of the fort at

83

Rough Castle and in Seabegs Wood. The Military Way seems to have formed the *via principalis* of all the forts bar three (Duntocher, Cadder and Bar Hill), which raises the question of how it fits into the constructional sequence of the Wall (see below p.133). By-pass roads seem to have been provided at all the forts to allow long-distance travellers a speedier journey without the necessity of calling at every fort en route.

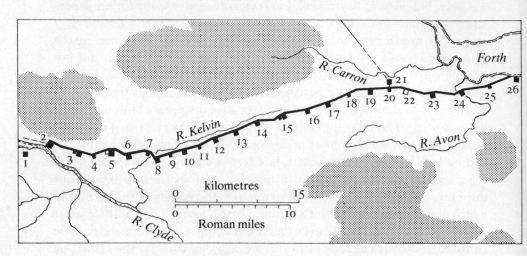

FIGURE 5.2   *The Antonine Wall with its forts and fortlets: 1 Bishopton, 2 Old Kilpatrick, 3 Duntocher fort and fortlet, 4 Cleddans fortlet, 5 Castlehill fort and fortlet, 6 Bearsden, 7 Summerston fortlet, 8 Balmuildy, 9 Wilderness Plantation fortlet, 10 Cadder, 11 Glasgow Bridge fortlet, 12 Kirkintilloch, 13 Auchendavy, 14 Bar Hill, 15 Croy Hill fort and fortlet, 16 Westerwood, 17 Castlecary, 18 Seabegs fortlet, 19 Rough Castle, 20 Watling Lodge fortlet, 21 Camelon, 22 Falkirk, 23 Mumrills, 24 Inveravon, 25 Kinneil fortlet, 26 Carriden.*

The Wall and its accompanying ditch and road ran from Bridgeness on the Forth to Old Kilpatrick on the Clyde, a distance of a little over 37 miles (40·5 Roman miles) (fig.5.2). The route which it followed is of obvious strategic significance, as was recognised over 60 years before by Agricola (see above p.39), its importance being further reflected in its proximity to modern arteries of east-west communications: the Forth-Clyde canal closely follows the line of the Antonine Wall for some 20 miles, the Glasgow to Edinburgh railway for rather less than half that distance. Its approximate position, then, was dictated by geography. Its exact location was also determined to a large extent by local topography. For tactical reasons the most desirable location was on or above a north-facing slope with a wide field of view. Thus for most of its course, the Wall follows the south side of the Kelvin and Carron valleys, enjoying an excellent view northwards to the Campsie Fells and the Kilsyth Hills; however, where it crosses the Kelvin, west of Balmuildy, the more broken terrain on the north side of the river and the proximity of the Kilpatrick Hills present considerable problems. Yet, nowhere along its length are there such outstanding geological features as the crags which dominate the central sector of Hadrian's Wall, although the conspicuous raised beach in the area of Kinneil and the prominent basalt masses of Croy and Bar Hill are used to advantage. Hardly surprisingly, then, the line is not straight. Indeed, even when allowance is made for a difference of terrain, comparison with Hadrian's Wall reveals that the northern barrier is significantly more sinuous in its course – doubtless the result of a more flexible approach to its design. Paradoxically, however, this same flexibility seems occasionally to have worked to its disadvantage as a defensible line (see below p.162f). Such tactical considerations apart, the Wall manifests throughout its length the hand of the Roman military planner, engineered from high point to high point like a Roman road and capable of either holding to prolonged alignments or, as in the Summerston salient, diverging abruptly from the established line.

In its course the Wall had to negotiate two rivers, the Kelvin and the Avon, as well as several smaller streams. The latter would have presented no particular problems, being dealt with presumably by the provision of rather larger culverts in the Wall base, but there are questions about the former which remain unanswered. Clearly, a bridge or ford must have been provided for the Military Way so as not to hinder communications. The former may have been provided at the crossing of the Kelvin, where stonework and timber were discovered in dredging the river near Balmuildy (Davidson 1952), although recent dendrochronological analysis of the timber indicates a medieval date; that a ford is a feasible alternative is suggested by Maitland (1757, 179) who records that the river was at one time actually forded in the vicinity of the fort. Possible evidence of a bridge across the river Avon is provided by a scatter of worked stones at an appropriate point on the river bed (DES 1973, 58), although this could also represent the remains of a built ford. Both crossings seem to have been guarded by forts. What is less certain is whether the Wall itself also crossed the river on some sort of bridge, or merely stopped at each bank. The former is assumed in the case of Hadrian's Wall (Bruce 1978, 39–40), the latter in the case of the Antonine Wall (Robertson 1979, 32 and 82). Clearly, it would have been important that some form of barrier be provided to prevent unwanted access through the Wall by river, though the continuation of a turf wall across a bridge is rather more difficult to envisage than the continuation of a stone one as an extension of the bridge parapet. It may well be, as Davidson originally suggested (1952, 93), that the reason for the close proximity of the Military Way to the rear of the Wall as it approaches

85

the river at Balmuildy was that it enabled the postulated bridge effectively to cover the gap in the barrier.

The sites of fifteen forts are known along the line of the Wall. There seems to have been no terminal station at the eastern end, its place being taken by the fort at Carriden situated on the coast just under one mile (1·6 km) to the south-east. The spacing between the forts (see Table 5.1), suggests that it was the intention to dispose them at approximately 2–3 mile intervals, in which case there are still forts to find at Kinneil, between Carriden and Inveravon, and at Seabegs, between Rough Castle and Castlecary, although repeated investigation has failed to locate the latter. There is considerable variation in the size of these forts (figs 5.3 and 4 and Table 5.1), from Mumrills at one extreme to tiny Duntocher, which is hardly worthy of the appellation. It is also clear from those sites where relevant excavation has taken place that the structural and probably, therefore, the chronological relationship between fort and Wall varied: some can be shown to be earlier, others later, others roughly contemporary. These differences were long considered to represent evidence of either a more flexible response to local conditions or merely the result of the varying speed of the construction teams involved (Robertson 1973, 22–3 and 27). Only recently has the additional significance become apparent (see chapter 6).

    With the exception of Carriden, already noted, and Bar Hill situated some 120 ft (36 m) to the rear, the Antonine Wall formed one side of each fort (figures 5.3 and 4), although in the case of Old Kilpatrick, Duntocher, Balmuildy and Castlecary it would be more correct to say that one side of their defensive perimeter was incorporated in the running barrier. There are no known examples of forts projecting north of the Wall line as occur commonly on Hadrian's Wall, and indeed it is clear from the later forts at Greatchesters and Carrawburgh that this structural relationship was already tactically out of fashion by the late 130s. The majority of the forts have turf ramparts on a stone base similar in construction to the Antonine Wall itself, although varying in basal width from c.12–20 ft (3·7–6·1 m) (Table 5.1). Balmuildy and Castlecary are the only two forts with a stone curtain wall. The free-standing corners of the known forts are rounded in the typical 'playing-card' shape, but evidence of corner towers has been recovered from only the two stone-walled examples and possibly Old Kilpatrick. Towers might be expected in the northern corners, to supplement the Wall defences, but there is as yet no evidence of these. All of the forts were also defended by a ditch or ditches on the three sides not covered by the Antonine ditch itself, even on the side where an annexe was appended, with the exception of Bearsden and Duntocher (figs 5.3 and 4). Variation in the number of ditches was presumably dictated by local topography or anticipated hostility and additional ditches are known to the north of the forts at Old Kilpatrick and Duntocher. In contrast, the

TABLE 5.1 *Forts*

Site	Area acres	ha	Annexe position	Annexe area acres	ha	Rampart width ft	m	Spacing in Roman miles
Carriden	4	1·6	—	—	—	—	—	
Inveravon	—	—	—	—	—	—	—	5·3
Mumrills	6·5	2·6	W	4·2	1·7	13	4	2·4
Falkirk	—	—	—	—	—	—	—	2
Rough Castle	1·0	0·4	E	1·9–1·4	0·8–0·6	20	6	3·3
Castlecary	3·5	1·4	E	2·8	1·1	8 (stone)	2·4	3·9
Westerwood	2	0·8	—	—	—	16	4·9	2·1
Croy Hill	1·5	0·6	—	—	—	20	6	2
Bar Hill	3·2	1·3	—	—	—	12	3·7	1·9
Auchendavy	c.2·8	1·1	—	—	—	—	—	2·2
Kirkintilloch	—	—	—	—	—	—	—	2·0
Cadder	2·8	1·1	S and E	c.7	2·8	15·5	4·7	2·6
Balmuildy	4	1·6	E	1·8	0·7	7·5 (stone)	2·3	2·5
Bearsden	2·4	0·9	E	1·2	0·5	14	4·3	3
Castlehill	c.2·6	1	—	—	—	—	—	1·6
Duntocher	0·5	0·2	W	0·8	0·3	13	4	2·1
Old Kilpatrick	4·2	1·7	—	—	—	14·5	4·4	2·5

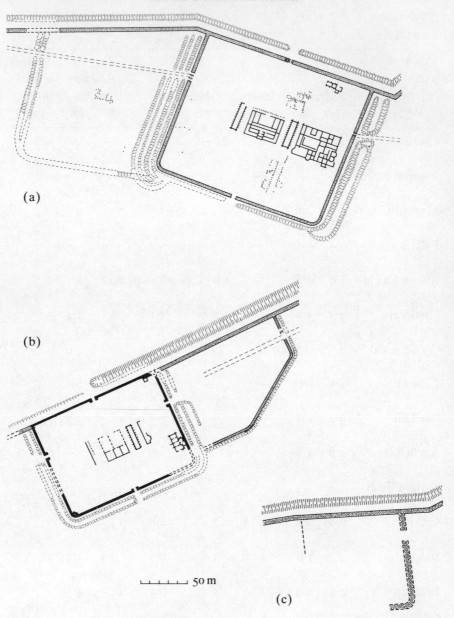

(a)

(b)

(c)

⊢ ⊣ 50 m

Antonine Wall ditch is reduced in width opposite the north front of at least three of the forts, Balmuildy, Castlecary and Mumrills. As far as can be ascertained, causeways through the Antonine ditch were left at all of the 'primary' forts, and also at Rough Castle and Cadder (see below p.106f). The break in the ditch at Croy Hill seems too far to the east of the fort to have been left merely for access, and may, therefore, represent the legion's unwillingness

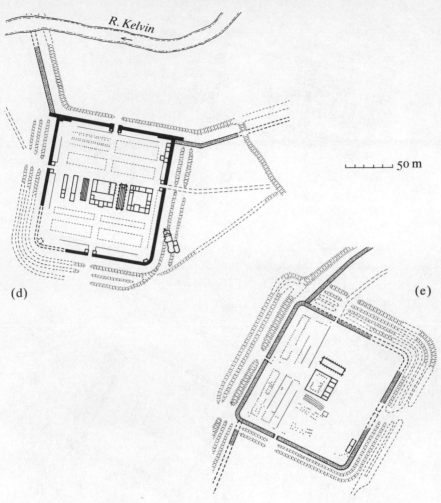

(d)

(e)

R. Kelvin

⌐⌐⌐⌐⌐ 50 m

FIGURE 5.3   Comparative plans of primary forts on the Antonine Wall:
a) Mumrills; b) Castlecary; c) Auchendavy; d) Balmuildy;
e) Old Kilpatrick.

to complete the ditch through solid rock, although, as Maitland observed
(1757, 175f), it is a remarkable lapse in view of their obvious persistence in the
immediately vicinity. Gaps through the other ditches were provided at all
forts, but not necessarily for all the gates. For example, the ditches do not
appear to have been interrupted at the south gates of Rough Castle, Westerwood and Croy Hill, or at the west gates of Bar Hill and Cadder, at least, not in
the first occupation of those sites (fig.5.4).

All the forts, with the exception of the smallest at Duntocher, had a gate
in each side. These were in every case simple single entrances, generally

89

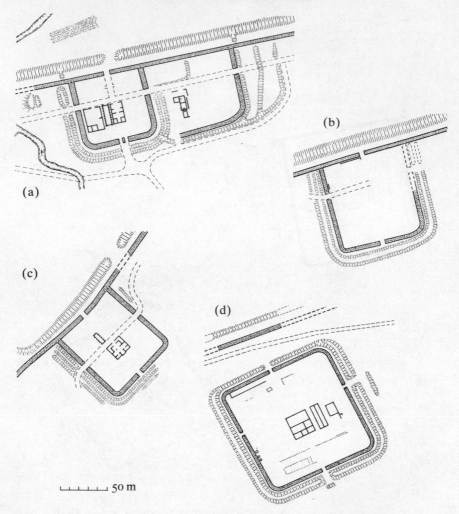

(a)

(b)

(c)

(d)

└┴┴┴┴┘ 50 m

FIGURE 5.4   *Comparative plans of secondary forts on the Antonine Wall:*
a) Rough Castle ; b) Westerwood ; c) Croy Hill; d) Bar Hill,
e) Cadder ; f) Bearsden ; g) Castlehill ; h) Duntocher.

without guard-chambers. Definite evidence of the latter has been found only
in the stone gate-towers at Balmuildy, although similar structures in timber
may be indicated by the post-holes at one side of the entrance behind the
rampart at Cadder, Old Kilpatrick and possibly Mumrills. With the exception
of the two stone-walled forts, and the strange foundations for the west gate at
Mumrills, the gateways were defined by post-holes revetting the sides of the
rampart. Whether these carried a tower that rose above the rampart, or merely
a bridge across the top of the entrance gap, is impossible to say. The former is

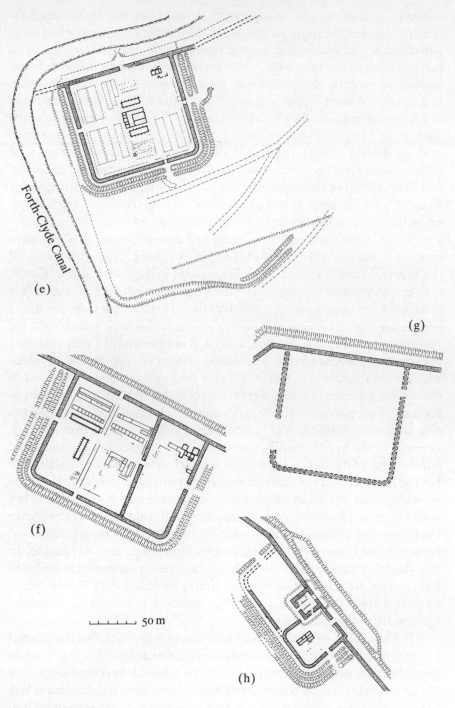

Forth-Clyde Canal

(e)

(g)

(f)

⊢ ⊣ ⊣ ⊣ ⊣ ⊣ 50 m

(h)

normally assumed on the analogy with standard practice in Roman fort-construction, but the apparent structural weakness of these gates when compared with first-century examples gives ground for doubt (Hanson 1982). The turf ramparts of the forts were presumably surmounted by a walkway and wooden breastwork, the stone walls by a crenellated parapet to facilitate defence should it ever have been necessary. That such provision was made in Roman defences is shown by its depiction on Trajan's Column (Cichorius 1900, scene XXXII), although there is little or no independent archaeological evidence for its existence on either Wall. A desire to increase the security of such a walkway may account for the later thickening of the rampart at Cadder and Duntocher, but the apparent evidence of similar rampart thickening at Rough Castle has been shown by more recent excavation to have been an erroneous interpretation (MacIvor et al. 1980, 236–7).

Seven of the excavated forts possessed annexes, most of which were attached to the east side of the forts (Table 5.1) (figs 5.3 and 4). The size of the annexe is usually at least half as large as or, in the case of Rough Castle, Cadder and Duntocher, even larger than the fort itself. In no instance is it certain how the annexe rampart related to that of the fort, but there is a strong impression that they were secondary, although this may reflect only the sequence of primary construction, and need not necessarily imply that they originated in different phases. This would seem to be supported at Bearsden where it has recently been recognised that the fort was originally planned to cover some 3·5 acres (1·6 ha), but then provided with a dividing rampart to separate off the eastern third to form an annexe before much, if any, construction of internal buildings had been undertaken (information from Dr D. J. Breeze). Similarly, at Mumrills, the annexe ditch apparently cut through the outer ditches of the fort on the west side (Steer 1961, 99 note 1). In all cases bar two the ditches of the fort continue along the side to which the annexe is appended, thus physically emphasising its separateness from the fort; but at Castlecary and Balmuildy, certain structures within the annexe are built over the intervening ditches. Precisely what function these enclosures performed is unclear (see below p.187f), as excavation within them has been limited. In four cases they enclose the fort bath-house, and recent excavation at Bearsden has provided fragmentary evidence of timber buildings also. Similar minor structures are doubtless represented by scattered post-holes at Mumrills, Cadder, Balmuildy and Duntocher.

It is inevitable, given the considerable divergence of size, that the internal layout of Antonine Wall forts would also have differed (figs 5.3 and 4). Certain generalisations, however, can be made. The buildings of the central range were almost invariably of stone construction. Even at Bearsden, which seems to lack both *principia* and *praetorium* of standard design, the granaries were built in stone, and at Duntocher, which is too small to have contained the normal range of structures, there is a small stone building in the centre. The only exceptions appear to occur at Mumrills, Cadder and Old Kilpatrick: at the first, the original timber *praetorium* was re-built in stone; at the second, a stone *praetorium* was replaced by a timber one, and at the third, one of the fort's two granaries was of timber from the beginning and never subsequently altered. The only other stone-built structures within the forts were the occasional internal bath-houses as at Mumrills, Castlecary, Bar Hill, Cadder and Balmuildy. Because the vast majority of the excavations within forts took place at least fifty years ago, the record of stone structures, which were more easily identified, is rather better than that of timber ones. Yet these, which include the barracks, stables and store-buildings, were the very structures which, in the absence of epigraphic evidence, might supply information about the nature of the garrison. Their form and disposition, and their significance in elucidating the history and purpose of each site will be discussed in chapters 8 and 9. Most of the forts, with the exception of Bearsden and possibly Rough Castle, demonstrate two structural periods in their internal buildings. The details and significance of this will be considered in chapter 7.

The anatomy of the wall also included a number of smaller fortifications, known as fortlets, one of which has long been known (Christison and Buchanan 1901, 337), while three more were discovered shortly after the last war as a result of either excavation (Robertson 1957a) or aerial reconnaissance (St Joseph 1951, 61 and 1955, 86). The significance of these discoveries, however, was not fully realised until the early 1970s (Gillam 1975), eventually being confirmed by fieldwork and excavation in 1977 and thereafter (Hanson 1979; Keppie 1980a) (see below p.108f). The sequence is not yet fully understood, but it seems likely that fortlets occurred at regular intervals, possibly about one Roman mile. Some nine fortlets are known at present (fig.5.5). The presence of others at Rough Castle, Castlehill and Bar Hill has also been suggested (see below p.121f), and more may be discovered in the immediate future as a result of ongoing survey (see Table 6.4). As yet, however, only three of the fortlets, at Wilderness Plantation, Duntocher and Kinneil, have undergone intensive excavation. In all three cases the remarkable similarity to the milecastles on Hadrian's turf wall was clear. All the fortlets where sufficient evidence is available have been identified as contemporary with or earlier than the building of the Wall. Their ramparts were built of turf on a cobble base which was similar to, though slightly narrower than that of the Antonine Wall (Table 5.2), and their southern free-standing corners are usually thought to have been rounded like the forts: this has been proved by excavation only at Seabegs and Croy Hill, although those of the fortlet at Duntocher may have been square (Robertson 1957a, 17).

From their axial dimensions, at least two different types of fortlet are evident (Table 5.2). The difference lies in the length of their north-south axis,

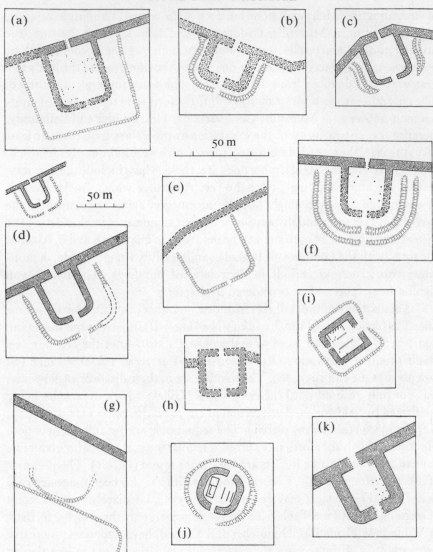

FIGURE 5.5 *Comparative plans of fortlets: a) Kinneil; b) Watling Lodge;*
c) Seabegs; d) Croy Hill; e) Glasgow Bridge; f) Wilderness
Plantation; g) Summerston; h) Cleddans; i) Duntocher;
j) Outerwards; k) High House, Hadrian's Turf Wall
milecastle 50.

the east–west axis remaining constant at about 60 ft (18·2 m) internally. The
most obvious group – Seabegs, Kinneil, Croy Hill and Wilderness Plantation –
measure approximately 70 ft (21·3 m) from north to south within a rampart
which displays a remarkable consistency of width from site to site. The second

group, at present made up of only two examples, at Duntocher and Cleddans, have a much wider rampart and are almost square in plan, the north-south axis being only just over 57 ft (17·5 m) in average length. Watling Lodge may belong to the same group of short-axis fortlets, to use Hadrian's Wall terminology, or it may represent a third type, for its dimensions are not sufficiently well known to be certain. On Hadrian's Wall the variation in fortlet types is assumed to be the result of different legionary builders, and a similar interpretation of the fortlets on the Antonine Wall is probable (see chapter 6).

TABLE 5.2 *Fortlets*

| | Dimensions | | | | Number of | Rampart width | |
| | N–S | | E–W | | ditches | | |
Site	ft	m	ft	m		ft	m
Kinneil	c.70·5	21·5	c.60·7	18·5	1 or 2	10	3
Watling Lodge	c.50+	15·5	c.60·7	18·5	1	c.15	4·6
Seabegs	71·5	21·8	59	18	2	10	3
Croy Hill	72	22	60·7	18·5	1	9·5	2·9
Glasgow Bridge	98 ft (30 m) within ditch				1	—	—
Wilderness Plantation	c.65	19·5	56–9	17·4–18	2	10	3
Summerston	108 ft (33 m) within ditch				1	—	—
Duntocher	57	17·4	59	18	1	12	3·7
Cleddans	c.57·7	17·6	59	18	—	11·8–13	3·6–4

What little is known of the interior of the fortlets indicates the presence of small timber buildings, probably barracks, again rather reminiscent of the milecastles on Hadrian's Wall. Unlike the majority of the latter, however, all of the fortlets known, with the possible exception of Cleddans, where excavation was not sufficiently extensive, were surrounded by one or more ditches. Gateways centrally positioned in the north and south ramparts to allow access through the Antonine Wall are assumed as axiomatic, though they have not been investigated in all cases. Only at Kinneil, Seabegs, Wilderness Plantation and Duntocher has more than one post-hole been discovered, although only from the south gate at the latter site. The spacing between the posts (1·5–3 ft (0·46–0·91 m)) and their probable total (6 or 7) is more reminiscent of the structure of the north gate of Turf Wall milecastle 50 than of any of the fort gates already described (fig.5.5). The probability of a tower over the north gateway is thus considerably increased. Causeways across the Antonine ditch in front of these gateways might be assumed, for at least two of the milecastles on Hadrian's Wall are thus provided (Simpson *et al.* 1935; Simpson and Richmond 1935), but apart from Watling Lodge, where the Roman road issued northwards to Camelon, none are attested. Indeed, the available evidence of aerial reconnaissance and field observation suggests strongly that this solitary case is the exception rather than the rule.

An important element in all first- and second-century frontiers which appears to be lacking on the Antonine Wall is a watch-tower system. This deficiency has been noted occasionally, but no one ventured to postulate the existence of a regular series until 1975 (Gillam 1975, 55–6). Of course, the north gates of the fortlets may have formed an element in such a system, if they rose to form towers, but a closer spacing than at mile intervals would be expected for efficient surveillance. Only very recently three small enclosures abutting on the rear face of the rampart were recorded by the Royal Commission on Ancient and Historical Monuments of Scotland on aerial photographs of the sector of the Antonine Wall on either side of Wilderness Plantation fortlet (1978, 112–3, 159 and pl.13B). It was originally hoped that such structures might prove to be members of a uniform system, extending along the entire length of the Wall. At the present moment, however, after the excavation of one example, Wilderness West, it seems certain that these hopes were vain (Hanson and Maxwell 1982), for that site appears to have consisted of little more than a single ditch and rampart of relatively slight proportions enclosing an area almost 20 ft (6 m) square which contained traces of neither structures nor occupation (fig.5.6). There was no evidence, either within the enclosure or in the fabric of the adjacent stretch of rampart, of post-holes or construction trenches that could be construed as part of a stone or timber watch-tower. The slightness of its defences, especially when compared with the massiveness of the Wall against which it abutted, made it clear that, whatever its purpose, it was of a very minor character, exhibiting no clear affinities with any known category of Roman site, not even with the humble beacon-stances shortly to be considered. Practically all that could be said of the excavated example was that it had evidently formed part of the original Wall plan, being constructed at about the same time as the curtain, and may have enjoyed only a brief period of use.

At an early stage it was also believed that there was a significance in the spacing of the Wilderness Plantation enclosures and in their relationship to the nearby fortlet as well as to the fort at Balmuildy (fig.5.7). Thus the central member of the group is situated only 98 ft (30 m) short of one Roman mile from the north gate of Balmuildy, and when first identified, the two eastern-most enclosures were thought to lie a third of a Roman mile apart. However, the more precise measurements of intervals along the line of the Wall between the enclosures and the fortlet which recent excavation and ground survey have

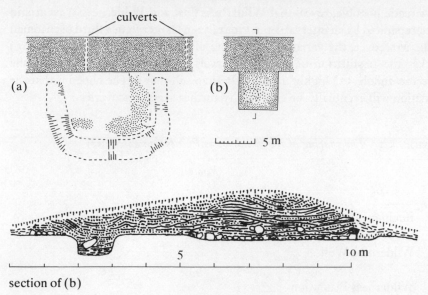

FIGURE 5.6 *Minor works on the Antonine Wall: a) Wilderness West enclosure; b) Bonnyside East expansion (not aligned to North).*

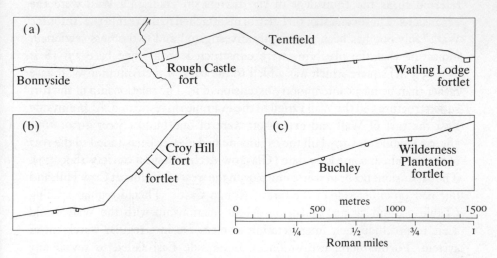

FIGURE 5.7 *The distribution of expansions (a and b) and minor enclosures (c) on the Wall.*

97

now made possible, reveal that Wilderness East and Wilderness West are, in fact, separated by an interval some 170 ft (52 m) larger than a third of a Roman mile. Moreover, the variation in spacing of the individual sites (Table 5.3) makes the postulation of regular intervals of one-sixth of a Roman mile (Breeze 1980b, 52) highly unlikely. Perhaps all that can be hoped is that the situation will eventually be clarified by further aerial discoveries.

TABLE 5.3 *The spacing of the Wilderness Plantation enclosures*

Site	m	Roman paces
Buchley		
	295	199
Wilderness West		
	285	193
Wilderness Plantation fortlet	c.260	176
Wilderness East		

Prior to the discovery of these enclosures, the elements which were also referred to as the equivalent of the turrets on Hadrian's Wall were the expansions. These consist of turf platforms attached to the rear of the Antonine Wall. Only one has been thoroughly investigated and two others sectioned, indicating that the platforms were constructed on a stone base 17–18 ft (5.2–5.5 m) square which was added to the back of the Antonine Wall base rather than being a contemporary extension of it. The relationship of the turf superstructure and the Wall varied in the examples investigated. At Bonnyside East the turf of Wall and expansion were of one build (Steer 1957, 164) (fig.5.6), while on Croy Hill the expansion had clearly been added to the rear of the curtain at some later date (Glasgow Archaeological Society 1899, 79). The expansions occur in pairs: one pair to the west of the fort at Croy Hill, and one pair on either side of the fort at Rough Castle. Their irregular spacing (Table 5.4 and fig.5.7) and inconsistent relationship with the Wall would seem to preclude their interpretation as elements in a regular watch-tower system. Furthermore, excavation at Bonnyside East failed to reveal any evidence of timbers to support a tower. The traces of burning which were there revealed, however, support Macdonald's interpretation of the expansions as signal-platforms or beacon stances (1934, 356–8). That such installations were actually employed by the Romans is admirably illustrated on the columns of both Trajan and Marcus Aurelius (Macdonald 1934, pl.lx), which further

TABLE 5.4 *The spacing of expansions*

Site	m	Roman paces
Croy West		
	135	91
Croy East		
	478	323
Croy Hill fortlet		
Bonnyside West		
	325	220
Bonnyside East		
	542	366
Rough Castle		
	734	496
Tentfield West		
	590	399
Tentfield East		
	708	478
Watling Lodge		

hint at one of the reasons for the beacons occurring in pairs: signalling by night would necessitate a strong blaze such as would be provided by a pile of logs; by day the same effect might better be achieved by a column of smoke from a hay-rick or similar material. Another suggestion is that by the use of two adjacent signalling-points more complicated messages might be transmitted. Never-theless, in the case of the first explanation one would have thought that there was no need for so wide a separation of stances either from each other or from the adjacent forts or fortlets which presumably accommodated the signallers; it must have been inconvenient and is not justified on the grounds of fire hazard. In the case of the second, it is strange that the province of Britain can furnish no other archaeological evidence for dual stances in the various signalling or surveillance systems which have so far been recognised.

In its developed form the Antonine Wall presented a major barrier to movement across the narrow Forth-Clyde isthmus. Comprising, as we have seen, a formidable ditch in front of an impressive turf-built rampart, the line was guarded at regular intervals by forts, large or small, interspersed with smaller posts and minor installations, the whole range of garrisons linked together by a broad metalled road. But as with Hadrian's Wall, simply to block off the isthmus itself would not have sufficed to check or control all movement.

PLATE 5.2   *The fortlet at Lurg Moor, Renfrewshire, from the air.*

It would have been a simple matter, especially on the west side, to outflank the Wall by sea and make a descent on the coast to its rear. Thus the frontier, though not the Wall itself, was extended to the west with a fort situated nearly 2·75 miles (4·4 km) beyond Old Kilpatrick on the opposite side of the Clyde at Bishopton. The position commanded a fine view across the Clyde estuary at a point where in Roman times there may have been a ford. The fort, which was discovered from the air (Steer 1949), was subsequently shown by excavation to have covered an area of approximately 4 acres (1·6 ha) internally and, on the basis of the finds, to have been occupied in the second century only (Taylor 1952, 87). A further 8 miles (12·9 km) to the west, again overlooking the Clyde estuary, lies a fortlet situated on the northern edge of Lurg Moor. The site is still visible as an earthwork defended by a ditch and rampart which enclose an area of 0·13 acres (0·05 ha) (pl.5.2). No excavation has taken place, but its function as part of the Antonine frontier system was confirmed by the discovery of second century pottery at the site (Robertson 1964a, 200). This may be one of a chain of such posts, but only one other has yet been located, some 6 miles (9·7 km) further south and west at Outerwards. Although in size (0·05 acres:0·02 ha) and general appearance Outerwards may resemble a large watch-post, excavation revealed a turf rampart on a cobble base enclosing stone and clay sill-walls of two small rectangular buildings which showed two periods of occupation (Newall 1976). These fortlets and the fort were connected by road, and possibly further links were provided by signal towers (Newall 1976, 111). The system is, however, but a pale reflection of that known along the Cumberland coast on the western flank of Hadrian's Wall.

On the south bank of the Forth estuary to the east of the Wall, forts are known some 11 miles (17·7 km) beyond Carriden at Cramond and a further 9 miles (14·5 km) away at Inveresk. Both were large forts, 4·8 acres (1·9 ha) and approximately 5·7 acres (2·3 ha) respectively, and both, positioned conveniently at the mouths of rivers, may have guarded harbour facilities. The continued importance of the former is confirmed by its selection in the early third century as one of the only two forts in Scotland to be occupied permanently during the Severan campaigns (Rae and Rae 1974). The significance of the latter site has long been surmised, for, despite little excavation, it has continually furnished evidence of an extensive civilian settlement outside the fort (see below p.189), and was clearly an important, possibly nodal, point in the Antonine road system.

To complete this general survey of the Antonine frontier system only one further element remains to be considered. The Antonine Wall represented a convenient line demarcating the area which, it was hoped, would develop into a peaceful and romanised part of the province of Britannia (see chapter 8). But it did not represent the northern limit of Roman interest in the province nor even of Roman occupation in the second century. A military presence was maintained as far north as the Tay with permanent installations or outpost forts strung out along an arterial road in much the same way that forts had been employed, and later continued to be employed, north of Hadrian's Wall.

All the forts actually situated on the Antonine Wall, and those fortlets

TABLE 5.5   *The outpost forts*

Site	Area acres	ha	Rampart width ft	m	Annexe position	area acres	ha	Spacing in Roman miles
Camelon	6	2·4	?41	15	N and S *c.* 2·3 and 8		0·9 and 3·2	21·8
Ardoch	6·2	2·5	*c.*15–20	4·6–6·1	N	*c.*25	10·1	6·9
Strageath	3·7	1·5	23·5	7·2	W	1·1–2·7	0·4–1·1	14·9
Bertha	*c.*9	3·6	20	6·1	—	—	—	

PLATE 5.3   *The fort at Ardoch, Perthshire, from the air.*

which have been examined, had gates through the Wall to the north. At only one point, however, do we have evidence of a main road passing through the Wall. Somewhat surprisingly, this occurs not at a fort, but at the fortlet of Watling Lodge. The road led first to the fort at Camelon less than one mile north of the Wall, then on to Ardoch, Strageath and finally Bertha at the confluence of the Almond and the Tay. On the grounds of spacing (Table 5.5), it seems probable that there would have been a further fort in the vicinity of Stirling guarding a crossing of the Forth. Three of the four known forts have been extensively excavated, though only one, at Strageath, in recent years.

Although there are differences between the outpost forts, there is also a striking homogeneity. All occupy the sites of first century forts; three of the four are larger than average; three of the four have large annexes appended; three of the four demonstrate two periods of occupation. There are indications of a greater concentration on the defences since, as outpost forts, they would be more exposed to unexpected attack. The surviving remains of the ditches at Ardoch form an extensive and complex system which continues to puzzle archaeologists (pl.5.3). Although not fully examined, and in places at least as complex as at Ardoch, the defences at Strageath also seem to have been extended in the Antonine period (Frere 1979, 37). In each case, the size of the ramparts, too, seems to have been rather larger than in the majority of forts on the Antonine Wall (Table 5.5), although details derived from the early excavations at Camelon and Ardoch may not be wholly trustworthy. Similarly, with gates the evidence available is insufficient to form even a general conclusion, save to note that all were of timber.

Internally the outpost forts exhibit appreciable variations of plan and, as one would expect of re-occupied sites, do not follow what seems to be the norm in the forts on the Antonine Wall. At Strageath all the buildings were of timber, while at Camelon all were apparently of stone. At Ardoch the only building of stone to be recorded in the excavation lay in the *retentura*, but none was apparent in the central range. In broad terms, however, the internal arrangements were standard and will be discussed in respect of the probable garrisons in chapter 8.

VI. THE BUILDING OF THE WALL

One of the most rapidly expanding areas of study relating to the Antonine Wall is that devoted to the examination of its structural evolution. To a certain extent this may be considered a belated attempt to apply principles developed by students of Hadrian's Wall to the more northerly frontier, and the reader may express surprise at the tardiness of their application. On the other hand, it must be remembered that such a process was only feasible on Hadrian's Wall when the existence and significance of a sufficient number of structural pointers had been recognised. Close perusal of Wall guides and text books (e.g. Birley 1961) will reveal how long it has taken in many cases for the significance of known features to be appreciated. Again, it should be emphasised that the construction of so much of the original Hadrianic barrier in stone has made the preservation and identification of those pointers a more frequent occurrence than could have been expected on the Antonine Wall. This did not prevent Sir George Macdonald from presenting a hypothetical reconstruction of the building scheme (1934, 359–400), but the magisterial quality of that account, combined with the relative infrequency of excavations on the Wall itself, particularly in the decades immediately following the publication of his hypothesis, has served rather to inhibit the sort of speculative enquiry that was demanded. In recent years, however, a sudden increase in the quality and quantity of information has had a liberating effect on the subject, and scholars have felt more free to examine the problem in a discursive vein.

For long it has been accepted that the original concept of the Antonine Wall was unitary; that, unlike Hadrian's Wall, which was still undergoing alterations at the end of Hadrian's reign, all the forts along its length were built as part of a single 'master-plan'. Macdonald was convinced that the presence of Flavian *praesidia*, which he believed to underlie each Wall fort, had 'fixed

104

the points at which the Antonine *castella* were destined to stand' (1934, 396), and this view has been largely accepted. More recently, however, this unitary approach has been challenged, particularly by John Gillam, who noted the differing structural relationships between forts and Wall, and postulated that the known dispositions represented a considerable modification of the original plan (1975). This, he suggested, pointing out the similarities between the few fortlets then known along the Antonine Wall and the milecastles of Hadrian's Wall, had been modelled upon the latter in its more developed form. Such a drastic departure from long held views did not, and still does not, attract universal acceptance and deserves careful and rather detailed consideration here.

Although the Wall forts display considerable diversity in size and plan, it can be seen that they fall into two recognisable classes (figs 5.3 and 4): those capable of accommodating a complete regiment – Carriden, Mumrills, Castlecary, Bar Hill, Auchendavy, Cadder, Balmuildy, Castlehill and Old Kilpatrick – and those clearly intended to house vexillations – Rough Castle, Westerwood, Croy Hill, Bearsden and Duntocher.

Three of the former group were certainly constructed before the curtain was built in their vicinity. Two of these, Castlecary and Balmuildy, are the only forts on the Wall provided with a surrounding stone wall. At Castlecary the northern angles of the fort were squared in anticipation of the arrival of the turf-built wall (Christison and Buchanan 1903, 278), but at Balmuildy wing-walls had been constructed, indicating that the curtain, when eventually it was built, was expected to be of stone also (Miller 1922, 6–7). The third fort, Old Kilpatrick, which guards the western terminus of the Wall, was constructed with all four corners rounded, but the disposition of its ditches shows that the builders knew that the Rampart would at length butt against the fort at its northern angle. In the event, so long an interval elapsed before this occurred that the occupants of the fort appear to have taken their own steps to complete the security of the defensive perimeter, and that work had to be undone before the curtain itself could be constructed (Macdonald 1932, 220–30).

Of the remaining six forts in this group, three, Castlehill, Auchendavy and Carriden, have undergone no excavation, so that their relationship to the Wall has not been conclusively demonstrated. In the case of the latter, however, since it stood detached from the line of the Wall, excavation would be unlikely to provide an answer, although as guardian of the eastern terminus of the Wall its construction may be imagined to have had a high priority. In contrast, there are reasons to suspect that Castlehill was a later addition. The presumed presence of both fort and fortlet on the site and their apparent close relationship (Keppie 1980b) is strongly reminiscent of the situation at Duntocher, where the fort was secondary (see below pp.106–7).

The evidence from the last three, however, is equivocal. At Mumrills it would seem that, at the very least, foreknowledge of the position to be occupied by the fort – the largest on the Antonine Wall – determined the course of the barrier in that sector; had it been otherwise, the Wall-builders would surely have sought a line of greater tactical advantage than that actually adopted, one which would have run much further to the north and commanded a better view of the Carse below. As it is, the need to site the southern defences of the fort on the edge of the scarp overlooking the Westquarter Burn was seen as paramount, and in consequence the barrier was compelled to describe a sudden re-entrant on gaining the summit of the Mumrills Braes. It is, however, not absolutely certain that the fort was actually built before the arrival of the curtain-building party. Re-investigation of the defences at Mumrills in the late 1950s revealed that the eastern rampart of the fort had not been bonded into the Antonine Wall but slightly overlapped its rear kerb where this had been terraced into the slope of the original ground surface. However, an examination of the short lengths of Wall on either side of the fort, suggested to the excavator that they had formed wing-walls, as at Balmuildy, but in this instance of earth revetted with clay (Steer 1961, 93–6). Bar Hill, like Carriden, stands free of the Wall and it has been suggested that it, too, might have been built early in the programme, for had it been a later addition it would surely have been attached to the rear of the Wall (Breeze and Dobson 1976a, 99). On the other hand, there seems no sensible reason why, if the fort had preceded or even been contemporary with the building of the curtain, the Wall would not have been made to abut its northern corners; to have done so would have meant a considerable saving of time and effort, and not to have done so would have cut off the fort from the territory to the north. Moreover, recent excavations have confirmed Macdonald's earlier discovery that the Bar Hill fort overlies what appears to be a semi-permanent work of probable Antonine date, like the similar example on Croy Hill (Hanson 1980b). The most attractive conclusion, therefore, is that the fort on Bar Hill is secondary and, furthermore, that somewhere close by lies an as yet undiscovered fortlet to provide access to the north (see below p.122). Finally, examination of the north-east corner at Cadder indicated that the base of the Antonine Wall continued past its junction with the east and west ramparts of the fort without a break, thus suggesting that the latter was secondary (Clarke 1933, 9–10). On the other hand, the Antonine ditch appears to have been broken in front of the northern gate of the fort thus indicating that, when it was dug, the existence of the fort had already been determined.

Of the smaller 'vexillation' forts, Duntocher is the only one which clearly preceded the construction of the Wall. However, it is also manifestly obvious that the fort itself is of secondary construction. The first structure on the summit of Golden Hill had been a free-standing fortlet of standard size (see above p.93f). and the fact that it was entirely enclosed by its ditch suggests that the builders knew how long it might be before the curtain was constructed thereabouts. At some time prior to the arrival of the Wall-builders, a small fort, o·5 acre (o·2 ha), was constructed immediately adjacent to the fortlet, the later work incorporating the south-eastern side of the first in its own rampart (fig.6.1) (Robertson 1957a, 14). The awkwardness with which the fort is accommodated to the sloping ground beside the fortlet makes it clear that when the latter was constructed it was not expected that it would eventually be superseded in this manner. It is also noteworthy that when the fort was built, the opportunity was not taken to demolish the smaller work and make the more advantageous ground available for the new construction.

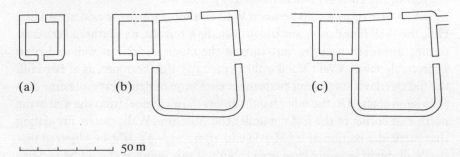

└──┴──┴──┴──┘ 50 m

FIGURE 6.1   *Diagrammatic presentation of the structural sequence at Duntocher: a) fortlet; b) the addition of the fort; c) the Wall abuts both fort and fortlet.*

The rest of the forts for which evidence is available are now generally characterised as being secondary both structurally and by intention (Breeze and Dobson 1976a, 99–100), although this is something of an over simplification. At Rough Castle the east and west ramparts of the fort butted against the south side of the Antonine Rampart clearly indicating that, in Macdonald's words, they had 'been laid down independently' (1934, 219). As far as can be seen from a contemporary photograph (Buchanan *et al.* 1905, fig.7), the rear kerbs of the Wall foundation continued unbroken past the point of junction with the base of the fort's rampart, although the photograph does not appear to demonstrate the same disparity between their turf superstructures. In this context it is interesting to note that the expansion of Bonnyside East, which is situated almost exactly half a Roman mile west of Rough Castle, exhibits a similar structural relationship with the Wall (Steer 1957). In addition, as at Cadder, there is an original gap in the Antonine ditch not quite directly in front of the north gate of the fort, as though the existence of the fort was anticipated when the ditch was dug. However, there is within the annexe a small ditched enclosure, which is apparently of early date, for it appears to be respected by the eastern ditches of the fort; its relationship to the larger work is strongly reminiscent of that observed between the two structures at Duntocher, and the possibility of a primary fortlet on the site, later to be replaced by a fort, has been noted (Gillam 1975, 54).

It has often been remarked that the fort at Westerwood sits awkwardly within its ditches. Macdonald believed that this indicated their prior existence, attributing them to Agricola (1934, 257–8). But his own excavations leave no doubt that the rampart of the fort was structurally secondary. The curtain had, as elsewhere along its line, been erected on a terrace dug into the subsoil to provide a secure and level foundation, while the much wider fort rampart had been laid upon the ground surface, so that at the point of junction it overlapped the rear of the curtain (Macdonald 1933).

A similar relationship between Wall and fort rampart is evident at Croy Hill; the Wall foundation was laid on a shallow terrace, its southern kerb continuing unbroken past the butt-ends of the much wider fort wall and at an appreciably lower level (Macdonald 1932, 247). Furthermore, as at Bar Hill, the fort overlay a small semi-permanent enclosure of definitely Antonine date (Hanson 1980b). On the other hand, the overflow channel from the well in the north-east corner of the fort ran under the Antonine Wall, clearly pre-dating that particular section of it (Macdonald 1932, 257–8). If it be objected that the Wall might possibly have been rebuilt at this point, it should be remembered that the channel issues through the Wall in the immediate neighbourhood of the butt-joint which is cited as proof of the secondary nature of the fort's defences; had such re-building taken place, it seems strange that the opportunity was not taken to bond Wall and fort rampart together. Furthermore, although there is no interruption in the ditch opposite the north gate of the fort, a plug of basalt 70 ft (21 m) wide was left undug some 200 ft (60 m) to the east. This feature has long been an object of puzzlement to antiquaries. Maitland was more willing to believe in the natural 'vegetation' of rock than in the possibility that the legionary diggers might have been defeated by the obduracy of Croy Hill's basalt (1757, 175–6). Macdonald saw the 'bridge' as tangible evidence of the factor which threw the original Wall-building plan out of sequence, delaying the construction parties so considerably that the remaining tasks had to be entirely re-allocated (1934, 398–9). A recent examination of the terminals of the ditch on either side of the present gap has shown that there is a change of alignment, the crest of the ditch-scarp lying some 4 m further south on the west than on the east. The impression gained is that the gap was intentional and may have marked the change-over between two construction parties; moreover, as hinted by the situation at both Cadder and Rough Castle, the gap suggests foreknowledge of the existence of the fort on the part of the ditch-diggers.

In contrast to the complexities and contradictions exhibited in the relationships between the Antonine Wall and its forts, that between it and its fortlets is straightforward. In all cases where evidence is forthcoming, the fortlets either preceded or were contemporary with the curtain wall. The two fortlets so far examined at the western end of the Wall, Duntocher (fig.6.1) and Cleddans, were originally both free-standing structures, although their northern corners were squared as if in anticipation of eventual junction with the Wall (Robertson 1957a, 17; Keppie and Walker 1981). On the other hand, excavation at Wilderness Plantation, Croy Hill, Seabegs and Kinneil have all demonstrated that those fortlets were bonded into the curtain (pl.6.1) (Wilkes 1974, 53; Hanson 1979, 19; Keppie and Walker 1981). It is possible, of course, that these fortlets had also preceded the building of the curtain and had been provided with wing-walls like many of the milecastles on Hadrian's Wall (Breeze and Dobson 1976a, 63); the position of Seabegs on a slight salient suggests that its location took priority over the convenience of a straight stretch of Wall, but a specific search for wing-walls at Kinneil failed to locate them. Whether wing-walls existed or not, it is certain that the fortlets were an integral part of the original plan for the Wall.

What conclusions can be drawn about the structural history of the Wall from this apparently disparate evidence? There can be little doubt that one fort, Duntocher, was not part of the original plan because of its relationship with the fortlet on the same site. For similar reasons it is tempting to include Castlehill, Rough Castle and possibly Croy Hill, although forts and milecastles in quite close proximity are attested on Hadrian's Wall. But, as has been pointed out above, the evidence for the structural relationship between the Wall system and the forts at Rough Castle, Croy Hill and Cadder is contradictory. If there was an overall change of plan, it is clear from the situation at Duntocher that, again as on Hadrian's Wall (Breeze and Dobson 1976a, 67-8), it occurred while construction work was still in progress. Since it is unlikely that all the elements of the building process – the laying down of the Wall base, the construction of the turf superstructure, the digging of the ditch, the building of the Military Way – would have managed, or were even intended, to keep pace with each other, it is inevitable that some forts should demonstrate different relationships with different elements of the system. This argument might well be taken to provide general support for the view that virtually all the forts on the Wall could have been part of the original plan, and that the differing structural relationships merely reflect the order of the work and not a change of concept (Robertson 1979, 30-1). However, if this were the case, it is difficult to understand why all the forts were not built as one with the Wall base as the fortlets seem to have been. Thus, at present the idea of a change of plan during the construction of the Wall does seem to provide the most satisfactory explanation for the evidence. Furthermore, the Gillam hypothesis presents the most plausible interpretation of the development of an otherwise unique

PLATE 6.1   *Excavation at Croy Hill showing the contemporary construction of the Wall and fortlet.*

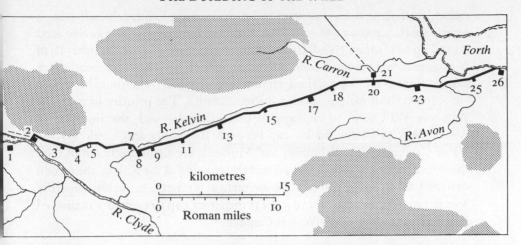

FIGURE 6.2   *The original plan of the Antonine Wall as understood at
present : 1 Bishopton, 2 Old Kilpatrick, 3 Duntocher fortlet,
4 Cleddans fortlet, 5 Castlehill fortlet, 7 Summerston fortlet,
8 Balmuildy, 9 Wilderness Plantation fortlet, 11 Glasgow
Bridge fortlet, 13 Auchendavy, 15 Croy Hill fortlet,
17 Castlecary, 18 Seabegs fortlet, 20 Watling Lodge fortlet,
21 Camelon, 23 Mumrills, 25 Kinneil fortlet, 26 Carriden.*

frontier. Given their geographical and chronological proximity, the gross
dissimilarities between the two Walls in north Britain have always seemed odd.
Until recently the numerous forts on the Antonine Wall could be explained
as an alternative to the regular system of milecastles on Hadrian's Wall. But
the continuing discovery of fortlets on the Antonine Wall, as Gillam pre-
dicted, makes such an interpretation untenable, and paradoxically, serves both
to increase the similarities and highlight the differences between the two
frontiers. That the design of the Antonine Wall should originally have been
influenced by the final form of its predecessor seems *a priori* likely; some overlap in the personnel responsible for the construction of the two Walls would
have been unavoidable, for Hadrian's Wall was still undergoing modifications
at the time of Antoninus's accession. Moreover, like the British High Command earlier this century, the Roman army will undoubtedly have prepared
for new conflicts on the basis of previous ones. That they were then prepared
to amend the system in the light of experience and local exigencies demonstrates an intelligence and flexibility that it has not been customary to attribute
to the Roman army.

Thus, as we understand it at present, the original plan for the Antonine
Wall will have included a regular system of milefortlets, together with forts at
Carriden, Mumrills, Castlecary, Balmuildy and Old Kilpatrick (fig.6.2). The

forts placed along a frontier tend to be situated approximately half a day's march apart, a distance of 7–9 Roman miles: for example, the twelve forts moved up to Hadrian's Wall from the Stanegate were disposed at intervals of 6–9 miles across a frontier some 80 Roman miles long. Thus on a frontier just over 41 Roman miles long, the optimum disposition of forts would have been six at intervals of marginally over 8 Roman miles. The primary forts on the Antonine Wall seem to conform to this principle, with the insertion of Auchendavy to fill the double gap between Balmuildy and Castlecary. As Table 6.1 shows, only Balmuildy and Mumrills are significantly out of their theoretical positions, the first to protect the crossing of the Kelvin, the second designed to occupy a site of superior tactical strength, probably originally selected by Agricola (see above p.39f); the larger gap so created was covered by a fort in advance of the Wall at Camelon.

TABLE 6.1 *The spacing between primary forts*

Site	Imperial miles	Roman miles
Carriden		
	7·1	7·8
Mumrills		
	8·4	9·1
Castlecary		
	7·5	8·2
Auchendavy		
	6·5	7·1
Balmuildy		
	8·5	9·2
Old Kilpatrick		

In order to assess the way in which the construction of the Wall was organised, we must now turn to other evidence and in particular the explicit testimony of the building records on stone. Of those which commemorate the construction of forts, only two, both found at Balmuildy (RIB 2191–2), allow us to date the relevant work to a specific governorship within the reign of Antoninus Pius. The name of Q. Lollius Urbicus which appears on each inscription indicates that they mark the completion of building work begun between AD 139 and 142; thus they confirm both the statement in the Augustan History which associates Urbicus with the building of the Wall (SHA Antoninus Pius V, 4), and the implication that Pius' acceptance of a second imperial acclamation in AD 142 (CIL X, 515) marked both the end of hostilities in Britain and the commencement of work on the Wall. However, they offer no immediate assistance by themselves in providing a more precise datum point to which we may relate the other phases of Wall construction. But it is nevertheless interesting to note that Balmuildy, so obviously a primary fort, should be the only one so far to have produced evidence of an origin in the time of Urbicus.

Perhaps more remarkable is the absence of a governor's name from the Distance slabs. At least 18 of these handsome examples of the legionary sculptor's craft survive (Table 6.2); their purpose was to record, in a more grandiose form than the centurial stones of Hadrian's Wall, the lengths of Wall completed by the legionary work parties engaged in building the Antonine frontier. As far as is known, they were set up at either end of each stint, possibly one stone in each face of the rampart, so that at each junction between two parties there could originally have been as many as four stones, two facing north and two facing south (Maxwell 1974, 328; Steer and Cormack 1969, 125). The identification of cramp holes in the back of several of the slabs suggests very strongly that they were set into masonry surrounds (Close-Brookes 1981); indeed it would have been difficult otherwise to have inserted them into a turf rampart without fear of subsidence. Furthermore, the trimming which is visible at the right-hand end of the Bridgeness slab (no.1) (pl.6.2) indicates that the surrounds may have been built in readiness beforehand to an agreed size and the slabs themselves occasionally pared to fit on site. This may also explain why slab no.5 lacks its right-hand ansate panel, although an alternative explanation is that the panel may have been supplied on a separate block. Each Distance slab bore, after the Imperial dedication, the identity of the legion and the exact length of frontier completed. On many of the slabs the inscribed panels are surrounded by carved figures representing the legionary insignia, scenes of victorious battle, deities and religious ceremonies (pls 6.2 and 3), while in two cases (nos 11 and 17) the inscription is interspersed between the purely decorative elements. During recent cleaning of two of the slabs (nos 1 and 6) traces of red paint were discovered on both the lettering and the sculptured scenes, a reminder of the colourful and imposing appearance they would originally have presented. It is quite common for Roman building inscriptions not to mention what had been constructed, for this would be self-evident from the location of the stone. Thus in the case of the Distance slabs it is not entirely certain whether they refer to the building of the frontier as a whole, or merely one element of it. However, two of the slabs (nos 12 and 15), both erected by the sixth legion, do specify that it was the construction of the rampart which they recorded (*opus valli*) (pl.6.4), and this accords both with what appears to have been the most time-consuming part of the work (see below pp.132–4) and with the centurial records on Hadrian's Wall.

Apart from their obvious relevance to the study of Wall-construction, the Distance slabs represent a unique body of evidence, graphically illustrating

PLATE 6.2   *Distance slab from Bridgeness (no.1).*

PLATE 6.3   *Distance slab from Hutcheson Hill (no.11).*

numerous aspects of Roman military organisation, iconography, religion and monumental art (Macdonald 1934, 359–400; Keppie 1979). On grounds of epigraphic content and treatment, as well as artistically and in terms of size, the stones may be divided into two separate groups which are also geographically distinct. The first comprises slabs nos 1–8, and possibly 19; the second nos 9–18 and probably 20 (Table 6.2). The most important difference between the two groups is that the first records the distance of the Wall constructed in *passus* or paces, while the second reckons the measurement in feet (*pedes*). It is also possible to show that the texts of the inscribed panels in the two groups which are attributed to the same legion are most probably the work

PLATE 6.4 *Distance slabs: a) Castlehill (no.8); b) Dalnotter (no.15).*

of different hands; for example, the horizontal bars of the letters A and H in slabs produced by *legio XX Valeria Victrix* from group 2 display a curious downward inflexion which is not used in those of the same legion in group 1. In terms of size those of the first group are appreciably larger, although spanning a diverse range, which includes the terminal slab (no.1) and an exceptionally small member (no.5). As the first group record the completion of longer distances and were, therefore, more widely separated, their larger size is understandable; consequently the occurrence on these inscriptions of the less abbreviated form of the imperial titles need occasion no surprise. Yet two or three stones of the second group could easily have included the same expansions had it been desired. A similar dichotomy is represented by the use of PER and the abbreviated P immediately before the number of paces or feet.

The approximate original findspot of as many as fifteen of the eighteen

Table 6.2 The Distance Slabs

Number (after Keppie)	Reference	Width/height in metres	Legion	Legionary strength	Distance F(eet)/P(aces)	Imperial titles	Findspot
1	2139	2·79 / 0·87	II	Legio	P 4652	unabbreviated	Bridgeness
2	2173	0·97 / 0·84	XX	Vex.	P 3000	unabbreviated	?Eastern half of Wall
3	2185	1·59 / 0·77	VI	Vex.		unabbreviated	Eastermains, Kirkintilloch
4	2184	0·59 / 0·44	XX	Legio	P 3660·8	none	Eastermains, Kirkintilloch
5	2186	1·01 / 0·635	II	Legio	P 3666·5	unabbreviated	Cawder House, Bishopriggs
6	2193	1·35 / 0·62	II	Legio	P 3666·5	unabbreviated	Summerston
7	2194	1·45 / 0·76	VI	Vex.	P 3666·5	unabbreviated	East Millichen
8	2196	1·49 / 0·76	VI	Vex.	P 3666·5	unabbreviated	Castlehill
9	2197	0·88 / 0·72	XX	Vex.	F 3000	abbreviated	Castlehill
10	2198	0·85 / 0·67	XX	Vex.	F 3000	abbreviated	Hutcheson Hill
11	Keppie 1979, 16	0·95 / 0·75	XX	Vex.	F 3000	abbreviated	Hutcheson Hill
12	2200	1·19 / 0·76	VI	Vex.	F 3240	abbreviated	Braidfield, Duntocher
13	2203	0·71 / 0·50	II	Legio	F 4140	none	?Duntocher
14	2204	0·63 / 0·54	II	Legio	F 3271	abbreviated	Carleith
15	2205	0·82 / 0·53	VI	Vex.	F 4141	abbreviated	?Dalnotter
16	2206	?0·85 / 0·68	XX	?Vex.	?F 4411	abbreviated	?Dalnotter
17	2208	0·73 / 0·69	XX	Vex.	F 4411	abbreviated	Old Kilpatrick
18	2199	0·75 / 0·56	XX	Vex.	F —	abbreviated	West of Castlehill
19	Keppie 1979, 20	?1·25 / 0·86	?XX	—	—	—	?Hag Knowe, Arniebog
20	2207	0·71 / 0·71	?XX	—	—	—	Ferrydyke, Old Kilpatrick

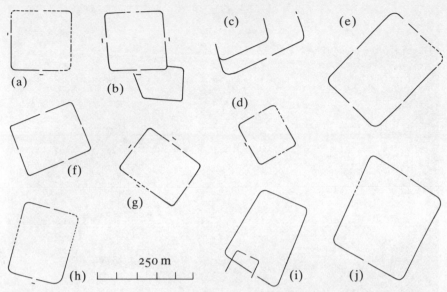

FIGURE 6.3 *Comparative plans of construction camps on the Antonine*
Wall: a) Kinglass Park; b) Little Kerse; c) Dullatur;
d) Easter Cadder; e) Buchley; f) Tollpark; g) Milnquarter;
h) Tamfourhill; i) Inveravon 2; j) Wester Carmuirs.

stones definitely identifiable as Distance slabs is either known or can be
inferred by reasonable conjecture. It will thus be evident that they provide the
best available means of ascertaining how the construction of the barrier was
organised (Macdonald 1921 and 1934, 393–400). But since Macdonald's time
aerial survey has provided another means of establishing the method of work
allocation, particularly in those sectors where no Distance slabs have survived.
Largely as a result of reconnaissance carried out by the Cambridge University
Committee for Aerial Photography, it has been possible to identify the sites of
temporary camps which may be interpreted as the bases used by the legionary
forces engaged in the building of the Wall (fig.6.3). Although no longer
surviving above ground, these structures may be recognised from cropmarkings that form in the vegetation overlying their long-buried ditches
(pl.6.5). As early as the 1950s it was realised that there was likely to be a
significant relationship between such sites and the building sectors of the Wall
(Feachem 1956a). At first it was observed that the camps at the eastern end of
the Wall were situated at or near the ends of what were then accepted as the
first three legionary 'rations'. More recently, the discovery of further examples
has led to the suggestion that each vexillation was housed in four labour camps,
two located at each end of the relevant sector, possibly because it was intended
that work in each stint should proceed from each end towards the middle

117

PLATE 6.5   *Construction camp at Tamfourhill from the air.*

(Maxwell 1974, 329). The reason for having two camps is unknown – nor is it certain that this was a universally observed arrangement – but conceivably one party might have been charged with building the rampart, the other with the digging of the ditch; or else the construction of stone base and superstructure might have been separate tasks (see below pp.132–4).

The camps situated in the vicinity of the Antonine Wall may be divided, on the basis of area, into four groups (Table 6.3) (fig.6.3). It may be significant that all the large camps of the fourth group, Buchley near Balmuildy, Wester Carmuirs to the west of Camelon, and Garnhall by Castlecary, are adjacent to what were undoubtedly primary forts; in size and proportions they compare closely with camp B at Castledykes (fig.1.5) (RCAHMS 1978, 127–8) which may have housed the construction gang, probably a vexillation of *legio II Augusta*, that built the nearby fort. Apart from an extremely large temporary work at Tollpark, not included in the list because it appears to underlie the Antonine Wall itself (St Joseph 1965, 80–1), these are probably the earliest Antonine temporary camps on or near the line of the frontier; two of them lie to the north of the Wall, a position especially significant in the case of Buchley since it could not have functioned efficiently as a labour camp once the Wall had been constructed.

The only other temporary site at which contemporaneity with the Wall-building phase may be demonstrated beyond doubt is Summerston. Excava-

118

TABLE 6.3   *Temporary camps in the vicinity of the Antonine Wall*

	Site	Approx. dimensions in metres	Area acres	hectares
Group 1	Easter Cadder	122 by 113	3·5	1·4
	Polmonthill	c.105 by 110	c.2·9	c.1·2
	Twechar	145 by c.105	c.3·9	c.1·5
	Dullatur 2	140 by 110–150	3·7–5·1	1·5–2·2
	Muirhouses	130 by c.128	c.4·1	c.1·7
	Dalnair	120 by c.150	c.4·5	c.1·8
Group 2	East Carmuirs	162 by 128	5·1	2·1
	Tollpark	165 by 128	5·2	2·1
	Milnquarter	165 by 128	5·2	2·1
	Little Kerse	152 by 143	5·4	2·2
	Kinglass	149 by 149	5·5	2·2
	Summerston	165 by c.140	c.5·7	c.2·3
Group 3	Inveravon 1	168 by c.168	c.6·9	c.2·8
	Inveravon 2	205 by 140	7·1	2·9
	Tamfourhill	185 by 150	7·0	2·8
	Dullatur 1	230 by 140–180	7·9–10	3·2–4·1
Group 4	Buchley	262 by 186	12·1	4·9
	Garnhall	259 by 174	11·0	4·5
	Wester Carmuirs	243 by 210	12·7	5·1

tion in 1980 revealed that the temporary camp was marginally earlier than the adjacent fortlet, whose south ditch was carefully aligned and decreased in width so as not to cut into the northern side of the camp (DES 1981). Otherwise, the presumed date of the remaining sites depends upon their spatial relationship to the Antonine Wall: with the exception of East Carmuirs, which lies adjacent to the fort at Camelon, the camps lie to the south of the frontier at a distance which ranges from 30 to 425 metres. In two cases, Inveravon 2 and Little Kerse, the camps are associated with minor works, that relating to the former being a slight enclosure that overlaps the south side of the main camp, the latter being a sub-rectangular annexe whose ditch contained pottery fragments of early Antonine character (McCord and Tait 1978) – further confirmation of the presumed date.

To these surviving examples should perhaps be added the testimony of early antiquaries concerning the existence of 'great forts' on the line of the Antonine Wall. In some cases the term must be taken to refer to the impressiveness of the visible remains, as at Rough Castle, or their extent, as at Balmuildy.

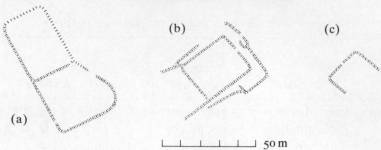

(a)

⊢―⊥―⊥―⊥―⊥―⊣ 50 m

FIGURE 6.4   *Semi-permanent enclosures along the Antonine Wall:
a) Croy Hill; b) Bar Hill; c) Mumrills.*

The sites thus described at Easter Cadder, Summerston and the east end of
Seabegs Wood may, however, more reasonably be identified as the temporary
camps known in the neighbourhood of these localities, and accordingly to our
list of camps perhaps should be added the 'great fort' at Langton to the east of
Falkirk (Sibbald 1707, 30).

It has recently been suggested that two further sites, the small enclosures
beneath the forts at Croy Hill and Bar Hill, were also construction camps
(Hanson 1979, 19) (fig.6.4). However, the enclosures do not resemble any of
the groups of camps outlined above, and both have provided hints of more
permanent occupation – a roadway at Croy Hill and footings for a building at
Bar Hill (Macdonald 1932, 265; DES 1980, 37). Exactly what function these
posts were intended to perform is uncertain, but their proximity to the sites of
known or presumed fortlets might indicate some connection between the two;
they could, for example, have housed the garrison of the fortlets during the
construction phase. The only other structure of similar type known along the
Wall is the small (0·3 acres: 0·1 ha) single-ditched enclosure on the very edge
of the escarpment to the south-east of the fort at Mumrills: it seems to have
been intended for more than temporary occupation (Steer 1961, 96) and is
situated close to the postulated site of a further fortlet at Beancross (Table
6.4).

The significance of the different sizes of camps is not immediately
apparent. The most numerous classes are the first two, which are equally
represented, with average areas of 3·9 acres (1·5 ha) and 5·4 acres (2·2 ha)
respectively; the average size of the third group, ignoring the uncertain example at Dullatur, is 7·1 acres (2·9 ha) and the fourth 11·9 acres (4·8 ha).
Given the approximate ratios of these sizes, bearing in mind estimates of the
density of occupation within temporary works (Hanson 1978b, 142–3), one
might argue that the groups were designed to accommodate units equivalent
to two, three, four and six cohorts respectively. However, if this were the case,
the two pairs of camps situated at either end of the first sector, which enclose a

total area of some 23·6 acres (9·6 ha), would have been capable of housing rather more than the full legion which is credited with construction of this sector on the Bridgeness slab. It seems more likely that the density of occupation within construction camps was rather less than within those built during a campaign (Maxwell 1980, 45–53), so that the four groups would have held closer to 50 per cent of the figures quoted above.

Macdonald believed that the Wall forts had provided the pointers to the allocation of construction work across the isthmus because their location had been determined already by Agricola. However, indications that not only were most of them not Agricolan in origin (Hanson and Maxwell 1980; Hanson 1980b), but many were not even part of the original plan, undermine his scheme. Given the additional evidence provided by the labour camps and the fortlets, it is time for a radical reappraisal.

It is virtually axiomatic that on Hadrian's Wall building allocations were related to the minor structures, the turrets and milecastles; to use C.E. Stevens terminology, the Wall was broken up into 'curtains' one third of a Roman mile long (1966, x). Prior to the disruption caused by the moving up of forts from the Stanegate, a number of legionary lengths are detectable along both the stone and turf sectors of the Wall. These work-lengths are all 5 or 6 Roman miles long, or rather 5 or 6 Wall miles, for the two do not always coincide (Birley 1961, 102). In fact, it is worth stressing the problems of mensuration at this point. There are three different standards of measurement: dead-level or map reckoning, always the shortest distance between two points; ground measurement, which will usually exceed map reckoning because of undulations in the topography; and 'notional' distances which relate to fixed points in a system, like the milecastles, and can be either longer or shorter than dead-level reckoning.

If, as now seems certain, we are correct in assuming that the system of fortlets on the Antonine Wall was both regular and primary, it would be reasonable to expect that they too might have provided a suitable framework for dividing up the work of curtain construction. The total length of the Antonine Wall by dead-level reckoning is 40·47 Roman miles, which is not a particularly convenient figure for subdivision. Measurement from the most easterly and westerly fortlets known, even taking into account the topographic variations, will not allow either terminus to fit into a convenient scheme of whole Roman mile intervals, for in both cases there is a distance of approximately two-thirds of a Roman mile between the end of the Wall and the estimated position of the first fortlet. However, the mid-point of the Wall lies within 50 Roman feet (14·8 m) of the fortlet at Croy Hill, which might suggest that rather than being laid out from one end, the positions of the fortlets were determined in relation to a central point. If this were the case, the notional length of the Wall would have been 42 fortlet intervals (Table 6.4), of which the end two were only two-thirds of a Roman mile long, that is a total of 41·33 Roman miles.

TABLE 6.4   *A suggested sequence of fortlets on the Wall from east to west*

1.	Grahamsdyke	22.	Girnal Hill
2.	Deanfield	23.	Bar Hill
3.	KINNEIL	24.	Shirva
4.	Nether Kinneil	25.	Auchendavy
5.	Inveravon	26.	Hillhead
6.	Polmont School	27.	Kirkintilloch
7.	Beancross	28.	GLASGOW BRIDGE
8.	Laurieston	29.	Bogton
9.	Callendar House	30.	Cawder House
10.	*Falkirk/Bantaskin	31.	WILDERNESS PLANTATION
11.	*WATLING LODGE	32.	Easter Balmuildy
12.	*Tentfield	33.	SUMMERSTON
13.	*Rough Castle	34.	Boclair
14.	*Milnquarter	35.	Manse Burn
15.	*SEABEGS	36.	Thorn Road
16.	Allandale	37.	Castlehill
17.	Garnhall	38.	CLEDDANS
18.	Tollpark	39.	DUNTOCHER
19.	Westerwood	40.	Carleith
20.	Easter Dullatur	41.	Mount Pleasant
21.	CROY HILL		

Sites which have been positively identified are indicated in CAPITALS.
* Non-standard intervals apparent in this sector.

As yet there is no clear support from the structural evidence for a further subdivision of the Wall into units one third of a Roman mile long to correspond with that known on Hadrian's Wall, but if we turn to the first group of Distance slabs, the most striking are numbers 5 to 8 which record the completion of 3666·5 paces or $3\frac{2}{3}$ Roman miles. In fact, if an allowance for error of only a fraction of one per cent is made, representing less than 15 paces in absolute terms, all the distances recorded in the first group of slabs are multiples of one third of a Roman mile. At first sight the second series of Distance slabs, those found between Castlehill and the Clyde, appear to provide no additional support. The recorded distances of the six stints (Table 6.5) have seemingly little in common with each other or with a scheme of division into thirds of a mile. Yet it should not be forgotten that all the

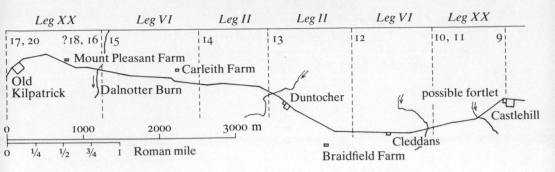

FIGURE 6.5   *Legionary work-stints from Castlehill to the Clyde (nos 9–20 indicate the find-spots of Distance slabs).*

structural evidence in this sector makes it clear that both forts and fortlets were constructed before the arrival of the Wall builders. It might be expected, therefore, that the legions would not include what were in effect lengths of curtain already in existence in the records of the distances that they subsequently constructed. The total length recorded on Distance slabs from this sector, allowing for duplicates, amounts to 22,203 Roman feet or some 60 paces short of $4\frac{1}{2}$ Roman miles. If a further allowance for the forts at Old Kilpatrick and Duntocher, the fortlets at Duntocher and Cleddans and the putative fortlets at Mount Pleasant and Carleith is included, the total figure falls only 31 paces short of $4\frac{2}{3}$ Roman miles. Moreover, the map measurement from the fort at Castlehill to the Clyde is 7553 yards (6907 m) or 4668 paces which is within $1\frac{1}{2}$ paces of $4\frac{2}{3}$ Roman miles. The correspondence between the two modes of measurement is sufficiently close to be convincing, although one problem remains. Ground measurement, as represented on the Distance slabs, ought to exceed map measurement because of topographic variations, whereas, even allowing for the ramparts of forts and fortlets, there remains a shortfall of $32\frac{1}{2}$ paces between the two. It seems unlikely that an additional sector of Wall construction has been omitted both because the shortfall is too small and because of the very close correspondence between the total work allocated to each legion (Steer and Cormack 1969, 125) (Table 6.5). Nor does this close correspondence allow us to suggest some miscalculation in the measurements given on the slabs. It is possible that the eastern end of the sector lay slightly to the west of the fort/fortlet at Castlehill, as the find-spot of Distance slab number 9 might suggest (Macdonald 1934, 382). However, it is tempting to see hidden in this shortfall the existence of further small structures along the Wall, the equivalent of the turrets on Hadrian's Wall, which, like the forts and fortlets, were completed before the curtain was built and were thus not included in the lengths recorded on the Distance slabs.

As Macdonald recognised (1934, 394), the abrupt change in the standard

TABLE 6.5 *Legionary allocations in the*
Castlehill-Clyde sector (Roman feet)

Legio II	Legio XX	Legio VI
4140	4411	4141
3271	3000	3240
7411	7411	7381

or measurement which occurs at Castlehill is indicative of two things: that a
re-allocation had taken place in order to complete an odd length as rapidly as
possible (fig.6.5): and, assuming that the building had started at one end, the
work had commenced in the east. However, since the evidence from the
Distance slabs is so much better in the west, we shall work from known to
unknown and attempt to define the work stints in reverse order (fig.6.6).

As already hinted at above, the original length of the last sector was
probably 4⅔ Roman miles from the north bank of the Clyde to the site of the
fortlet at Castlehill. Slabs 8 and 9, which mark adjacent ends of two sectors,
were both found at Castlehill (Macdonald 1934, 378 and 382–3), the latter
having been deliberately displaced from its original position. The former
records the construction of Wall-curtain for 3666½ paces to the east by *legio*
VI (pl.6.4). The opposite end of this stint was marked by a second stone of the
same legion (no.7), found some way to the west of the western march of the
lands of Summerston and a little to the north of East Millichen farmhouse
(Macdonald 1934, 377). A position about 500 yards (450 m) or one third of a
Roman mile west of the newly discovered fortlet at Summerston would fit the
recorded location very well. The presence of a temporary camp at Summerston, immediately adjacent to the fortlet there (see above pp.118–19), provides further confirmation of the end of this sector.

The next slab (no. 6) recording the same distance as the previous two,
but at the hands of *legio II*, was found in the immediate vicinity of Summerston
and would originally have been placed cheek by jowl with number 7
(Macdonald 1934, 374–6). A further 3⅔ Roman miles by map measurement
would take the Wall to a point slightly beyond the fort at Cadder. Allowance
for ground measurement would bring the point to within one third of a Roman
mile of the putative fortlet, marked by a re-entrant in the Wall, at Cawder
Lodge, approximately one Roman mile east of Wilderness Plantation. The
precise location of slab number 5, which must mark the eastern limit of this
stint, is unknown, but it first came to light at Cawder House (Macdonald
1934, 369) whither presumably it was taken as an object of antiquarian
interest.

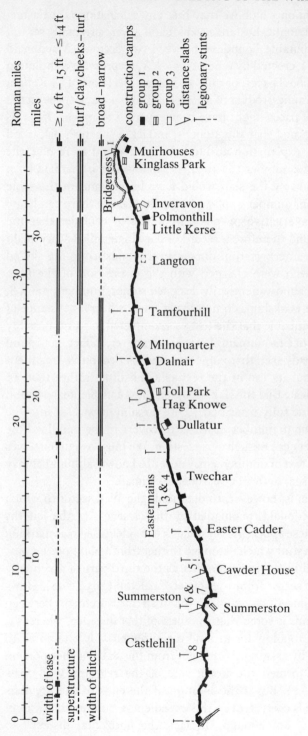

Figure 6.6 *Postulated original legionary work-stints as defined by the Distance slabs and temporary camps plotted against structural variations in the Wall and ditch (after Keppie, with additions).*

The next fixed point on which we may base any calculation is at Eastermains where, beyond all doubt, Distance slabs 3 and 4 were originally set up, thus marking the indisputable boundary between two sectors (Macdonald 1934, 367–9). Number 4, erected by men of *legio XX*, records the completion of work amounting to 3660·8 paces, or only 29 Roman feet short of 3⅔ Roman miles; number 3, a handsome product of *legio VI*, exhibits a blank space on the die where the number of paces might have been expected to appear. For this reason it might be suggested that the stone is, in fact, a 'waster', discarded before completion – an explanation adduced by Macdonald to resolve the problems relating to stone number 18 (1934, 387); however, if that had been the case, it is highly unlikely the slab would have been found in the same location as its companion, number 4, of whose functional use there can be no shadow of doubt. An alternative proposal would be to consider that the inscription is complete and therefore a record of one single mile (Macdonald 1934, 381); yet such an interpretation does a severe unjustice to the skilled craftsmen of *legio VI* who were charged with the disposition of the text, particularly because the almost identically designed stones, numbers 7 and 8, probably from the same workshop, do not display such a flagrant instance of asymmetry. It is more probable that the text was completed in paint, possibly pending the availability of a monumental mason who never, in fact, got round to the task; we have already seen that paint was used for decorative treatment of the Distance slabs, but its use in the text as a substitute rather than an embellishment may indicate that the slab occupied a less conspicuous position in the rampart than those fully inscribed. Quite possibly it was set into the north face as a companion to number 4, whose discovery in the middle of the Antonine ditch lends credence to such a suggestion. We must resign ourselves to accepting that the full text of number 3 may never be known, although it may be possible, as we shall see, to form a reasonable estimate.

The crucial problem is, however, to determine the Wall sector to which each slab referred. Macdonald, persuaded by the closeness of the lengths recorded on stone 4 to those appearing on stones 5 to 8, identified it as marking the eastern terminus of a stint which extended thither from a point on the west side of the modern road to Bogton, or rather as the third part of an equally divided 11 Roman-mile sector from the fort at Castlehill (1934, 399). However, as Macdonald himself recognised, the map measurement between Castlehill and Eastermains is somewhat in excess of that distance, whereas it ought to be rather less, to allow for ground measurement. He attempted to overcome this problem by assuming omission from the slabs of that portion of the rampart which formed the north side of the relevant Wall forts (Macdonald 1934, 380–1), but if the location of the ends of the previous stints determined above is correct, even this expedient, assuming that it is an acceptable procedure, is not enough. In fact, the horizontal distance to

Eastermains from Cadder is only slightly less than four Roman miles. It is thus possible that slab 4 with its figure of 3660·8 paces may refer to work completed to the east of Eastermains rather than to the west as Macdonald supposed. Thus Eastermains can be identified as lying 4 Wall miles east of the original position of stone 5 at Cadder, and 2⅓ milefortlet intervals east of Glasgow Bridge, the additional fortlet positions falling a little way to the west of Kirkintilloch Peel and in the Hillhead area on the eastern outskirts of Kirkintilloch. This distance might have constituted a single stint, but it is conveniently split into two equal parts by the temporary camp of group 1 (Easter Cadder) situated on the west bank of the Park Burn midway between Glasgow Bridge and Kirkintilloch (Table 6.6) (fig.6.6).

The three and two-thirds Wall miles from Eastermains recorded on slab 4 would take the Wall to a point on the lower eastern slopes of Bar Hill, in the neighbourhood of Girnal Hill; a more precise definition of the location would be that it lay precisely one Wall-mile west of the recently discovered fortlet on Croy Hill, in other words, at the site of another fortlet still to be identified. One of the intervening fortlet positions would have coincided with the site of the fort at Auchendavy; the other two should be found at Shirva, where by strange coincidence a considerable number of Roman grave stones, as well as an inscribed legionary tablet, have also been found, and on the north-west shoulder of Bar Hill about 250 yards (230 m) west of the fort itself. One further item of evidence, however, will not readily fit into the framework outlined above; the temporary camp of group 1 at Twechar lies almost in the centre of the 3⅔ mile stint to the east of Eastermains. However, if slab 4 is taken to refer to a sector to the west of Eastermains, a similar situation would arise with the camp at Easter Cadder.

The distance from Girnal Hill eastwards to the next group of temporary works of the labour-camp type at Dullatur is approximately 2 Roman miles; yet another fortlet may be presumed to have existed hereabouts, in a corresponding position on the Wall, by East Dullatur House. A sector of precisely this length would conveniently make up an equally balanced total of legionary rations distributed between six legionary parties, one large and one small from each legion, over the 17 Roman miles from Castlehill to Dullatur; an arrangement reminiscent of the later subdivision of the western terminal sector, but on a larger scale.

Between Dullatur and the eastern terminus of the Wall the Distance slabs offer evidence for only three sectors: that between the River Avon and Bridgeness (no.1), an unprovenanced sector of 3000 paces completed by *legio XX* and, possibly, a sector of unknown length beginning or ending at Arniebog. It has been generally held in recent times, following Macdonald, that the Avon-Bridgeness sector was one of a triplet, all of which were constructed at the same time by equally-matched legionary vexillations (Feachem

1956a; Maxwell 1974, 329; Keppie 1974, 151–5). However, the positions of the temporary camps which may be identified as labour camps only give reliable support for this hypothesis in the Polmont-Bridgeness sector and cannot be used to confirm its applicability between Polmont and Seabegs, to which latter point the combined lengths are assumed to have extended. On the contrary, the discovery of a temporary camp of group 3 at Tamfourhill (pl.6.5) only fractionally over two miles from the camp of group 3 at Milnquarter, casts serious doubt upon the hypothesis.

It seems likely, therefore, that the composition of the Dullatur-Avon sector is less straightforward than has been supposed. Measuring some 15 Wall-miles in length, it appears on the evidence of the disposition of temporary camps to have been built by parties working closer together than in the Avon-Bridgeness sector (fig.6.6). The camp at Tollpark lies only 2·2 Roman miles from Dullatur and Dalnair a further 2·4 Roman miles beyond that, suggesting that the next two stints were of the order of two to three Roman miles in length. Macdonald placed the probable Distance slab number 19 at Arniebog some 300–400 yards (275–365 m) east of the fort at Westerwood (1934, 398). However, it is clear from a contemporary account that it was discovered on an eminence (Hag Knowe?) almost mid-way between Westerwood and Castlecary, and would, therefore, support the suggestion of a two mile sector to the east of Dullatur (Gibb 1901, 25). The similarity between the kneeling figure on the Arniebog slab and those on one of the stones from Hutcheson Hill recording work by *legio XX* (no.11), might indicate that the same legion was responsible for work in this area also. A second camp in the neighbourhood of Seabegs at Milnquarter, only marginally over one Roman mile east of Dalnair, probably represents the western labour camp of the next adjacent stint which would then run on to the vicinity of Watling Lodge where a camp of group 3 at Tamfourhill marks the end of another sector of 2 or 3 miles. Beyond that there are no further construction camps known until Little Kerse and Polmonthill over 5·5 Roman miles away, although this distance may have been split by the postulated camp at Langton (see above p.120). Thus a subdivision of the 15 Wall-mile stretch into stints of 2, 3 or 4 miles would seem to harmonise not only with the evidence of the temporary camps, but also with the otherwise unallocated Distance slabs (nos 2 and 19).

The final or rather first stint from Bridgeness to the Avon appears to be one of the most clearly defined. The location of the Bridgeness slab is well known and the distance recorded, 4652 paces or just under $4\frac{2}{3}$ Roman miles, accords well with the presumed location of the end of the stint at the River Avon, for it exceeds the dead-level distance by just under 100 paces (148 m) as one might expect, given the local topography.

In the absence of Distance slabs from all the stints thus defined, it is not possible at present to determine with certainty which legion was responsible for each one. However, further clues may be forthcoming in the structural evidence. The attribution of work lengths on Hadrian's Wall is based either on the centurial stones or on the identification of consistent minor differences in the design of the milecastles and turrets which distinguish the work of a particular legion, the differences manifesting themselves in the proportions of the milecastles and the construction of their gates as well as in the entrance position and internal layout of the turrets (Hooley and Breeze 1968, 98–102; Hunnysett 1980). Although no such detailed system can yet be outlined for the Antonine Wall, where the differences are not so clean cut, there are indications that the milefortlets fall into at least two well defined groups (see above p.93ff) one of which, the long-axis type, may be attributed to *legio II Augusta* on the basis of the occurrence of two examples within stints which the Distance slabs make clear were the responsibility of that legion. The short-axis fortlets at Cleddans and Duntocher, although in sectors built by different legions according to the Distance slabs (fig.6.5) arc sufficiently similar to suggest that they were in fact the work of the same party. This lends further support to the view that the stint from Castlehill to the Clyde was intended to be completed by one legion, and suggests, given that the two sectors to the east are credited to the VI and II legions respectively, that *legio XX* might originally have been assigned to the task. Other short-axis fortlets at Watling Lodge and possibly Glasgow Bridge might then also be attributed to the same legion (Table 6.6) Ironically, it would appear that the legion responsible for short-axis milecastles on Hadrian's Wall built long-axis fortlets on the Antonine Wall and vice versa.

The allocation of work defined above and set out in Table 6.6 demonstrates a surprising asymmetry. The 13 sectors cannot be equally divided between the three legions either in terms of the number of stints or the total length of construction assigned. Equality of work completed is a striking aspect of the later-re-allocation of the westernmost sector (Table 6.5), and is further hinted at in slabs 4–8, but it should not be pressed too hard as a principle; the legionary contingents were not of equal strength, and much other work – the building of forts, the digging of the ditch, the construction of the Military Way – which might have engaged those less heavily burdened by rampart building, is not recorded on the Distance slabs.

We are not certain how the work was organised within a legionary sector. The apparent alternation of large and small stints allotted to each legion has been taken to indicate that each may have been divided up into a larger and smaller working group (Macdonald 1934, 398). It is not yet possible to use the evidence of the labour camps to support this suggestion, but they do indicate

TABLE 6.6 *Building sectors and legionary responsibility as planned*

Sector	Distance in wall-miles	Legion*	Distance slab no.	Fortlet type
Old Kilpatrick				
	$4\frac{2}{3}$	XX		Short-axis
Castlehill				
	$3\frac{2}{3}$	VI	7 and 8	
East Millichen				
	$3\frac{2}{3}$	II	5 and 6	Long-axis
Cadder				
	2	XX		Short-axis
Easter Cadder				
	2	VI	3	
Eastermains				
	$3\frac{2}{3}$	XX	4	
Girnal Hill				
	2	II		Long-axis
Dullatur				
	2	XX	19	
Tollpark				
	3	II		Long-axis
Dalnair				
	3	?VI		
Tamfourhill				
	3	XX	2	Short-axis
?Langton				
	4	?VI		
Polmonthill				
	$4\frac{2}{3}$	II	1	Long-axis
Bridgeness				

* Allocation to legions is based upon either epigraphic evidence or milecastle structural type.

that within a legionary sector the workforce was split into 2 or possibly 4 parties working towards each other from opposite ends. Given the importance of the fortlets in the setting out of the frontier, and the obviously primary nature of the Wall base, one might postulate two parties: one charged with the construction of the foundation, the minor structures and the Military Way; the other with the curtain itself. There are certainly indications that the build-

PLATE 6.6   *Section of Wall base excavated at Bantaskin showing possible division between work gangs.*

ing of Hadrian's Wall was organised along similar lines (Bruce 1978, 23–4). The relationship between the ditch and a number of secondary forts indicates that its excavation lagged behind the other work and may have been organised as a separate process. Certainly, the re-use of the labour camp at Dullatur does point to sequential activity there (Keppie 1978b, 9–12).

Within these various groups the work will undoubtedly have been further subdivided by century. Although we lack the vast number of centurial stones known from Hadrian's Wall (Stevens 1966, Appendix 1), we do occasionally find structural evidence which suggests that the same system was employed. Towards the eastern end of the lengthy stretch of Wall excavated recently at Bantaskin, a distinct change in the nature of the stone base was noted (pl.6.6), while the section of base uncovered at Easter Balmuildy was markedly different in character from that revealed just over a mile away at Buchley, although both lie within the sector of Wall attributed to *legio II Augusta* on Distance slabs 5 and 6 (Keppie 1976, 69 and 67; Hanson and Maxwell 1984). Variations in ditch width may be similarly explained: attention has already been drawn to a possible division between gangs working on the ditch at Croy Hill (see above p.108). A recent analysis of such structural variations failed to demonstrate any clear-cut relationship with the known or assumed legionary stints (fig. 6.6); rather the differences are more likely to relate to the activities of individual work-gangs within each stint (Keppie 1974, 162–3).

How long the frontier took to construct depends, obviously enough, upon the speed at which such work could be achieved. This in turn depends upon the magnitude of the task and the number of men available. While neither of these factors is known exactly, some estimation can be attempted.

Assuming that the broader dimensions of the ditch extended for some 13 Roman miles in the central sector, with a reduction of approximately 25 per cent across the rest of the isthmus, the total volume of earth to be excavated was of the order of $1\frac{1}{4}$ million cubic yards (955,000 m³). The work rate for nineteenth-century labourers quoted by Bruce was some 20 cubic yards (15·3 m³) per man day, although it was suggested that no more than 8 cubic yards (6·1 m³) would have been appropriate for the soldiers digging the ditch of Hadrian's Wall (1851, 94). Such a work rate seems excessive by modern standards, particularly bearing in mind the intractable nature of the subsoil across Croy Hill, and is not supported by the rates for healthy males using modern tools recorded during construction of the experimental earthwork on Overton Down (Jewell 1963, 51). A figure of 5 cubic yards (3·8 m³) per day might be a reasonable daily average for well-trained soldiers allowing for the inevitable delays caused by the need to drive the ditch through solid rock, and is more or less in accord with more recent builder's estimation procedures (Rea 1951, 48). This would suggest a total of approximately 250,000 man days for completion of the ditch.

Taking the estimated dimensions of the rampart as discussed in chapter 5 (p.77ff), the size of individual turf blocks as a half by one-and-a-half by one Roman foot (Vegetius II, 8), and allowing for the limited use of turf in the first 11 Roman miles of Wall, the total number of turf blocks required would have been of the order of 25 to 30 millions, which represents the stripping of some 800–950 acres (325–385 ha) of turf. Using Hobley's figures, based upon the reconstruction of a turf rampart at the Lunt (1971, 28), and calculating that the number of productive hours in a working day is unlikely to exceed six, this translates into between 850,000 and 1 million man days. Given the problems encountered in obtaining suitable turf indicated by its limited use at the eastern end of the Wall, and allowing for the material then required to make up the core, the time factor might have been increased by 25 per cent. If there was also a breastwork on top of the rampart, this can hardly have required less than 1 million cubic feet (28,000 m³) of timber if posts 4 inches (100 mm) square were set at 5 feet (1·5 m) centres and infilled with split timbers. Although there is no reason to suspect that timber was anywhere in short supply (Hanson and Macinnes 1980), the felling, transportation, conversion and erection process might have added a further 60,000 man days to the building programme.

The above calculations for the time taken to construct the curtain have not included its stone base. Assuming an average width of 14 feet (4·3 m) and depth of 6 inches (150 mm), the volume of stone required would have been of the order of 52,000 cubic yards (40,000 m³). By no means all of this needed to be worked, or even necessarily quarried, for the bulk of the stonework consists of rough cobbles. Some might have been derived from watercourses or obtained by surface collection, made easier if an area had already been subject to agriculture, but at least some quarrying is implied by the worked kerbstones. The whole process, including transportation, might have added a further 60,000 man days.

TABLE 6.7 *Man days for Wall building*

Stone base	60,000
Military Way	60,000
Fortlets	50,000
Turf superstructure	1,250,000
Timber breastwork	60,000
Ditch	250,000
Total	1,730,000 man days

Construction of the Military Way might well have gone hand-in-hand with that of the Wall base, for both were employing similar materials, and at Bonnyside the road seems to have preceded the erection of the turf super-structure of the Wall (Steer 1957, 164). The smaller pebbles or gravel which made up the surface of the road were obtained from local small quarry scoops, some of which are still in evidence at the rear of the Wall to the west of Rough Castle, but the larger foundation stones would presumably have been obtained in the same way as the stones which make up the Wall base, and a similar number of man days for the labour involved might be suggested.

Finally, the building of the fortlets would have represented the construction of a further 2460 m of rampart, their north fronts having been included in the calculation for the building of the curtain itself. For the most part, however, the ramparts of the fortlets do not exceed 75 per cent of the curtain's width, so the work involved would have amounted to only 35,000 man days for both base and superstructure, to which might be added a further 15,000 for the erection of the internal buildings.

The total figure for the building of the fortlets, Wall, ditch and Military Way, but excluding any forts, amounts to just less than 1¾ million man days (Table 6.7). We do not know exactly how many men were involved in the construction of the frontier. The Distance slabs suggest that *legio II* was present in full force, but only vexillations from the other two legions (Table 6.2). Clearly, every legionary soldier present could not be actively engaged in construction work; from the full complement of *legio II* perhaps 75 per cent or just over 4000 men might have participated. The size of the vexillations from legions *VI* and *XX* is uncertain, but if our calculations for the capacity of labour camps is correct (see above p.120f), each would have been of the order of about 1500–2000 men. Taking the lower total figure, the work could have been completed in only 250 days or just over 8 months which, if the time available in any one year for building equalled that for campaigning, would have taken $1\frac{1}{3}$ seasons.

Thus the timetable of work might be reconstructed somewhat along the following lines. The acclamation of Antoninus as Imperator in AD 142 should be seen as official confirmation that the fighting in North Britain had been brought to a successful conclusion. But before any construction work could be undertaken, it would have been necessary to survey the isthmus in order to determine the precise line of the frontier, the location of the primary forts and fortlets and to allocate the work amongst the legions. Construction of the primary forts at Old Kilpatrick, Balmuildy, Auchendavy, Castlecary, Mumrills and Carriden would have enjoyed a high priority, as we have seen, so that a garrison could be established as soon as possible. But forts were also required to consolidate the hinterland, to secure the eastern and western flanks of the Wall and provide outposts to the north. It might be supposed that this work could have been undertaken by those parts of legions VI and XX not present in the Wall-building contingent, for they are recorded constructing forts at Camelon, Cappuck and possibly Newstead (RIB 2210, 2119 and 2122–4). But the limited evidence points to the involvement of *legio II* also, for it is attested at Cramond (RIB 2137) and may have been responsible for the construction of Castledykes (RCAHMS 1978, 127). The construction of over 20 forts, including the six along the Wall, and a dozen smaller posts was surely sufficient to have occupied all the legionary troops available for a full season, though some alleviation of this task seems to have been afforded by auxiliary building (RIB 1276). One might suggest, however, that many of these forts could have been built during the time when the isthmus was undergoing detailed survey, leaving the rest to be completed the following season by those not involved in Wall-building, thus allowing work to commence on the Wall itself as soon as possible. It is unlikely that there would have been time to tackle much more than the first three stints in the east, that is from Bridgeness to Watling Lodge, though the laying of the base, the building of the Military Way and possibly the construction of fortlets may have been able to progress rather further.

The second season will have seen a resumption of work on the Wall with the intention of bringing it to a conclusion before the onset of winter put a stop to building activities. But 143 AD also saw a re-assessment of the role of the frontier (see below p.165), possibly related to the arrival of a new governor (?Cornelius Priscianus: Birley 1981, 115–6). Before those laying the base had reached Castlehill, or even sooner, and probably before the ditch diggers and

PLATE 6.7   *Building inscription of* legio II Augusta *from Cawder House.*

rampart builders had reached Rough Castle, a decision was taken to strengthen
the defences of the Wall by the addition of further garrisons. This entailed the
construction of some 10 or 12 new forts which must have considerably diverted
the legionary builders from their allotted tasks, though there is no reason to
suggest that work on the rest of the Wall would have been halted entirely. All
the legions seem to have been involved in the new fort-building activity; *II
Augusta* is attested on a building stone at Cadder and in conjunction with *XX
Valeria Victrix* at Bar Hill (RIB 2188, 2171 and possibly 2209) (pl.6.7), while
the latter legion alone was responsible for the construction of the fort at
Bearsden (Hassall and Tomlin 1977, 433–4), and *VI Victrix* is recorded on
three building stones from Croy Hill (RIB 2161–3). It is possible that auxiliaries may have helped with the work, for they are attested on building inscriptions from Rough Castle and Bar Hill (RIB 2145 and 2170). But until the time
of Trajan at least, building work was the preserve of the legions; Bar Hill and
Castlecary, where a further auxiliary building inscription is known (RIB 2155),
both provide records of legionary constructions, so that unless the work had
been shared between legionary and auxiliary contingents at the same site, it
seems more likely that all of the auxiliary dedications refer to rebuilding in the
second Antonine period when the standard of masonry is notably inferior (see
below p.155).

The construction of the additional forts will undoubtedly have prolonged the building of the Wall well into a third season, especially if the decision had been prompted by local hostilities, since they would first have had to be suppressed. Thus the end of the third season may have been in sight with the Wall still uncompleted. It is precisely into such a context that a re-allocation of the final sector into smaller stints would make sense, in order to bring the work to a speedy conclusion by the winter of AD 144 with the optimum use of available manpower.

VII. THE HISTORY OF THE WALL

The history of the Antonine Wall, particularly the date of its final abandonment, has been one of the most complex and hotly debated topics in recent study of the Roman occupation of northern Britain. The dispute has been caused by the apparently contradictory nature of the evidence: for example, the dates derived from studies of the imported samian ware pottery did not tally with those based on the indigenous coarse wares; the coin hoards provided a different chronological picture from that derived from coins found on excavations. Various ingenious explanations have been put forward at one time or another, but the key to the problem did not appear until the publication of a detailed study of the samian pottery from sites throughout Scotland (Hartley 1972), and the subsequent re-dating of the coarse pottery to bring it into line (Gillam 1974). A broad consensus has at last been reached, although much of the detail, and in particular the causation of events, remain open to dispute.

Chronology. Most of the Roman forts in Scotland which have been examined, including those on the Antonine Wall, have provided evidence of two distinct periods of occupation, normally referred to by archaeologists as Antonine I and II. These are attested either epigraphically, where two different auxiliary units are recorded from the same site, as at Mumrills, Castlecary and Bar Hill (Table 8.2), or structurally, where buildings within a fort can be shown to have been rebuilt, usually along similar lines (Table 7.1), but sometimes to an entirely different plan, as at Mumrills (fig.7.1). The ephemeral traces of a third occupation which have been detected at some Antonine Wall sites will be discussed in chapter 10.

The approximate date for the beginning of the primary occupation is securely fixed by an historical reference (SHA Antoninus Pius V) and two

TABLE 7.1   *Structural evidence for two periods in Wall forts**

Site	Defences	Central range	Barracks / stables
Mumrills	New ditches on E side, re-used stones in culverts through rampart.	*principia* and *praetorium* rebuilt on new foundations	—
Rough Castle	Alterations to E defences of annexe	E wall of *praetorium* on new foundation, two types of walling.	—
Castlecary	—	Two distinct types of workmanship.	—
Croy Hill	—	Minor alterations in *principia*, two main road surfaces.	—
Bar Hill	—	Minor alterations in *principia*.	
Cadder	Two floor levels in E gate.	Pits beneath *principia*, two series of post-holes in *praetorium*.	Additional post-holes, some packed with re-used masonry, and raised floors.
Balmuildy	—	Minor alterations in *principia* and *praetorium*.	Two drainage systems and hints of an earlier street system.
Duntocher	—	Two stone buildings on different alignments, two series of post-holes, two phases of roadway.	
Old Kilpatrick	—	Two foundations, one above the other, raised floor level and sealing of post-holes in *principia*.	Two different methods of construction.

* Evidence from bath-houses has been excluded because they are subject to alterations at frequent intervals which need not necessarily reflect different periods of occupation within the fort.

important building inscriptions from Balmuildy (RIB 2191 and 2192) which place the construction of the Wall in the governorship of Lollius Urbicus (AD 139–142). The end of this occupation came at some time late in the 150s during the governorship of Julius Verus (c.AD 154–8), for rebuilding is attested at Heddon-on-the-Wall between the Hadrianic forts of Benwell and Rudchester in AD 158 (RIB 1389), and the fact that Verus is mentioned on inscriptions from Corbridge, just south of Hadrian's Wall, and Brough-on-Noe in Derbyshire presumably indicates re-occupation at those sites too (RIB 1132 and 283).

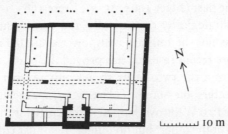

FIGURE 7.1   *The* principia *at Mumrills showing two structural phases.*

It was pointed out in 1964 that the break in the occupation of the Antonine Wall was only brief (Steer 1964, 25–7). The inscriptions from Rough Castle, Castlecary and Bar Hill (RIB 2145, 2155 and 2170) all record building by auxiliaries, and thus ought to relate to the second period of occupation of the Antonine Wall (see below p.156), yet all are dedicated to Antoninus Pius. Furthermore, the number of sites on the Wall at which buildings of the second Antonine occupation followed almost exactly the same lines as their predecessors (Table 7.1) looks like more than coincidence: the original foundations must have been readily visible still. Indeed, were not two units attested at Bar Hill, the structural changes evident would barely warrant the assertion of two distinct periods of occupation, so that one must presume a minimal gap between them. Further it is possible that some of the barrack blocks at Bar Hill, Rough Castle and Cadder may have continued in use through both periods of occupation on the Wall (see below pp.165–9).

The archaeological evidence from two sites in the hinterland also suggests only a short interval between their two Antonine occupations. At Crawford alterations to the defences prior to the second occupation involved the backfilling of at least part of the earlier ditch circuit, but little or no silt had accumulated in these ditches. Unless they had been deliberately cleaned out prior to being backfilled, which seems unlikely, one can only conclude that the ditches had not been left unattended sufficiently long for the quite rapid natural silting process to take effect (Maxwell 1972, 178). A similar situation was noted 30 years ago at Newstead (Richmond 1950, 14), but since the site continued in occupation as an outpost fort of Hadrian's Wall, its history cannot be taken to reflect that of the Antonine Wall. At Camelon, however, situated less than a mile north of the Wall, there was no detectable gap in the occupation of the southern annexe, although different phases of construction were evident (Maxfield 1979, 32).

Furthermore, the evidence which has now accumulated for the early date of the final abandonment of the Antonine Wall (see below) removes any possibility of a long period of re-occupation of Hadrian's Wall in the 150s, unless the two Walls were occupied simultaneously. Such an explanation has been put forward in the past (Steer 1964, 25–9; Frere 1967, 156), but would make no sense either strategically or tactically and can be summarily dismissed. There simply was not the military manpower available in Britain to make it possible, and more recent research has proved the point. A comparison of the samian pottery from the two Walls shows only a 5 per cent overlap in the distribution of potters' die-stamps (Hartley 1972, 22–6). In other words, the occupation of the two Walls overlapped sufficiently for the repair of one prior to the evacuation of the other, but no longer. A similar conclusion may also be drawn from the chronological distribution of coins from sites on both Walls (Shotter 1976, 88–90).

Detailed study of the samian ware has also indicated that the second occupation of the Antonine Wall was short-lived. Hartley concluded that, with the exception of one or two sites, notably Newstead, which were held as outpost forts for Hadrian's Wall, no forts in Scotland were held for more than a few years after AD 160 (1972, 36–8). Gillam has now brought the dating of the coarse pottery into line, although this has wider ramifications for the interpretation of the later second and early third century occupation of Hadrian's Wall which it would be out of place to discuss here (Gillam 1974, 8–12) (but see below pp.193–212).

The numismatic evidence, however, appears to remain internally contradictory and thus will be considered in more detail. There are three types of coin find: stratified site finds, stray finds and hoards, of which the most important are the site finds. There is only one stratified coin known from any fort on the Antonine Wall which is later than the reign of Antoninus Pius himself, and that is a denarius of Lucilla, his daughter, minted between AD 164 and 169 (Miller 1928, 34). One or two later coins have been picked up as stray finds in the vicinity of forts: an *as* of Marcus Aurelius of AD 174–5 from Mumrills, an unspecified coin of Commodus from near Kirkintilloch and a possible Commodan coin from Bar Hill (Robertson 1957b, 244–5). But these could have been dropped by a Roman patrol or a local native at any time thereafter; they certainly cannot be taken to indicate occupation of any of the forts at that time. In a recent statistical assessment of all the coin finds, excluding hoards, known from the Wall, Shotter has concluded that evacuation prior to AD 170 would be consistent with the data (1976, 84–6). A similar absence of later second-century coins is notable at all the Roman forts in Scotland which did not form part of the outer screen for Hadrian's Wall or figure in the Severan campaigns (Robertson 1975a, 384–5).

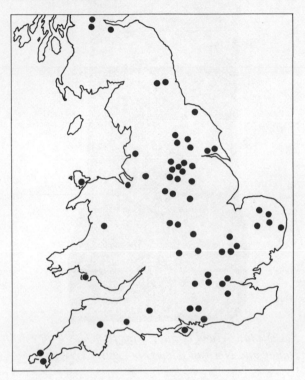

FIGURE 7.2 *The distribution of coin hoards in Britain deposited in the mid-second century (after Robertson).*

The coin hoards, however, appear to tell a different story. A number of hoards are known in Scotland which must have been deposited in the later second century. One from Rumbling Bridge, Kinross-shire, not far north of the Antonine Wall, has figured prominently in the argument for the continuing occupation of the Wall at least into the reign of Commodus (Robertson 1957b). Unfortunately, we have no way of knowing either who deposited the coins or whence they derived. While a nearby Roman military source is a possibility, it is by no means the only one. It is not unreasonable to suggest that the coins could have been amassed by a native, either by trade or plunder. The examples of much later large hoards such as the famous Falkirk hoard or the fourth-century hoard from Fort Augustus in Inverness-shire are readily explained in this way without being taken to imply Roman occupation of the area at that time (Robertson 1978, 207–9). Thus the hoard evidence alone is not

PLATE 7.1   *Possible late second century altar from Castlecary dedicated by Italian and Norican soldiers in* legio VI Victrix.

sufficiently certain to counterbalance that from other coin and pottery finds.

Furthermore, there is strong epigraphic evidence for the reoccupation of forts on and to the south of Hadrian's Wall in the early 160s. Building activity during the governorship of Calpurnius Agricola (*c*.AD 162–6) is attested at Corbridge (RIB 1149), Chesterholm (RIB 1703) and Ribchester (RIB 589), while his presence is also indicated at Carvoran (RIB 1809). The significance of these inscriptions was recognised almost 30 years ago by John Gillam, although the accepted dating of the destruction deposit at Corbridge led him to the assumption that this activity fell between the two Antonine occupations of Scotland rather than marking their end (1953).

The only sites in Scotland where later second-century occupation is demonstrable were those which acted as outpost forts for the newly re-occupied Hadrian's Wall. In the west the original outpost forts at Birrens (Robertson 1975, 284), Netherby (RIB 975) and Bewcastle (Goodburn 1978, 421 and 474) continued to be held, while in the east Roman surveillance certainly reached as far north as Newstead (Hartley 1972, 53–4) and possibly beyond. An altar from Castlecary (RIB 2148) (pl.7.1) hints at occupation there later than the 160s, but is not supported by other evidence (see below p.197).

The overall chronological picture is now relatively clear. Inevitably future work will produce refinements, but it seems unlikely that the main periods of occupation indicated in Table 7.2 will be seriously challenged. It should be stressed, however, that not all forts or other structures, especially on Hadrian's Wall, show all the phases indicated. Nor need the history of any one necessarily correspond in detail with any other.

TABLE 7.2   *Periods of occupation on the two Walls*

Hadrian's Wall		Antonine Wall	
Structural Phase	*Date*	*Structural Phase*	*Date*
IA	122–142		
		I	142–c.158
	158		
		II	c.158–164
IB	164–185		
II	185–197/208		

Analysis. If the broad chronology is now generally agreed, the interpretation of exactly what happened and why remains a matter of dispute. There are, at opposite extremes, two approaches to the analysis of the history of this period, which might be termed the pro-Roman and the pro-native. The first tends to explain all events as the result of Roman policy, quite often dictated not by what was happening in Britain but by actions on the broader imperial stage; the second prefers to see events influenced almost entirely by local considerations. Thus the pro-Roman view is inclined to see all troop movements as calculated policy decisions reflecting either requirements elsewhere in the empire or, less popularly, merely with whim of the emperor, while the pro-native view prefers to explain them as the result of direct military interaction between Roman troops and the local inhabitants. The history of the northern frontier in the second century provides ample scope for such scholarly disagreements, for in the space of no more than a quarter of a century the frontier was moved from the Tyne-Solway to the Forth-Clyde line and back, twice.

The reasons for the original abandonment of Hadrian's Wall and the building of the Antonine Wall at the start of Pius' reign have been discussed already in chapter 4. The occupation appears to have continued without incident, as far as our sources tell us, for some 15 years before it was brought to a close. Traditionally, the end of the first occupation of the Antonine Wall has been seen as the result of enemy action, with evidence of apparent destruction recorded from the early excavations at a number of Wall forts. In recent years, however, archaeological interpretation has become more sophisticated. The bare evidence of buildings having been destroyed does not mean that the enemy were responsible. The nature of the destruction, which is less than fully described in older excavations, is crucial to an interpretation of the events which led to the evacuation. Local tribesmen, for example, are unlikely to have taken the time and trouble to dismantle buildings totally as a token of their victory over Rome; fire is the obvious means of achieving such an end with the minimum of effort, especially when most of the buildings in a Roman fort were either wholly or partly built of timber, and evidence of destruction by fire alone is thus more likely to represent hostile action. But even if one ignores the possibility of accidental fires, it is becoming increasingly clear that deliberate demolition, which included the burning of timbers, was a common occurrence at the end of occupation of a Roman fort, and must surely have been standard practice for a departing garrison (Hanson 1978a, 302–4). Fortunately, some attempt can be made to distinguish between these possibilities. Extensive burning *in situ* is more likely to reflect hostile action than limited burning of dismantled structures. Thus although the early excavators were in the habit of concluding that their sites had suffered disasters of varying magnitude, in their need to interpret the information from their excavations according to the historical theories of the time (*vide* Miller 1922, 105; 1928, 57), a closer examination of the published reports makes it difficult to substantiate this on the basis of the excavated data. Only at Mumrills is there clear evidence of a building, the commandant's house, having been burnt down. Ironically, the excavators concluded that the fire must have been accidental, for the timber building was replaced by a much larger stone-built structure which is best associated with the first rather than the second period of occupation on the site (Macdonald and Curle 1929, 439–40; see also p.174 below). This conclusion would seem to be confirmed by the evidence obtained during excavations some years later which suggested the deliberate slighting of the defences at the end of the first period of occupation (Steer 1961, 90). Further evidence of Roman demolition has been forthcoming in recent excavations at Bearsden where a claw tool and a number of bent nails had simply been left behind when the site was abandoned (Breeze 1979b, 25). Elsewhere, as observed above, and notably at Bar Hill, it seems possible that some barrack buildings may even have continued in use into the second period of occupation. An examination of the Distance slabs also implies that the withdrawal was both deliberate and unhurried. The records of their discoveries in modern times indicate that many had been deliberately concealed; a suggestion which is further supported by the excellent state of preservation of so many of the stones, which can hardly have been long exposed to the ravages of the Scottish climate (Keppie 1975, 60–1). It is not known for certain, however, whether this occurred at the end of the first or second period of occupation.

If we turn to sites which do not lie on the line of the Wall, the pattern is generally similar. North of the Wall, at Strageath, excavations over the last decade or so have produced evidence of deliberate demolition in the form of deposits of burnt daub and charcoal from bonfires lit by retiring troops (Frere 1979, 41), while at Camelon no destruction whatsoever was apparent in the southern annexe of the fort during recent excavations there (Maxfield 1979). Further south, on Dere Street, the human bones and military equipment recovered from pits at Newstead are sometimes quoted as indicative of successful native insurrection (Frere 1978, 177), but this need not be the case. Only three of the 25 Antonine pits contained anything out of the ordinary. One of those was almost certainly a votive deposit, since it contained an upright birch branch some nine feet long down the centre. The other two should probably be interpreted in the same way as earlier pits from the site (see above, p.46f), that is, as rubbish deposits. Further south, at Cappuck, no evidence of destruction was noted and in several sites on the western route the pattern is largely the same. At both Castledykes and Crawford buildings of the first Antonine period continued in use through the second (Robertson 1964b, 82; Maxwell 1972, 173 and 177), while the fortlet at Barburgh Mill, where no re-occupation took place, was deliberately demolished and the ditches partially backfilled (Breeze 1974, 142-3). Only at Birrens is widespread enemy destruction postulated (Robertson 1975b, 283), although some doubt has recently been cast on that interpretation (Breeze 1977a, 459); the destruction itself is undeniable, for a layer of masonry debris, burnt clay and wood was spread consistently across the site. But Birrens could hardly have been abandoned as part of the return to the more southerly frontier, for it was an integral part of that system, and there is evidence of it being rebuilt in AD 158 (RID 2110) at exactly the same time as the section of Hadrian's Wall at Heddon. It does not seem particularly logical for the Romans to destroy the fort by fire in what appears to have been an untypically haphazard manner if this decision was part of a policy which involved reconstruction at the same site. Were that the case, there ought surely to be evidence of careful demolition.

The withdrawal from Scotland in the late 150s cannot then have been the result of hostile tribes from the north sweeping the Romans before them. Even accepting the destruction at Birrens, only very localised hostility is evident. The concentration of Roman installations in the Annan and Nith valleys indicates that that area had been considered a possible trouble-spot, although the reduction of the garrison in the second Antonine occupation suggests that the problem had originally been overestimated. The long accepted explanation of the withdrawal is that there had been an internal revolt in the province to the south, amongst the Brigantes of northern England – a view originally expressed by Haverfield in 1904. The starting point for this hypothesis was a number of building inscriptions erected in the governorship of Julius Verus (AD 154-8) at Birrens (RIB 2110), Corbridge (EE ix, 1383 correcting RIB 1132) and Brough-on-Noe (RIB 283), and the slab from Newcastle recording the arrival of legionary vexillations (RIB 1322). Since all these forts lie in the territory normally assigned to the Brigantes, an explanation was thought to have been provided by the much debated brief sentence in Pausanias, although this now seems more likely to refer to events earlier in Antoninus' reign (see above pp.62–3).

PLATE 7.2   *Issue of Antoninus Pius AD 155 depicting Britannia supposedly subdued.*

There are, however, a number of factors which, when added together, point to unrest within the province at about this time. A coin issue of AD 154–5 depicts a seated figure of Britannia, the personification of the province, who has been described as looking dejected or defeated, her head propped on her right hand (Toynbee 1924, 152) (pl.7.2). While such provincial issues are abundant during the reign of Hadrian and need not necessarily mirror anything that was happening in the relevant province at the time, Britain is the only province so commemorated in Antoninus' reign, once at the beginning and again in 154–5 AD. Thus it seems likely that the later coins do refer to a specific event, even if one rejects the possibility of assessing Britannia's demeanour, and hence the state of the province, from a coin. In addition, the inscription from Newcastle referred to above, which records the arrival of legionary troops from the German provinces during the governorship of Verus, is strongly suggestive of troop reinforcements being sent either after or in anticipation of trouble. These two items alone might not be sufficient to sway the balance in favour of an internal revolt, but together with the evidence of the coin hoards, they acquire considerable authority. Hoarding, which is generally accepted as a good indicator of troubled times, reaches a pronounced peak under Marcus, Antoninus' successor, with a notable concentration of hoards in the territory of the Brigantes (Robertson 1974b, 27 and 31) (fig.7.2). The close dating of hoards is often difficult when records of them derive from antiquarian sources, so it is uncertain whether the majority of hoards attributed to Marcus relate to his own reign or to the period in Antoninus' reign when he was issuing coins as Caesar. But even if all the hoards derive from the

160s rather than the 150s, they provide archaeological confirmation of the trouble referred to in Marcus' reign (SHA Marcus VIII, 7–8) which, since internal disorder tends to break out only after a period of discontent, may well have had its origins rather earlier.

Ideally one would like to be able to demonstrate this archaeologically, by pointing to sites where destruction at the appropriate date is attested, as has been done for the Boudican revolt of AD 60. There is, however, little evidence of destruction at Roman forts in Brigantian territory which can be safely attributed to the mid-second century. But since most of the Pennine forts seem to have been unoccupied at this time, this need occasion no surprise. Even where destruction is indicated, as at Lancaster (Wilson 1972, 312) and possibly Ambleside and Hardknott (Hartley 1980, 5), it is difficult on the basis of pottery dating alone to be sure that it occurred in the 150s rather than the 160s. Ironically, the clearest evidence of destruction at a number of forts appears to date rather later in the century (see below pp.198–9).

If the forts do not show signs of destruction, we must turn to the other manifestations of Roman occupation, the towns and villas, to see whether there are any indications that they suffered at this time. Few of the villas that are known in Brigantian territory seem to have been occupied sufficiently early in the second century to have been affected (Branigan 1980b, 21). One, at Kirk Sink, Gargrave, was founded shortly after the middle of the century (Wilson 1975, 238), while a second, at Welton, was occupied without disruption through the middle of the century, both of which imply settled conditions. Urban centres in the area are not numerous and excavation has been limited, but there is no evidence of destruction at this time. Even the construction of defences, as at Aldborough, seems to come later in the century (Charlesworth 1971, 159).

The conclusion must be, therefore, that a revolt of any magnitude in the territory of the Brigantes in the 150s is unproven, but that unsettled conditions may have continued from the mid-second century onwards with sporadic outbreaks of hostility. Nonetheless, the perceived threat seems to have been sufficient to cause a certain amount of indecision about the northern frontier. It is not acceptable, however, to blame the vacillation on the governor, Verus (Breeze 1975, 76). It is totally contrary to the tradition of direct imperial control over foreign policy to suggest that the governor had exceeded his brief in ordering the troops out of Scotland. If Verus was responsible for the evacuation of Scotland, as the dating evidence seems to make clear, he was acting on the instructions of Antoninus himself. But that evacuation was short-lived and the re-occupation of the Antonine Wall virtually immediate. The nature of the problem in northern England had been overestimated, Antoninus had overreacted and was now eager not to lose the prestige of his original conquest unnecessarily.

It is difficult to say exactly how rapidly the return to Scotland took place. The impression gained from excavations at Crawford and Camelon was that the gap was almost imperceptible. The evidence, or rather the lack of evidence, from Hadrian's Wall supports this. Apart from the inscription from Heddon-on-the-Wall (RIB 1389), there is nothing which indicates re-occupation at this time. The occupation of Hadrian's Wall is subdivided by archaeologists into structural phases (see Table 7.1) but these are at present insufficient to fit the known fluctuations on the northern frontier: the postulated re-occupation of Hadrian's Wall in AD 158 does not seem to be represented in the structural phases evidenced in the forts and milecastles. It might be argued that the re-occupation of the Wall was begun in AD 158 and continued as a gradual process. This would explain the missing structural phase, but represents a return to the doctrine of simultaneous occupation of the two Walls which is both *a priori* unlikely and totally at variance with the analysis of the samian ware. We are left with the conclusion, therefore, that the evacuation of Scotland under Verus was so brief that there was hardly time for any reconstruction on Hadrian's Wall. In this context the rebuilding at Corbridge assumes some importance. It has long been noted that with the exception of the Trajanic period, the history of the fort at Corbridge reflects not that of the Tyne-Solway frontier, but that of the occupation of Scotland (Gillam 1977, 73–4). Re-occupation of Corbridge under Verus (EE IX 1383 correcting RIB 1132) is, therefore, more likely to herald the return to Scotland than the occupation of the more southerly line. Thus, if the beginning of the reconstruction of Hadrian's Wall is attested in 158 AD (RIB 1389), the return to Scotland was underway before the end of the same year, since that probably marked the end of Verus' governorship (Birley 1981, 120–3).

The second Antonine occupation of Scotland is marked by a considerable reduction in the overall garrison (fig.7.3). In the south-west most of the smaller posts appear to have remained unoccupied and the route through Nithsdale left completely unprotected. Excavation at the forts at Carzield, Loudoun Hill and Raeburnfoot, the fortlets at Barburgh Mill and Durisdeer and the tower at Beattock Summit indicate only one period of occupation. Elsewhere in the Lowlands the fort at Lyne has provided evidence of only one period of occupation which the excavators related to the second rather than the first Antonine period (Steer and Feachem 1962, 217). The pottery upon which this assumption was based would not now be assigned quite so late as was then assumed (Hartley 1972, 34 *re* Cettus and Cinnamus), so a reduction in garrison, with the fort replaced by a fortlet in the second period, is probable at Lyne also. Our knowledge of the forts along Dere Street is limited, but the garrison at Newstead appears to have been reduced, the mixed contingent of legionaries and auxiliary cavalry being replaced by an *ala milliaria* (Richmond 1950, 19–24), although it remained the most important site in Scotland. The

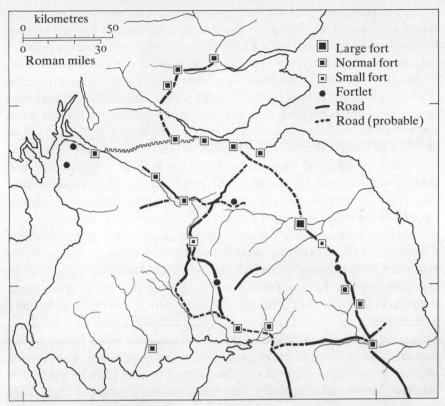

FIGURE 7.3 *Permanent military installations in North Britain during the second Antonine occupation.*

small fort at Cappuck was further reduced in size, though we do not know the precise effect upon the garrison (Richmond 1951, 145), while the road post at Chew Green seems to have been given up, for it revealed only one period of occupation, which presumably belongs to the first Antonine period (Richmond and Keeney 1937, 142).

A similar pattern of reduction is evident on the Wall and its outpost forts. At least one fort on the Wall was not re-occupied, while others demonstrate a reduction in the size or fighting potential of their garrison (see below p.171). There has been insufficient excavation at any of the milefortlets to be certain whether they were re-occupied at this time, but the interiors at Seabegs (Keppie and Walker 1981) and Wilderness Plantation (Wilkes 1974, 57) were cobbled over. However, this could have occurred during the first occupation, when the tactical plan for the Wall was changed. To the north of the Wall, the fort at Ardoch was reduced in area by approximately 25 per cent (pl.5.3), while one of the equitate cohorts at Strageath seems to have been replaced by a second infantry unit.

This reduction in garrison hardly lends support to the suggestion that the return to Scotland was in answer to a northern threat, nor that the original evacuation had been precipitated by any serious native pressure. Expediency may have dictated the diminution of the garrison if the Pennine forts continued to be occupied as has been suggested (Hartley 1972, 39). If true, this would imply that unsettled conditions, rather than open rebellion, were continuing in northern England, since troops were left behind, but the threat was not considered sufficiently serious to prevent the return to Scotland. Nor should it be thought that the re-occupation was intended to be other than permanent. The new troop dispositions were akin to those evident in the first century and may well represent a more rational appraisal of requirements. Nonetheless, within five years the situation had altered quite dramatically and once more the troops were withdrawn.

Again, the nature of the evacuation is in dispute. In the past, evidence of a second great disaster at Antonine Wall forts has been alluded to and generally attributed to that attested historically in the 180s (Macdonald 1934, 479), to that postulated in the 190s (Gillam 1953, 375), or to that thought to have occurred in the early years of the third century (Jarrett and Mann 1970, 203). The revised chronological framework, which will allow none of these interpretations, highlights the dangers of circular reasoning when archaeological data are made to fit historical or pseudo-historical events. Before any assessment of the causes of the final abandonment of Scotland can be made, it is essential that the archaeological evidence is examined without any preconception or bias.

At no site is there unequivocal evidence of hostile action causing the end of the occupation. The early excavators seem to have equated limited survival of structural evidence with destruction by the enemy, whereas, if this does reflect activity in Roman times rather than the gradual denudation of the site over the centuries, it is more likely to represent deliberate demolition by the respective garrisons. Where there are more positive data, they point to a similar conclusion. Although there are indications of destruction by burning of structures outside the fort at Mumrills, the area was tidied up and the material used to fill the annexe ditches (Steer 1961, 91–2). Similarly, the deliberate filling of the wells at Old Kilpatrick (Miller 1928, 23) and Bar Hill (Robertson *et al.* 1975, 14) with structural debris is the action of a Roman demolition squad, not of a band of hostile natives.

Both from the outpost forts and from those in the hinterland a similar picture is emerging. At Strageath the discovery of a broken spade-blade in a post-hole of the second Antonine period is strongly suggestive of demolition by the army (Frere 1979, 41). Disturbed post-holes, bent nails and pits full of demolition debris hint at a similar fate for the fort at Crawford (Maxwell 1972, 164 and 170), while the mass of pottery in an annexe ditch at Castledykes is strongly reminiscent of the clearing-up process seen at Mumrills (Robertson 1964b, 275). At Cappuck, on the other hand, the fortlet defences seem to have fallen gradually into decay (Richmond 1951, 145), though this may relate to later occupation there (Hartley 1972, 40).

It is difficult on the above basis to believe that the final abandonment of the Antonine Wall was in any way connected with hostility in Scotland, particularly when a number of forts in quite isolated positions, including Newstead and possibly Castlecary, were maintained as outpost forts for the restored Hadrianic frontier. Nevertheless, there is reference in the literary sources to the threat of war in Britain in the early 160s and the dispatch of Calpurnius Agricola to deal with the problem (SHA Marcus Aurelius VIII, 7–8). Agricola's presence is attested on inscriptions at a number of forts, all located in northern England (see above p.142). Pottery evidence indicates the reoccupation of many other forts in the same area around this time, if they had not already been refurbished by Verus a few years earlier (Gillam and Mann 1970, 25). There is no specific evidence of destruction in northern England which can definitely be associated with Agricola's governorship but the significance of the coin hoards as indicators of civil unrest has been noted already (see above p.146f). That such unrest continued below the surface for some time is hinted at by a reference to a further threat of war in Britain later in Marcus' reign (SHA Marcus Aurelius XXII, 1) and the transfer of a large contingent of newly conscripted auxiliary cavalry from the Danube frontier to reinforce the army in Britain (Dio LXXI, 16). Nonetheless, it is hard to accept that affairs in Britain alone were sufficiently serious to have brought about the northern withdrawal. Rome was at her peak of power under the Antonine emperors and could have dealt with the situation very readily were not other problems more pressing. Almost from the beginning of his reign Marcus was faced with serious upheaval: the Chatti invaded Germany and Raetia and a major war erupted in Parthia. The presence in Britain as governor at the time of Marcus' accession of M. Statius Priscus, one of the most able generals of his day, suggests that the threat of war was being taken seriously, but his rapid transfer to Parthia highlights the relative strategic importance of the two extremes of the empire. Trouble in northern Britain did not constitute a serious threat to the heart of the empire, nor did Marcus rely upon any northern conquest for his prestige with the army or the people of Rome. Under these circumstances the withdrawal from Scotland not long after Marcus' accession can be seen as a rational policy decision intended to reduce pressure on stretched resources (Breeze 1975, 77), but stimulated by an undercurrent of unrest within the province. Thus the Antonine Wall marked the northern frontier of the Roman empire for little more than 20 years from AD 142 to 164.

VIII. THE WALL IN OPERATION

The questions most often asked about the Antonine Wall are also the most difficult to answer, for they concern its purpose and how it functioned. Since no explicit literary evidence has survived to provide the answers, any attempt to reach a reasoned conclusion must combine a detailed study of the remains (chapters 5 and 6) with a general knowledge of defence strategies and an understanding of the nature of the Roman army (chapter 1).

In principle, military frontiers are designed, and later develop, to meet threats of a particular intensity (Luttwak 1976, 61–6). In other words, to take the two extremes, to face small-scale infiltration on the one hand or massed attack on the other. To deal most efficiently with the latter requires the concentration of mobile units within easy striking distance of the area of supposed threat. The utilisation of natural barriers is common because they reduce the number of places through which a large force may gain entry to the defended area. Thus strongpoints can be strategically positioned near mountain passes, river crossings, or simply at convenient points along natural routes. Since advance warning of hostile movement is essential to allow time to concentrate the forces where they are needed, some system of outposts or mobile patrols and a good communications network are necessary.

Thus, before we can attempt any assessment of the workings of the Wall, we must ascertain the nature and disposition of garrisons throughout the frontier zone. The evidence for this varies both in form and reliability. Epigraphy is the best source of detailed information about troops, but it is not always easy to use. All too often the inscriptions cannot be precisely dated. Where extensive excavation has taken place within a fort, it may be possible to assess the type of garrison from the number and size of its barracks and stables. Cavalry barracks are generally smaller and have fewer *contubernia* than in-

152

fantry barracks (Breeze and Dobson 1969, 27–30). Unfortunately, we do not possess the total plan of any Antonine fort, while complete plans of barrack blocks are rare, and no building has been identified as a stable with any certainty. As a last resort, fort size provides a crude general indication of the number of troops likely to have been in garrison, but the more we learn of the internal arrangements of forts, the more we realise the dangers of extrapolating from limited data.

The garrison of the Wall will be considered first (Table 8.1). As originally planned, it appears there were to be, along its entire length, only six forts, now referred to as the primary forts. There is no detailed information from Carriden, the most easterly example, which is known only from air-photographs. However, its estimated size would indicate that it was capable of holding a full quingenary garrison, possibly even a part-mounted unit. In contrast, there is a comparative wealth of evidence from Mumrills, the largest fort on the Wall, where two different units are attested epigraphically, the *ala I Tungrorum quingenaria* and the *cohors II Thracum quingenaria equitata* (RIB 2140 and 2142). The size of the fort, some 6·5 acres (2·6 ha) in internal area, seems over-generous for a *cohors quingenaria* but ideally suited to house an *ala*, which would have been the highest ranking auxiliary unit on the Wall. That such a prestigious garrison was the first in residence is suggested also by the large size of the headquarters building, which was considerably reduced in size in the second period of occupation as more suited to a quingenary cohort (Macdonald and Curle 1929, 426–8) (fig.7.1). Unfortunately, the evidence from the commandant's house does not fit this interpretation quite so readily, for it was at its most impressive in the second period (Macdonald and Curle 1929, 436–8).

Castlecary, too, has produced a comparative wealth of epigraphic evidence. Two large auxiliary regiments are attested there, as well as vexillations from both the second and the sixth legions. It is often assumed that the legions were in garrison at some time during the Antonine period (Wright 1968, 194; Breeze and Dobson 1976a, 97), even though sufficient auxiliary units are known for the two periods of Antonine occupation of the site; but there is no need to equate legionary altars with a legionary garrison, for they can be readily explained as dedications by the Wall- or fort-builders.

There is no shortage of legionary dedications from the line of Hadrian's Wall (Table 8.2), but no one would suggest that they all represent legionary occupation even though one, from Housesteads (RIB 1583), specifically states that soldiers of *II Augusta* were *agentes in praesidio* (on garrison duty). Indeed, the very fact that this is precisely specified implies that it was an unusual situation. The outposting of legions to undertake menial garrison duties would have been a waste of their considerable training and expertise. The fact that the inscription mentioning *cohors I Tungrorum* (RIB 2155) was a building record

TABLE 8.1 *The probable garrisons of forts on the Wall*

| | Internal area | | Garrison | |
Site	acres	hectares	Antonine I	Antonine II
CARRIDEN	c.4	1·6	*cohors quingenaria*	
Inveravon	small		—	
MUMRILLS	6·5	2·6	*ala I Tungrorum quingenaria*	*cohors II Thracum quingenaria equitata*
Falkirk	—			—
Rough Castle	1·0	0·5	detachment of uncertain unit	detachment of *cohors VI Nerviorum quingenaria*
CASTLECARY	3·5	1·4	detachment of *cohors I Fida Vardullorum milliaria equitata*	detachment of *cohors I Tungrorum milliaria*
Westerwood	2	0·8	detachment of unknown unit under legionary centurion	
Croy Hill	1·5	0·6	detachment of unknown unit	
Bar Hill	3·2	1·3	*cohors I Hamiorum quingenaria*	*cohors I Baetasiorum quingenaria* or a detachment thereof
AUCHENDAVY	c.2·8	1·1	*cohors quingenaria* or unknown detachment under legionary centurion	
Kirkintilloch	—			—
Cadder	2·8	1·1	*cohors quingenaria*	*cohors quingenaria peditata*
BALMUILDY	4	1·6	detachment of *cohors milliaria*	*cohors quingenaria peditata* or detachment of *cohors quingenaria equitata*
Bearsden	2·4	0·9	cavalry detachment	no garrison
Castlehill	c.3·2	1	detachment of *cohors IIII Gallorum quingenaria equitata*	—
Duntocher	0·5	0·2	detachment of unknown unit	
OLD KILPATRICK	4·2	1·7	*cohors quingenaria equitata* or *cohors milliaria*	detachment of *cohors I Baetasiorum quingenaria*

Primary forts are indicated in CAPITALS

Table 8.2 *Legionary altars and tombstones from Hadrian's Wall*

Site	Altars	Tombstones
Wallsend	centurion of *VI Victrix*	
Newcastle	two dedications by *VI Victrix*	
Benwell	two centurions of *XX Valeria Victrix* and one of *II Augusta*	
Rudchester	centurion of *VI Victrix*	
Carrawburgh	vexillation of *VI Victrix*	
Housesteads	soldier and centurion of *VI Victrix* and two dedications by soldiers of *II Augusta* (one indicating that they were on garrison duty)	
Great Chesters	two centurions, one of *XX Valeria Victrix*, the other unspecified	erected by a centurion of *VI Victrix*
Carvoran	centurion of *VI*, *II* and *XX*	soldier of *XX Valeria Victrix*
Birdoswald	centurion of *VI Victrix*	
Birdoswald to Castlesteads	soldiers of *II Augusta* and *XX Valeria Victrix* and vexillation of *VI Victrix*	
Castlesteads to Stanwix	soldiers of *VI Victrix* and *II Augusta* (the latter with their centurion)	
Stanwix to Burgh-by-Sands	legate of *VI Victrix* (to record successes beyond the Wall)	
Burgh-by-Sands to Drumburgh	vexillation of *VI Victrix*	

suggests that this was probably the secondary garrison, since the original programme of fort-building must surely have been assigned to the legions; and such an inference is supported by the somewhat inferior nature of the masonry from the later period (Christison and Buchanan 1903, 304–6), which may reflect the contrast between legionary and auxiliary building-standards. The early excavations did little to reveal the barrack accommodation within the fort, though it is clear that it is far too small to have held either of the milliary units known if at full strength. The dedication by the original garrison, *cohors I Fida Vardullorum*, indicates that it was under the command of a *praefectus* rather than a *tribunus*, possibly in recognition of its reduced size (RIB 2149).

TABLE 8.3. *Inscriptions from Antonine Wall forts assignable to legionaries or auxiliaries**

SITE	LEGIONARY			AUXILIARY		
	Building	Altar	Tombstone	Building	Altar	Tombstone
Mumrills					ala I Tungrorum	II Thracum
Rough Castle					VI Nerviorum	
Castlecary	cohors VI, unspecified legion	3 by VI Victrix, one by II Augusta, one by unspecified vexillation		VI Nerviorum I Tungrorum		I Fida Vardullorum
Westerwood		wife of centurion of VI Victrix				
Croy Hill	3 by VI Victrix	VI Victrix	3 soldiers on possible tombstone			
Bar Hill	II Augusta and XX Valeria Victrix	II Augusta		I Baetasiorum	I Hamiorum I Baetasiorum prefect of unspecified unit	I Hamiorum
Auchendavy	II Augusta	4 by centurion of II Augusta	at least one of II Augusta†			
Cadder	II Augusta					
Balmuildy	2 by II Augusta				tribune of unspecified unit	
Bearsden	XX Valeria Victrix					
Castlehill					IIII Gallorum I Baetasiorum	
Old Kilpatrick						

* All auxiliary inscriptions are by cohorts unless otherwise indicated.

† Davies (1976) has argued that the second possible tombstone is a dedication by an *ala* alone or in conjunction with a legionary vexillation.

There is some debate over the identification of the next primary fort. Bar Hill has been much favoured, but Auchendavy is here preferred for reasons expressed in chapter 6 (above p.106). Despite a number of inscriptions from this site, which include a remarkable series of altars (Table 8.3), no unit is named. It has been suggested that the altars which were erected by a legionary centurion, M. Cocceius Firmus, were official dedications by him in his capacity as commander of the fort (Breeze and Dobson 1976a, 97; Macdonald 1934, 431), for the circumstances of their discovery recall those of the well known examples from Maryport (Jarrett 1965). On the other hand, Birley has noted that the failure to specify the unit belies the official nature of the dedications, whose number and wide religious scope can best be explained as the result of Firmus' earlier career in the Rome garrison rather than as the result of annual dedications over a period of years (1953). Thus the altars may indicate no more than the presence of the second legion in its capacity as the unit probably responsible for the building of the fort (RIB 2180). Although the additional presence of at least one legionary tombstone (RIB 2181) is strongly suggestive of a legionary garrison, such an interpretation is not absolutely essential; for example, the discovery of a legionary tombstone in the vicinity of the fort at Carvoran on Hadrian's Wall (RIB 1826) has not led to the suggestion that it ever had a legionary garrison. There has been no excavation at Auchendavy, but its size would be just about sufficient to house a *cohors quingenaria peditata*.

Balmuildy is without doubt a primary fort and has produced two very important legionary building dedications, but no certain indication of its garrison. An altar dedicated by Caecilius Nepos (RIB 2189) found in the fort bath-house refers to him as *tribunus* rather than by the usual title *praefectus*, which ought to indicate that he was in command of a milliary unit (Cheesman 1914, 36). This was probably the original garrison, although, as at Castlecary, the fort is hardly big enough to have housed such a large unit. At first glance the blocks of buildings within the *praetentura* and *retentura*, which would appear to relate to the second period of occupation (Miller 1922, 107–8), seem best suited to accommodate a *cohors quingenaria peditata*. However, this would represent a rather generous allocation of space, and the simplest interpretation of the post-holes in the one block that was thoroughly examined would suggest the presence of a small barrack block and an ancillary unpartitioned building, rather reminiscent of the barrack and possible stables or stores-buildings known from recent excavations at Bearsden (Breeze 1979b, 22) (figs 5.3 and 4). Thus the possibility of a cavalry presence should not be discounted.

The only inscription known from Old Kilpatrick, the most westerly of the primary forts, is a formal dedication to Juppiter Optimus Maximus by *cohors I Baetasiorum*, apparently under the command of a legionary centurion while the prefect, Publicius Maternus, was absent (Barber 1971). This has posed a number of problems. The centurion involved, Julius Candidus, names his legion as *I Italica*, which had been stationed on the Danube frontier since the late first century and is not otherwise attested in Britain. A possible explanation for his presence on the Antonine Wall might be the early third-century campaigns in Scotland when the emperor Severus brought vexillations from various legions. Superficial support for a post-Antonine date for the altar seems to be provided by the position of the abbreviation I.O.M. on the capital rather than the die, a notable third-century trait (Kewley 1973). Yet if this criterion were pressed, several perfectly acceptable Antonine altars from other Wall sites would require unnecessary redating (see below p.184). Moreover, both the absence of ligatures and the fineness of the lettering point to a second century date (information from Dr R.S.O.Tomlin). In fact, rather than introducing unnecessary complications, it would be simplest to regard Julius Candidus' position as similar to that of both Flavius Betto and Flavius Verecundus, who were in charge of detachments of auxiliary units at Rough Castle and Westerwood respectively. There is also a more direct parallel at Maryport in Cumbria, where the centurion in charge of *cohors I Hispanorum* under Hadrian was from *legio X Fretensis*, at that time stationed in Judaea (RIB 814). Since *cohors I Baetasiorum* seems to have formed the garrison of Bar Hill in the second Antonine period, it might be expected that it had formed the primary garrison at Old Kilpatrick. However, the comparatively large size of the fort and the proposed restoration of its internal plan suggest that sufficient accommodation would originally have been available for a cohors milliaria or a *cohors quingenaria equitata*. Thus a detachment of *cohors I Baetasiorum* may have been the secondary garrison at Old Kilpatrick under Candidus, which would explain the reduction of barrack accommodation in the second period (Miller 1928, 15–16), while the remainder of the unit was at Bar Hill under the prefect, Publicius Maternus.

The nature of the evidence quoted above makes the detailed assessment of the original or intended garrison of the Wall very difficult. However, if the assumptions made above are correct, the total garrison of the primary forts would have been of the order of 4000 (Table 8.1), including those manning the fortlets. Of the latter only Duntocher, Wilderness Plantation and most recently Kinneil have been excavated on sufficient scale to provide evidence of internal buildings. But assuming fortlets at approximately one-mile intervals and garrisons similar to those postulated for the milecastles on Hadrian's Wall (Breeze and Dobson 1972, 189), the number of men required is unlikely to have exceeded 1000 and was probably nearer 500. Given the small size of the forts at Balmuildy and Castlecary in relation to their postulated original garrisons, it would not be unreasonable to assume that a proportion of each unit was to be permanently outstationed in these fortlets. On the other hand, the primary forts on Hadrian's Wall, where a similar relationship may have existed between the occupants of milecastles and the main garrison, were not apparently reduced in size on that account. Be that as it may, the overall garrison strength of the Antonine Wall would thus have been approximately the same as that of Hadrian's Wall, with slightly less than half of the number of men covering almost exactly half the distance.

The primary forts are, for the most part, situated in good strategic positions: the two coastal forts require no further justification; Mumrills and Castlecary straddle the lines of access leading to the only known road to the north, and both seem to lie in the vicinity of earlier Agricolan forts; Balmuildy guards one of the only two major river crossings on the Wall line at the southern end of Strathblane, an obvious route to the north between the Kilpatrick Hills and the Campsie Fells. This suggests that the attention of the garrison would not have been focussed solely on the immediate locality. The outpost forts, in particular the concentration of troops in Strathearn along the old Gask frontier line, highlight the area from which the major threat was anticipated, and to these installations we shall now turn (Table 8.4).

TABLE 8.4 *The garrison of the northern outpost forts*

	Internal area		Garrison	
Site	acres	hectares	Antonine I	Antonine II
Camelon	6·0	2·4	*cohors milliaria* or *ala quingenaria*	
Ardoch	6·2	2·5	uncertain but probably two units	uncertain but reduced
Strageath	3·7	1·5	*cohors quingenaria equitata* and *cohors quingenaria peditata*	two *cohortes quingenariae peditatae*
Bertha	c.9·0	3·6	unknown but possibly two units	

The only inscription known from Camelon records building by *legio II Augusta* (RIB 2210), although this need not be taken to imply that a vexillation of that legion was in garrison. The large size of the fort and the known barrack dispositions suggest that it was intended to house either a *cohors milliaria* or an *ala quingenaria*. There is no epigraphic evidence of the second century garrison at Ardoch and it is impossible to extract with confidence from the early excavation report (Christison *et al.* 1898) the plan of the internal buildings at any single period. The size of the first Antonine fort, however, would allow ample room for a milliary equitate unit. Even the later fort, though reduced in size, would still have provided sufficient space for such a unit, so there is a

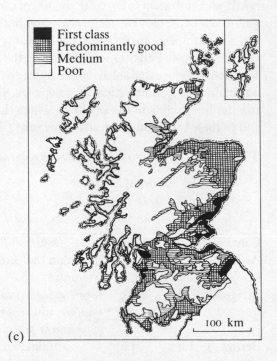

	Normal fort
	Fortlet
	Palisaded enclosure
	Broch
	Dun
	Hillfort

First class
Predominantly good
Medium
Poor

100 km

(c)

strong possibility that the fort contained more than one regiment, at least in the first period of Antonine occupation. A similar suggestion has been put forward for Strageath despite its comparatively small size. On the basis of extrapolation from extensive sampling of the northern half of the fort, the excavator concluded that the fort had housed a *cohors equitata* and a *cohors peditata* in the first Antonine period, followed by two *cohortes peditatae* in the second (Frere 1979, 40). In the case of the most northerly of the outpost forts, Bertha, we have only the very minimum of evidence. Occupation of the site in the Antonine period is attested by occasional finds of pottery and an altar dedicated to *discipulina* and identified as of second-century type (Wright 1959, 136–7). Unfortunately, the latter makes no mention of the garrison but, if the estimated

160

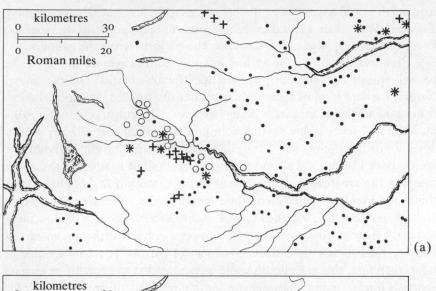

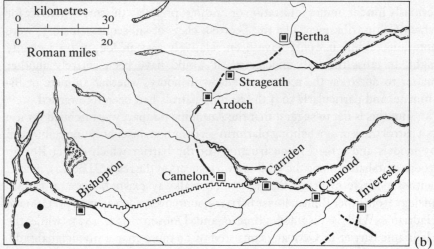

FIGURE 8.1 *The Antonine Wall in its strategic context : a) the distribution*
of native settlement sites ; b) the Antonine Wall and its outpost
forts ; c) modern land use classifications in Scotland
(after Coppock).

size is correct, it is the largest fort north of Newstead and one might again
anticipate the presence of two units brigaded together.

So far, troop dispositions (Tables 8.1, 8.4) seem to indicate what might
be termed a typical Roman offensive frontier, which looked out towards the
anticipated source of trouble and allowed major forces to be brought to bear
with considerable speed some distance north of the Wall line. The presence of
the only certain cavalry regiment at Mumrills guarding the southern end of the

road north would have allowed further troops to be brought rapidly into play if needed. Why, then, was it deemed necessary to build a curtain wall some 40 Roman miles long physically connecting the six forts across the isthmus ?

Frontiers designed to meet low-intensity threats require the troops to be well spread out with adequate facilities for observation and patrolling. Natural barriers to movement are useful, but the smaller the threat the less restricting a river or mountain range becomes. The construction of a man-made linear barrier is one obvious solution, though no barrier has yet been devised which will stop a sufficiently determined and resourceful individual or group. Both Hadrian's Wall and the Antonine Wall fit neatly into the above category. Both represent considerable obstacles to movement, both had troops thinly and evenly disposed along their length in the milecastles and fortlets and, almost certainly, both had provision for close surveillance of movement across the frontier from turrets or watch-towers, with the further provision of a back-up road to ease the lateral movement of patrols. It seems sensible to infer, therefore, that the curtain walls were intended to prevent, or at least seriously hinder, minor infiltration or raiding; precisely the sort of activity for which Celtic tribesmen, like the Scottish clans of subsequent history, were notorious. While it would have been relatively easy in fog, or on a cloudy night, to cross the wall undetected, it would have been entirely another matter to do so on the return journey with booty, whether animate or inanimate, and particularly so if the Roman patrols had been forewarned.

But this is not to suggest that the Antonine rampart was intended for use as a patrol track or as a fighting platform – a common misconception reinforced by models and artists' reconstructions of the barrier which depict Roman troops marshalled along the Wall top with spears at the ready. There is, in fact, neither positive evidence that any such walkway existed, nor any certain analogy from other Roman linear barriers; moreover, such an interpretation of Hadrian's Wall is disputed (Breeze and Dobson 1972, 187), while the Hadrianic barrier in Germany consisted of no more than a wooden palisade, which must preclude any such provision. The existence of the so-called Military Way which ran just behind the Antonine Wall all along its length would have partly obviated the need for a patrol track. Indeed, the Romans, recognising that this arrangement was an improvement on the relationship between the original Stanegate road and Hadrian's Wall, constructed a similar Military Way on their return to the Tyne-Solway frontier. As for the defensive capabilities of the Antonine Wall, a close examination of the line taken reveals a number of stretches where better positions could have been chosen if defence had been a major consideration. At Kinneil, instead of being sited on the very edge of the raised beach, a dominant position which would have done away with the necessity for a ditch, the Wall lies at least 30 to 50 m back, which would have allowed any would-be attackers to regain their breath and regroup under cover. A similar situation is evident in the line chosen immediately to the east of Inveravon and at the western end of Polmont Wood, as well as at Summerston, Crow Hill and Duntocher. At a number of points the Romans appear actually to have reduced the defensive potential of the Wall. At Watling Lodge, in Callendar Park, Tentfield Plantation and across Croy Hill the construction of a counterscarp bank must have created safe or dead ground immediately beyond the ditch, while the very wide berm on Croy Hill negates the defensive potential of a strong topographical position. Nor does it make sense, if static defence of the Wall was the intention, to provide gateways at such close intervals, for entrances are always a weak point in any defensive circuit. Finally, it should not be forgotten that, although the army was quite capable of defending its forts if under attack (Cichorius 1900 scene 32), its training in the first two centuries AD was mainly directed towards operations in the field (see above pp.26–9).

The provision of defence against low intensity threat was largely a Hadrianic innovation. As we have already noted, although a very experienced soldier, Hadrian was not a warrior emperor like Trajan his predecessor. He was responsible for no major wars or additions to Roman territory; rather he cultivated a defensive policy, even giving up some conquests in the East (SHA *Had.* V, 1). This is not to suggest that Hadrian lacked concern for the frontiers of the Empire; on the contrary he was renowned for his tours of inspection and spent almost half of his reign visiting the provinces (Dio LXIX, 9, 1). He realised the likely effect of static garrison duty on the efficiency of the army as a fighting machine and went to considerable trouble to ensure that it was kept in a state of skilled readiness by means of training manoeuvres (CIL VIII 18042; Dio LXIX, 9, 1–5). Thus we see an emperor concerned not with the expansion but with the rationalisation of the frontiers, the object of his reign being the efficient use, rather than mere aggrandisement, of power. The establishment of linear frontiers was intended to delimit the Empire, to facilitate control and promote romanisation. An attempt to find a solution to the problems of small-scale raiding, which is implicit in the construction of linear barriers, indicates a concern for the peaceful development of the provinces so defined. Other Hadrianic provincial policies, notably the encouragement given to urbanisation all over the Empire, lend support to this interpretation. In Britain the period was one which saw an upsurge in the foundation and development of towns (Wacher 1974, 375–404; Webster 1980).

The only literary reference to the role of any linear frontier refers to that of Hadrian's Wall: it was to separate the barbarians from the Romans (SHA *Had.* XI, 2). But there is nothing to indicate that the tribes north of Hadrian's Wall were any more barbarous than those immediately to the south of it. This surely implies, as Birley noted many years ago (1956, 28), an intention to romanize all the people within the new frontier, for it was the very act of building the Wall which created the distinction. Thus it may be claimed that both the Hadrianic and Antonine frontiers had a social purpose as well as a military one, which may go some way to explaining the occasionally poor tactical use of terrain exhibited by the designers of the latter.

We may seem to have wandered some way from our discussion of the military function of the Antonine frontier, but if, as does appear to be the case, the Antonine Wall in its original form was virtually a copy of Hadrian's Wall as it had developed by the end of Hadrian's reign, is it not logical to assume that both were intended to fulfil precisely the same function? The oration of Aelius Aristeides, delivered at Rome at about the time of the completion of the Antonine Wall, seems to confirm that this was the case:

> Here you built walls to defend you, and then erected towns bordering on them, ... filling them with colonists, giving these the comforts of arts and crafts, and in general establishing beautiful order. (XXVI, 81)

But the Antonine Wall, like Hadrian's Wall, was not intended simply as a barrier, for it was liberally provided with gateways in the fortlets situated approximately one mile apart along its entire length. While these would allow their garrison to sally forth to apprehend a hostile band, or facilitate the repair of the north face of the rampart and the cleaning out of the ditch, they would also provide for its main day-to-day function of controlling civilian traffic. As on the German frontier (Tacitus *Hist.* 4, 64; *Germania* 41), people entering the province would have been disarmed, and imported goods would have been subject to customs duties. Furthermore, rights of passage for local tribesmen would have been essential, for the building of the Wall had cut a swathe some 50 m wide right across the isthmus, without regard for tribal domains or lesser land divisions. That the tribal lands of the Dumnonii probably extended both north and south of the isthmus has already been pointed out (see above p.10). Unfortunately, there is so little evidence of pre-Roman Iron Age settlement immediately around the Wall that the area has been dismissed as archaeologically barren (RCAHMS 1963, 35) (fig.8.1). Yet it is an area of predominantly good land (Coppock 1976, fig. 6), which supports the greatest settlement concentration in modern Scotland. In more recent years excavation at Croy Hill and Camelon has indicated the displacement of native occupation in the vicinity of those forts (Hanson 1979, 20; Proudfoot 1978), though native pottery has also been recovered from older excavations, as at Mumrills (Macdonald and Curle 1929, 544–6); indeed, at Castlehill, just to the east of Bar Hill, the outer defences of a native hillfort were swept away to provide a seating for the Antonine rampart. Pollen evidence from Bearsden suggests that that fort was built in an area of established grazing land (Breeze 1979b, 22), and it is possible, as remarked above (p.68f), that the use of other materials than turf to build the curtain in the easternmost sectors of the Wall points to the prevalence of arable farming on that side of the country.

There is a similar lack of evidence of native settlement sites around Hadrian's Wall, yet excavation continues to show that a number of forts, for example Stanwix, Carrawburgh, Rudchester, Newcastle and Wallsend, were constructed on land which had already been cultivated.

It is, therefore, conceivable that the local disruption caused by the construction of the Antonine Wall was so great that armed hostility broke out, although this seems unlikely in view of the Wall's subsequent history. More probably, the advanced situation of the new frontier brought it rather closer to the main source of disaffection amongst the Caledonian tribes, whose presence immediately north of the isthmus may have been underestimated as a potential threat. Alternatively, it has been suggested that the army was experimenting with new methods of frontier control both in Lowland Scotland and on the Antonine Wall (Breeze 1980b, 48–50); certainly the new dispositions on the Wall are less obviously part of a bureaucratic blue-print. Whatever the reasons, the Wall appears to have been still under construction when major changes were made and further forts added (above p.105ff). The positioning of forts along the Wall at approximately two-mile intervals represents a closer spacing of garrisons than on any other Roman frontier. The effect on overall troop concentrations was considerable (Table 8.1).

Of these secondary forts, only Bar Hill, Cadder and possibly Castlehill were of sufficient size to hold a complete unit. Two units are attested at Bar Hill: *cohors I Hamiorum quingenaria peditata*, a unit of Syrian archers, on an altar and a tombstone (RIB 2167 and 2172), and *cohors I Baetasiorum quingenaria peditata* on an altar and a building inscription (RIB 2169 and 2170) (Table 8.3). The order in which these two regiments were in residence is disputed, but the fact that the Baetasii are recorded on a building inscription ought to imply that they were responsible for the rebuilding of the fort, for a legionary building inscription, which is more likely to relate to the original construction, is also known (RIB 2171). The presence of arrowheads at the bottom of the well in the *principia* and the absence of other relics of the Hamii lend support to the suggestion that they were the primary garrison (Steer 1964, 26–27). The known barrack accommodation, which apparently underwent no rebuilding, is not quite adequate for a quingenary infantry unit, even though the area of the fort is sufficiently large to have housed one. It seems strange that one of the secondary forts, whose construction must have delayed the whole programme of Wall building, should have been extended to cover 3·2 acres (1·3 ha) if only a fraction of that area was to be occupied by buildings; the more so when other such forts varied considerably in size, down to as little as half an acre (0·2 ha), presumably as a direct reflection of their garrison strength. The failure of the early excavators to recognise buildings across the whole of the *praetentura* might suggest that some had gone out of use in the second period and had been systematically dismantled, while the ones that were uncovered continued in use through both periods of occupation. This would allow the whole of *cohors I Hamiorum* to have occupied the fort in Antonine I, while *cohors I Baetasiorum* was divided between Bar Hill and Old Kilpatrick in Antonine II.

There is no epigraphic evidence for the garrison at Cadder, though the barrack accommodation known from excavations conducted fifty years ago suggests the presence of a *cohors quingenaria peditata*. Little evidence of two phases of construction was recovered from the area outside the central range and a large part of the *praetentura* was apparently unoccupied. However, most of the plan was derived from selective trenching (Clarke 1933, 48), a notoriously difficult method when applied to buildings of post-hole construction. When a larger area was exposed, a clear change of plan was noted, with a reduction in the size of the building concerned (Clarke 1933, 50). It is tempting once again to suggest that the open space in the *praetentura* might originally have contained buildings which were dismantled, and that those barracks which were examined might have served through both periods of occupation. Indeed, the excavator noted that the blocks in question were floored with gravel which overlay a depth of occupation material containing Antonine pottery, while elsewhere it could be seen that structural timbers had been replaced (Clarke 1933, 49–51).

No excavation has ever taken place at Castlehill, but an altar discovered during ploughing just to the east of the fort records a dedication by the *praefectus* of the *cohors IV Gallorum quingenaria equitata* (RIB 2195) (pl.8.1). The size of the fort, known only from aerial photography (St Joseph 1951, 61–2; Keppie 1980b), however, seems hardly adequate for an equitate unit, part of which may therefore have been permanently outstationed. If this unit also formed the garrison of the fort at Bearsden, as has been suggested (Breeze 1979b, 23), then it must have been the primary garrison at both forts, since Bearsden was not occupied in the second Antonine period.

The remaining secondary forts so far identified are all too small to have housed a complete auxiliary unit. The largest and most recently excavated at Bearsden has revealed a most unusual situation. No headquarters building was found and only two barrack blocks have been recognised. The small size of the latter suggests the presence of cavalry *turmae*, although no certain stables have been located. In addition, there is an over-provision of granaries. Whatever the explanation for these anomalies, the fort seems unlikely on present evidence to have held more than four *turmae* at most (information from Dr D.J. Breeze). The internal arrangements of the smallest fort, at Duntocher, are not at all clear, but it can hardly have held much more than a century.

It is sometimes suggested that some of the forts, especially the smaller ones like Croy Hill, may have been garrisoned by legionary detachments. But

PLATE 8.1   *Altar from Castlehill dedicated by* cohors IIII Gallorum.

neither the presence of the legions as builders nor their commemoration of that fact on inscriptions should occasion any surprise (Table 8.3). There is absolutely no need to equate legionary building with legionary occupation of secondary forts any more than of primary ones (above p.153ff), as is made clear by the evidence from Bar Hill where auxiliary garrisons are known for both periods but legionary construction is attested. On the same principle, as already noted, altars or other legionary dedications need not confirm the presence of the legions in any other capacity than as builders. There are, however, one or two exceptions. The dedication of an altar at Westerwood by the wife of Flavius Verecundus, a centurion of the sixth legion, implies that he was a member of the fort garrison, for it would be unusual for a centurion to take his wife and family with him in other circumstances (Wright 1968). But there is no need to postulate that he was in command of a legionary vexillation. In fact, the best parallel is provided by Flavius Betto, a centurion of the twentieth legion who dedicated an altar while in command of a detachment of *cohors VI Nerviorum* at Rough Castle (RIB 2144) (pl.8.2).

PLATE 8.2   *Altar from Rough Castle dedicated by Flavius Betto, centurion of* legio XX Valeria Victrix.

No archaeological evidence is available from either Croy Hill or Wester-wood to provide clear evidence as to the exact size and nature of their garrisons, but the overall area of the two adjacent forts might indicate room for a quin-genary unit split between them. Such a procedure is attested at Rough Castle where the barrack accommodation was incapable of housing more than half of *cohors VI Nerviorum* (MacIvor *et al.* 1980, 281). Yet this unit is also attested on an inscription recording the building of the *principia* (RIB 2145), which ought to imply that it was present during the second rather than the first period of occupation, an inference which is supported both by the find-spot of the stone, still within the *principia*, and the inferior secondary workmanship noted in the central range (Buchanan *et al.* 1905, 470 and 481). However, more recent excavations elsewhere in the fort have failed to confirm the presence of two periods of barrack accommodation. Furthermore, there are indications that part of the *praetentura* was devoid of major structures, con-taining only scattered post-holes; yet space was sufficiently at a premium within the fort for the *praetorium* to have blocked the intervallum road (MacIvor *et al.* 1980, 241 and 279). These apparent contradictions might be resolved by suggesting that the occasional post-holes in the eastern *praetentura* represent the remains of buildings which went out of use at the end of Antonine I and were cobbled over in Antonine II, for some at least of the cobbling in that area is contiguous with a secondary surfacing of the *via praetoria*. The remaining barracks, as perhaps was the case at Bar Hill and Cadder (above p.165f), would have been re-used in the second period. There is no need to blame the excavators of 1903 for the total destruction of the remains of barracks from the Antonine II occupation (MacIvor *et al.* 1980, 241); indeed such shallow sleeper-trenches as are necessarily postulated to fit such a theory would have been an unusual method of construction at this time (Hanson 1982). Even allowing for buildings across the whole of the *praetentura*, however, there would still be insufficient room for a complete unit to have formed the original garrison.

Although the construction of this and other secondary forts represented a rapid and major alteration to the overall plan of the Wall, which brought about a tripling of the number of forts along its length, there was not a corresponding increase in the total garrison because so few of the new forts were large enough to accommodate full units. The increase in the number of men was probably of the order of 75 per cent to around 7000, which is almost exactly three-quarters of the garrison on Hadrian's Wall. In other words, expressed proportionately, the Antonine Wall had a garrison one and a half times as strong as that on Hadrian's Wall, a figure rather less than previous estimates (Breeze and Dobson 1976a, 96). Whatever the reason for this increase it reflects the greater concentration of forces seen throughout Lowland Scotland in the first Antonine period (see above pp.72–4).

In the original plan of the Wall the troops were relatively evenly distributed along its length. In its final form, however, a greater concentration at its western end is apparent. Six of the forts in the western half of the Wall were of sufficient size to hold full auxiliary units (though not all did so), as opposed to only three of the forts in the east. Of course, the eastern sector was further protected by the outpost forts and may, in fact, have been facing basically friendly tribes. The total absence of permanent installations in Fife and the location of the Gask Ridge frontier during the later first century have been taken to indicate that the tribes on the north shore of the Firth of Forth, forming part, at least, of the Venicones, were then philo-Roman (Hanson 1980a, 24 and 32). Similar arguments could be put forward for the situation in the second century, were it not for the location of two large forts at Cramond and Inveresk on the south shore of the Forth estuary (fig.8.1). Three different units have been associated with Cramond. The Ingliston milestone (RIB 2313) has recently been re-dated to early in the reign of Antoninus Pius, after the rediscovery of an additional fragment (Wright and Hassall 1973, 336–7; Maxwell 1982c). Cramond being the nearest known Roman fort of that date, the unit attested on the milestone, *cohors I Cugernorum quingenaria peditata*, is generally attributed to this site, but the association is somewhat tenuous. Moreover, the large size of Cramond is more appropriate to a milliary cohort, and such a unit is known from an altar dedicated by *cohors II Tungrorum milliaria equitata* (Davies 1968, 96 correcting RIB 2135). The third unit known, *cohors V Gallorum quingenaria equitata* (RIB 2134) may represent the second Antonine garrison at Cramond, but a third-century date is also possible. Despite a wealth of occasional finds from the site, there is no epigraphic evidence of the garrison of the second coastal fort at Inveresk. However, its overall size and the estimated disposition of its barrack accommodation led Richmond to postulate an *ala quingenaria* (Richmond and Hanson 1980, 296). Thus there was a considerable force available beyond the eastern end of the Wall, presumably intended to limit any outflanking movements, although the existence of an extensive extra-mural settlement at Inveresk and its association with the most important civil official in the province hints at a function beyond the purely military (see below pp.189–91).

The threatening proximity of the Campsie Fells and the Kilsyth Hills is put forward to explain the greater concentration of garrison strength at the western end of the Wall (Breeze and Dobson 1976a, 96), despite the distinct lack of native settlement sites in the area (fig.8.1). Yet such concern does not appear to be reflected in arrangements for the protection of the equally 'threatened' coastline to the west. Unlike the concentration of forces along the Cumberland coast which continue the Hadrianic system, the only fort known at present on the left flank of the Antonine Wall is at Bishopton, overlooking the ford across the Clyde at Dumbuck. Nothing is known of its garrison, although on the basis of size alone it ought to have been capable of holding a quingenary cohort. The two small fortlets beyond Bishopton at Lurg Moor and Outerwards are unlikely to have held more than a few dozen men between them. Unless further forts or fortlets come to light, it would seem that the tribes of the western Highlands north of the Clyde were not deemed to constitute a particularly serious threat.

The Antonine Wall system could thus operate at a number of levels. It was not intended to act as a passive military cordon, since a mobile enemy force could easily have penetrated it by gaining crushing numerical superiority at its chosen point of attack. Rather, potential hostile activity would have been detected, ideally, by the outpost network or by patrols and in the worst case by visual surveillance from the Wall itself, whereupon a force assembled from one or more of the Wall-forts could have sallied forth to deal with the trouble if it was not too serious. The auxiliary troops would probably have attempted to do no more than contain or delay a major invasion until the arrival of reinforcements from the rear. In this connection, one of the oddities of the strategic arrangements of the northern frontier under Antonius Pius is the limited availability of legionary support. The established legionary bases at Chester and York lay too far to the south for immediate involvement, although some legionary troops were stationed at Newstead, and it is possible that similar vexillations were brigaded together with auxiliaries in one or other of the larger outpost forts. Nevertheless, unless no major threats were expected, it is hard to understand why the whole of *legio II Augusta* was not transferred from Wales to Scotland, for the establishment of a tribal capital at Caerwent under Hadrian (Wacher 1974, 375–6) would seem to deny the need for a legionary presence only eight miles to the west at Caerleon. In fact, the dispersed concentrations of troops along the Wall suggest that the main concern of the garrison was with medium intensity threats, while small-scale infiltration and raiding might be discouraged by the very presence of the Wall, an impressive psychological barrier. Hostile elements bold enough to attempt a crossing, would have been picked up by the patrols behind the barrier. The strategic function of the Wall in the Antonine scheme of things was thus essentially dependent upon all the other elements in the frontier zone, particularly the outpost forts and the hinterland garrisons; if it had a leading role to play, it must be considered first among equals.

As we have seen above, troop dispositions on the norther frontier changed again on the return to the Wall in the second Antonine period (Table 8.1). At least two of the primary forts demonstrate a reduction in the size or fighting potential of their garrison; at Mumrills the prestigious cavalry regiment was replaced by an equitate cohort, while at Castlecary an equitate regiment was superseded by a purely infantry unit, although both were nominally of milliary strength. A number of the secondary forts also provide hints of similar reductions in their garrisons: it has been suggested above that the barrack accommodation at Rough Castle, Bar Hill and Cadder was possibly reduced in the second period of occupation, while the fort at Bearsden does not appear to have been re-occupied at all (Breeze 1979b, 24–5). What effect these troop withdrawals had on the overall efficiency of the frontier, and whether the changes reflect a shift in frontier policy, cannot be determined. Given the relatively small numbers involved, it seems unlikely, for although the Wall was primarily a military frontier built by and for the army, the motives behind its construction were wider than mere military necessity. As already suggested, it was intended to fulfil political and socio-economic roles, to encourage the native peoples within the area now clearly defined to accept Roman rule and grow towards self-government. This is precisely what can be observed to have happened south of Hadrian's Wall by the third century AD. In Cumbria the construction of Hadrian's Wall appears to have had a stimulating effect upon native settlement (Jones 1979, 62–6), while civilian settlements grew up around a number of frontier forts, most notably Chesters, Housesteads and Chesterholm (Salway 1965, 77–90; Birley 1977, 31–79). Two sites, Corbridge and Carlisle (Salway 1965, 45–60; Charlesworth 1978, 117–23), developed sufficiently to deserve the description of towns, the latter becoming by the mid third century the administrative centre of the local tribe, the Carvetii (Wright 1965, 224). Similarly, the possible expansion of native settlements north of Hadrian's Wall which seems to have occurred in the mid second century has been attributed to the stimulus of the Antonine occupation (Jobey 1966, 6 and 1974). Major developments take time, however, and the Antonine Wall was not occupied long enough for its beneficial influence to take root. Yet this is not to deny that the seeds had been sown.

IX. LIFE ON THE WALL

Our interest in the exceptional military achievements of the Romans on their most northerly frontier should not blind us to the fact that the army of occupation was composed, like all armies, of ordinary human beings, of simple men who experienced the same needs and put up with the same constraints as soldiers of any age. Only a small proportion of the period during which the Romans maintained a presence in Scotland was actually passed in open warfare; we need not, therefore, picture the garrisons as perpetually on the alert for impending assault or rebellion. On the contrary, their most formidable enemy was probably boredom, and although a regular round of fatigues, routine training and field exercises no doubt helped to pass the time (Davies 1974 and see chapter 1), there would certainly have been frequent opportunities for the soldiers of the frontier garrison, from the highest rank to the lowest, to attempt a critical appraisal of their life-style. After a reluctant admission of the omnipotence of Jupiter Pluvius in these northern latitudes, the soldiers' first and last thoughts would probably have been on the subject of accommodation and food, not to mention the demands of other equally urgent appetites. With regard to the first two at least, it is probable that the garrison was more favourably situated than were their counterparts in national or imperial armies of much later eras – until comparatively recent times, in fact. Indeed, it was this concern with the not-specifically military side of garrison life which enabled the Roman Empire to exploit to the full the fighting efficiency of its troops.

The commanding officers – the prefects, tribunes and occasionally legionary centurions – dwelled apart from their troops in separate residences (*praetoria*) which are modelled on the typical town-house of the Mediterranean world: inward-looking structures, in which the various suites of rooms gave on

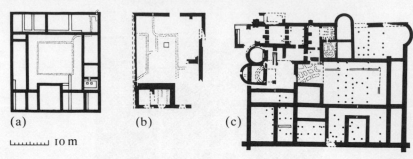

(a)   (b)   (c)

⌊⎽⎽⎽⎽⎽⎽⌋ 10 m

FIGURE 9.1   *Comparative plans of* praetoria *from Wall forts: a) Balmuildy; b) Rough Castle; c) Mumrills.*

to a central courtyard (fig.9.1). Here the commandant might enjoy a tolerable degree of privacy and reasonable comfort, with separate living-quarters, bed-rooms and a dining-room or reception room, together with office-accommodation and facilities for entertaining visitors of rank. In many of the forts – especially those that were capable of accommodating the major part of a full regiment – the *praetoria* were evidently buildings of some architectural pretensions; most were constructed, or at least founded, in stone, although some, the later building at Cadder and the earliest at Mumrills for instance, were timber-framed. Whatever the material, it is nevertheless safe to assume that the accommodation which such buildings provided was the most luxurious on the Wall, incorporating glazed windows and hypocausted heating-systems, which afforded at least partial insulation from the rigours of a northern climate. Even with only limited excavation of *praetoria*, it is evident that they varied considerably in size and plan (fig.9.1). Those at Mumrills and Balmuildy, being among the largest and best preserved, display most convincingly both the details of structural evidence and the complexity of the constructional sequence by which they obtained their final form. Each contained the facilities of civilisation that any Roman gentleman would have expected: at Balmuildy the commandant was provided with rooms heated by hypocaust and possessed his own private latrine, flushed by the rainwater collected in the drains around the central courtyard; at Mumrills an extensive bathing suite had been inserted into the south-east corner of what was already the most elaborate *praetorium* in any fort on the Wall.

Much less is known, unfortunately, about the accommodation provided for the auxiliary centurions and their men. The barracks in which they were quartered, being constructed of timber, have less successfully withstood the ravages of time and later occupation. Nevertheless, it should not be thought that their more spartan way of life was not accompanied by some degree of domestic comfort. Although built of timber framing set in individual post-holes, as most of them were (Hanson 1982), and lacking such refinements as

174

hypocausts and window glass, the average barrack-building might be as comfortable as many a more modern house. Clad in wattle-and-daub panels or clap-board and provided with gravelled or beaten earth floors, such quarters evidently possessed a degree of thermal insulation that would have kept them relatively cool in summer, and in winter would have conserved such heat as might have been given out by fires burning on stone-flagged hearths, like those excavated at Mumrills. The number and size of barracks within each fort depended upon the strength and composition of the garrison, and the plan of the barrack-block might itself differ in detail from examples not only in other forts, but even on the same site. Nevertheless, all adhered basically to the same principle of design, the block consisting of a larger room or suite of rooms for the officer in charge, whether centurion or decurion, with a row of smaller rooms (*contubernia*), from eight to ten in number, for the rank and file. Each of the latter might be divided into two parts, the outer half serving as a suitable place for storing and cleaning weapons and equipment, while the inner was used as a combined bedroom and mess, with the small hearth referred to above providing facilities for heating and small-scale culinary operations.

The size of accommodation varied considerably (fig.9.2). On the Antonine Wall the largest barracks to have been identified are those at Old Kilpatrick which extend to 174 ft (53 m), and those at Camelon, uniquely built in stone, are only a little shorter. The barracks at Balmuildy range from 130 ft (40 m) to 147 ft (45 m) in length, while those at Cadder and Bearsden are only 120 ft (36·5 m) and 118 ft (36 m) respectively. In few examples, however, is it possible to identify the internal partitions separating either the officer's quarters from the mens', or the individual *contubernia*. At Bar Hill, however, it has been suggested that the individual blocks measured 135 ft (41 m) overall and were divided up as follows: a room or suite 30 ft (9 m) square for the centurion and ten *contubernia* measuring approximately 24 ft (7·3 m) by 11 ft (3·4 m) on average (Robertson *et al.* 1975, 16–19). In some examples the line of the centurion's quarters, which projected beyond that of the men's, was continued as the outer edge of a verandah, but evidence for such a feature, usually described as a standard element in Roman barrack blocks, is in fact less commonly recorded on Wall sites than one might expect. At Bearsden, for instance, of the two buildings confidently identified as barracks, only one appears to have possessed a verandah, and that extended only half-way along the building, while in neither case did the centurion's quarters project (Breeze 1979b, 22–3). This site, however, being occupied by a minor vexillation of an auxiliary unit, may not have been constructed to the same high standards that would have been demanded at a major base. Indeed, the barracks were quite irregular in construction and much narrower than the examples from Bar Hill described above. Averaging less than 13 ft (4·0 m) in width, they were divided into a small officer's quarters providing between 225 and 250 sq.ft (21–25·5 m²) of

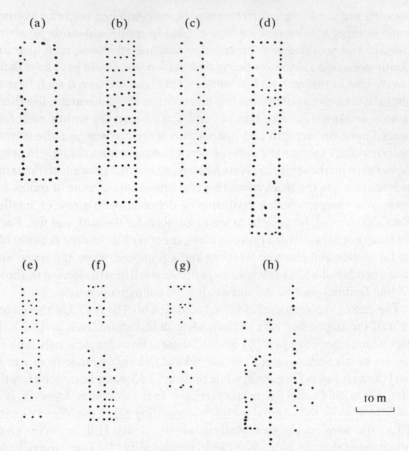

(a)   (b)   (c)   (d)

(e)   (f)   (g)   (h)

10 m

FIGURE 9.2   *Comparative plans of timber barracks from Wall forts:*
a) Cadder; b) Bar Hill; c) Balmuildy; d) Old Kilpatrick;
e) and f) Bearsden; g) Rough Castle; f) Mumrills
(a and b restored in part).

living area – less than a third of that available in the Bar Hill barracks – with
eight *contubernia* averaging about 155 sq.ft (14·4 m²) – just over half the Bar
Hill equivalent (information from Dr D.J.Breeze). Such comparisons are,
nevertheless, meaningless unless the strength of the accommodated unit is
known. At Bar Hill, where each block was probably allotted to a century of
eighty men belonging to a quingenary infantry cohort, the individual soldier's
allowance of floor space would have amounted to approximately 33 sq.ft
(3·1 m²). At Bearsden, on the other hand, it seems probable that each block
housed a single *turma* of troops from a composite regiment (possibly the
cohors IV Gallorum attested at the adjacent fort on Castlehill), in which case
their individual allotment would have been slightly larger than that for the

176

troops at Bar Hill, as one might expect for the better paid cavalry troopers. The smaller officer's quarters may indicate the presence of a *duplicarius* rather than the more senior cavalry officer, the decurion.

Although, as far as we know, the Roman soldier on the Wall did not have to pay rent for his quarters, there were certain standard deductions from his pay to cover equipment, possibly certain types of clothing, and food (Watson 1969, 103 and appendix A). The soldier was also encouraged to save, for a banking system, administered by the standard-bearers, was provided for men of each unit. Such spending money as was left was probably used to acquire extra comforts that made life on the frontier more enjoyable, and amongst these food and drink were presumably the most popular and accessible (see below). Not that the basic military food supply was nutritionally deficient (Davies 1971). The staple diet of the Roman soldier in garrison would have consisted of corn, bacon and cheese with various sorts of vegetables, and sour wine (*vinum acetum*) to drink; additional savour was available in the form of salt and olive oil.

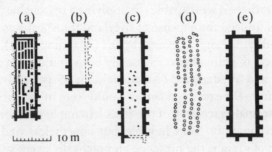

(a)   (b)   (c)   (d)   (e)

10 m

FIGURE 9.3   *Comparative plans of granaries from Wall forts: a) Rough Castle; b) Croy Hill; c) Castlecary; d) and e) Old Kilpatrick.*

The most conspicuous evidence of the food supply on the Antonine Wall is represented by the remains of granaries in which the units' corn and other perishable foodstuffs were stored, providing sufficient capacity in each case probably for a full year's supply (Tacitus *Agricola* 22; Bulmer 1969). Additional provision seems to have been made at Balmuildy and possibly Bar Hill where small granaries were inserted into the corner of the headquarters building at some later stage in the occupation, possibly to make up for the loss of the extra provision formerly available at Bearsden; the latter may have served as a supply depot in the first period of occupation on the Wall (Breeze 1979b, 23). It has been calculated that each man in the garrison would have required one third of a ton of corn per year, so that the size and solidity of such granaries come as no surprise (fig.9.3). Their presence is attested on all but the very smallest sites – Duntocher and the fortlets – and even Rough Castle and Croy Hill have standard examples. All the stone granaries are strongly buttressed, not, as is generally supposed, to enable the walls to withstand the outward thrust of the grain, but to give added support to the roof, as the walls were probably pierced at frequent intervals by large, louvred windows to ensure adequate ventilation within. As a further ventilation measure and a guard against rising damp the floor of the granary was suspended on rows of pillars or else on dwarf walls disposed longitudinally.

No less remarkable than the care which was lavished on the design and construction of the granaries is the organisation which must have been required to stock them. On the assumption that the Wall garrison numbered approximately 6000–7000 troops, the amount of corn supplied to them annually for human consumption must have been in the neighbourhood of 2000–2500 tons, to which should be added an unknown quantity of grain for animal feedstock, as well as meat supplies. How much of the grain and livestock was obtained locally and how much brought in from more southerly districts cannot be determined, but the presence of the frontier garrison could well have stimulated the farming industry of the Lothian and Berwickshire area, in particular, to a point where it was capable of supplying a reasonable proportion of the army's needs. Indeed the expense of overland transport was so high as to discourage long-distance supply except by sea (Manning 1975).

Physical traces of grain have occasionally been found in great quantities, as at Castlecary and Westerwood (Macdonald 1934, 453 and 256), but its general absence from the excavated *horrea* would seem to indicate, as much as anything, that the final evacuation of the forts left ample time for the removal of this precious commodity. More humble, but nonetheless vital evidence for the consumption of grain is the presence on practically every site of any permanence of hand-mills; some, like the handsome speciments from Balmuildy were made of local sandstone grit, others of volcanic tuff imported from the German quarries at Andernach and Niedermendig. Most of the grain thus ground was probably baked into bread; the identification of wheat debris from sewage deposits in a ditch beside the latrine at Bearsden seems to confirm that wholemeal bread was a major element of the soldiers' diet (Dickson *et al.* 1979, 51). Cereal could, of course, be used as the main ingredient of a wide variety of dishes – porage, gruel, soups and pastas, all of which would doubtless have been the better for seasoning, whether it be of the fish-sauce type (*garum* or *muria*) so beloved of Roman troops, or a fragrant herb, spice or seed; poppy and coriander seeds, for example, were probably thus used at Bearsden (Breeze 1979b, 24). For the larger-scale cooking requirements there were domed clay ovens, usually set into the rear face of the fort rampart, as at Balmuildy and Duntocher; one oven was probably used by a set number of barracks, each having access to it on a fixed roster. The method employed was to bring the oven to the required temperature by means of a fire built inside, and then, having raked out the ashes, to bake the meals placed within it by the remanent heat. For smaller repasts the hearth within the inner portion of the *contubernium* would have sufficed.

In addition to the standard rations, the troops indulged themselves in a wide variety of the produce of local fields, rivers and forests. Some of these would possibly have been obtained from land under the direct control, if not actually worked by, the garrisons; some requisitioned or bought from the native tribesmen living nearby, and some again the spoils of the hunt and drive. The bone remains from Bar Hill and Balmuildy show that the garrison, at least occasionally, dined off beef, mutton or pork, with wild boar and red deer making due contribution to the daily fare. Mumrills revealed a similar range of menu with the addition of chicken, while the garrison there and at Bar Hill evidently amplified their diet with shellfish – oysters, mussels and whelks. Fruit, nuts and wine may seem to smack rather of the gourmet's table than the army barrack-room, but all were available to the soldiers of the Wall; raspberries and figs have been identified at Bearsden, locally grown hazelnuts and walnuts are known from Bar Hill, and the implicit testimony of numerous amphora fragments on every site, indicating doubtless the consumption of *vinum acetum*, is supplemented more explicitly by graffiti: VINN on an amphora from Bar Hill (Robertson *et al.* 1975, 139–40) and $\Gamma\Lambda YK[Y\Sigma\ OINO\Sigma]$ (sweet wine) on another from Mumrills (Wright 1964, 184). Distinguishing marks like these were presumably intended to indicate vessels containing vintage wine as opposed to sour. Such delicacies had, of course, to be paid for and may either have been the special reserve of officers or the liquid enhancement of some special feast, perhaps that of Fors Fortuna. The preparations for such a feast are vividly illustrated on one of the military records from the fort at Vindolanda, just to the south of Hadrian's Wall (Bowman 1974). From the same source it is evident that on these occasions the day-to-day diet was abandoned in favour of more exotic or extensive menus, including such delicacies as goat, sucking-pig, ham and venison, with vintage wine eked out by Celtic beer (*cervesa*). If the biscuits which finished off the meal were hard-tack (*bucellatum*), at least the cheese might have been fresh and home-made, squeezed in a cheese-press like the examples found at Castlecary and Mumrills.

All archaeological excavations in Roman forts along the Wall produce vast quantities of pottery, mostly representing domestic culinary activity. Flagons, storage jars, heavy mixing bowls (*mortaria*), and cooking-pots identified by the soot deposits ingrained on their outer surface, are the most common items (pl.9.1). Table ware varies in quality from simple coarse-ware platters and cups to the fine red-gloss, imported Samian ware, though possibly only the officers could afford to use that (Breeze 1977b, 134–5).

If the soldiers of the Wall were well-equipped, decently accommodated and at least adequately fed, it was the intention of the Roman high command that they should stay that way. Consequently, as much attention was paid to

PLATE 9.1   *Typical assemblage of domestic pottery from Bearsden fort.*

the health of the garrison as to their creature comforts. An army medical service was therefore provided, as capable of curing their less dramatic illnesses as of tending them when wounded in action (Davies 1970). Although little material evidence survives to indicate its activity specifically in the Wall zone – no Wall fort has yet provided evidence of a hospital – the ability of the Roman army to maintain an effective military presence in a form which necessitated large bodies of men being garrisoned together over a long period of time, clearly indicates that the basic interdependence of health and hygiene was fully appreciated. The concrete evidence for this aspect of military administration is, fortunately, much better preserved, consisting as it does of the drainage systems, baths and latrines that have been identified in all the major, and not a few of the minor, establishments on the Wall.

The bath-houses (*balnea*) being required to incorporate hypocausted heating systems were for the most part built of stone (fig.9.4), but, as at Bearsden, the disrobing room and vestibules may have been of wood, which at some sites has possibly led to them being missed in early excavations. Although some are appreciably more complex than others – notably those at Castlecary, Mumrills and Balmuildy – the majority consist in essence of a row or suite of rooms in which the bather progressed from stage to stage of the bathing ritual, for a visit to the bath-house served a social and recreational as well as an ablutionary purpose. From the *apodyterium* where he shed his clothes, the soldier proceeded in turn to the *frigidarium* or cold room, and thence through the *tepidarium* or warm room to the moist heat of the *caldarium*; retracing his steps in due course he might finally sample the sweltering dry

180

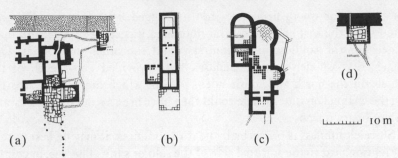

(a)   (b)   (c)

(d)

⌞⌞⌞⌞⌞⌞⌟ 10 m

FIGURE 9.4   *Comparative plans of bath-houses and latrines from Wall forts:*
a) Bearsden bath-house and latrine; b) Balmuildy fort
bath-house; c) Balmuildy annexe bath-house; d) Castlecary
latrine.

heat of the *sudatorium*, served by its own channelled hypocaust and furnace, before closing the pores with a quick plunge in the cold bath of the *frigidarium*. Fragments of what may have been iron strigils used by bathers to scrape their soiled bodies have been found at Bar Hill and Balmuildy, and most baths have produced evidence in the form of gaming counters to show how the leisure hours were whiled away. Hence the double appositeness of dedications in the form of altars (Table 9.1) and statuettes to Fortuna, the goddess of good fortune, who might also be invoked to turn away all harm from suppliants whilst in their most defenceless state. The water required for the baths was doubtless derived from many sources, but few excavations have sought or revealed these in their entirety. Although external supplies fed by pipe or simple aqueduct may be presumed in some cases, much of the water would have had to be provided from reservoirs fed by buckets from the fort's well, as one may imagine occurred at Bar Hill, or by judicious channelling of collected rain-water. At Croy Hill the water-supply for the fort was provided by tapping a natural spring in the north-east corner of the fort. After use, the water was in most cases returned to the drainage system and employed to flush the fort latrine. Several examples of these humble but essential establishments are known on the Wall, the best preserved examples being those found in the annexe at Bearsden and in the north-east corner of the fort at Castlecary (fig.9.4). The latter was a stone-built structure, measuring some 15 ft (4·6 m) by 12 ft (3·7 m) internally and occupying a position in the fort where its unavoidable odours would be dispersed most readily by the prevailing winds, and whence the effluent might pursue the most direct course into the Antonine Ditch; a conduit 2 ft (0·6 m) wide was provided through the thickness of the fort's stone wall for that purpose, and as so large an opening might conceivably afford a clandestine, if malodorous, means of access into the interior, precautions appear to have been taken to bar the conduit with rudimentary bollards of stone or wood, firmly set into its flagged floor. The building was entered from the east and the central floor area was stone paved, with open channels for the soldiers' use running round the other three sides. One imagines that wooden seating facilities were provided above each of the channels on the north and south sides, both of which drained towards the west; the channel on the east side could then have been a source of clean water for ablutionary purposes.

Since cleanliness is proverbially next to godliness, it may be best to turn our attention next to the spiritual side of the soldier's life. There is, of course, no archaeological evidence which can furnish a picture of the individual's private thoughts in religion or show how much he believed the essence behind the ritual of state-directed or personal observances. There are, however, a considerable number of dedications of one sort or another which show that at least the officers and commandants thought it well worth the expense of having a tablet or altar carved in stone to thank or propitiate the divine powers (Table 9.1). As one might expect, there are the official dedications to Jupiter Optimus Maximus and the ruling gods of the Olympian pantheon, Mars, Minerva, Diana, Apollo and Mercury, as well as the deities or heroes whom soldiers might admire, Hercules and Victory. Yet the soldiers of this frontier, like all troops stationed in foreign parts, felt a healthy respect for, and indeed practised veneration of, local divinities. Silvanus-dedications at Bar Hill and Auchendavy, and offerings to the Nymphs at Duntocher and Croy Hill, with its natural springs, represented an attempt to conciliate the good favour of local spirits as much as Greco-Roman godlings; and more explicit reference was made at Auchendavy and Castlehill – to the Genius Terrae Britannicae and to Britannia herself. The presence of *equites*, or soldiers with previous experience of cavalry service, is indicated by dedications to the Campestres and Epona at Castlehill and Auchendavy, but the altar to Neptune erected at Castlecary does not necessarily point to a recent or impending voyage, since Neptune was also god of streams and inland water; and, as Sir George Macdonald pointed out (1934, 422), that particular element might have been all too much in evidence in the lowlying ground beneath Castlecary in Roman times.

Some of the dedications tell us a little about the origins or circumstances of the donor; thus, the epithet Magusanus applied to Hercules on the altar set up by Valerius Nigrinus, *duplicarius* of the Tungrian cavalry regiment stationed at Mumrills, suggests that the Tungrians still worshipped the hero in a form known to their forefathers in the lower Rhine. Again, the relief carving of Jupiter Dolichenus consecrated at Croy Hill honours the father of the gods in a form which derives from the worship of Baal as practised in the relatively insignificant town of Doliche in distant Commagene, a district of Syria. Macdonald used this evidence to suggest that the stone had been

PLATE 9.2   *Altar from Carriden dedicated by the occupants of the* vicus.

erected in the reign of Commodus, since worship of Jupiter Dolichenus was then believed to have been fostered particularly by that emperor (1934, 416). However, the orientalising of Roman religion had been under way for a good while before that, and the prevalence of legionary centurions with eastern origins in the Antonine army (Birley 1979, 78) might be sufficient grounds for the appearance of Syrian influence at an earlier date than the late 170s or 180s. After all, Caristanius Justianus, who dedicated the altar to Silvanus at nearby Bar Hill, commanded a cohort of Syrian archers and was himself probably descended from a family resident in Pisidian Antioch.

Perhaps the most curious case, however, is that of M. Cocceius Firmus, a centurion of *legio II Augusta*, who may have commanded the garrison at Auchendavy (but see above p.157). He erected no fewer than four altars to as many as ten separate deities. The same man seems to have figured later in the annals of Roman legal history as the recipient of a refund from the Imperial treasury in respect of a slavewoman who had been kidnapped from him by foreign brigands. It is quite possible that this abduction took place while the

TABLE 9.1 *Religious dedications from Wall forts*

Dedicatee	Dedicator	Provenance	Reference
1. Jupiter Optimus Maximus (with Victoria Victrix)	M. Cocceius Firmus centurion *legio II Augusta*	Auchendavy	RIB 2176
2. Jupiter Optimus Maximus	*vikani* of Velunia(s) under supervision of Aelius Mansuetus	Carriden	Richmond and Steer 1957 (pl.9.2)
3. Jupiter Optimus Maximus (Dolichenus)	unknown	Croy Hill	RIB 2158
4. Jupiter Optimus Maximus	unknown	Duntocher	RIB 2201
5. Jupiter Optimus Maximus	*cohors I Baetasiorum* commanded by prefect Publicius Maternus, under supervision of centurion Julius Candidus of *legio I Italica*	Old Kilpatrick	Barber 1971 (pl.10.2)
6. Apollo (and Diana)	M. Cocceius Firmus	Auchendavy	RIB 2174
7. Apollo	unknown	Bar Hill	RIB 2165
8. Britannia with Campestres (Matres)	Q. Pisentius Justus Prefect of *cohors IV Gallorum equitata*	Castlehill	RIB 2195
9. Campestres (Matres) with Mars, Minerva, Hercules, Epona and Victory	M. Cocceius Firmus	Auchendavy	RIB 2177
10. Diana (and Apollo)	see no.6		
11. Epona (with five other deities)	see no.9		
12. Fortuna	vexillations of *legiones II* and *VI*	Castlecary	RIB 2146
13. Fortuna	Caecilius Nepos, tribune	Balmuildy	RIB 2189

14. Genio Terrae Britannicae	M. Cocceius Firmus	Auchendavy	RIB 2175
15. Hercules Magusanus	Val. Nigrinus, *duplicarius ala Tungrorum*	Mumrills	RIB 2140
16. (Hercules) Hero	see no.9		
17. Mars (Camulus)	unknown	Bar Hill	RIB 2166
18. Mars	unknown	Balmuildy	RIB 2190
19. Mars (with five other deities)	see no.9		
20. Mars	G. D.. B..	Croy Hill	RIB 2159
21. Matres	vexillations of *legiones II* and *VI*	Castlecary	RIB 2147
22. Matres	Cassius, *signifer*	Mumrills	RIB 2141
23. Mercury	soldiers from Italy and Noricum in *legio VI Victrix*	Castlecary	RIB 2148
24. Minerva (with five other deities)	see no.9		
25. Neptune	*cohors I Vardullorum* commanded by Trebius Verus, prefect	Castlecary	RIB 2149
26. Nymphs	vexillation of *legio VI Victrix* commanded by Fabius Liberalis	Croy Hill	RIB 2160
27. Quadriviae Caelestes (with Silvanus)	Vibia Pacata, wife of Verecundus, centurion of *VI Victrix*	Westerwood	Wright 1968 (pl.9.3)
28. Silvanus	possibly M. Cocceius Firmus	Auchendavy	RIB 2178
29. Silvanus	L. Tanicius Verus prefect	probably Bar Hill	RIB 2187 and Keppie 1978a
30. Silvanus	Caristanius Justianus prefect of *cohors I Hamiorum*	Bar Hill	RIB 2167
31. Victory (and Jupiter Optimus Maximus)	see no.1		

32. Victory	*cohors VI Nervio-* *rum* under com- mand of Fl. Betto, centurion of *legio* *XX*	Rough Castle	RIB 2144 (pl.8.2)

centurion was on active service in Scotland (Birley 1953), and, if so, provides an interesting illustration of the adventures which might befall a soldier serving on this northern frontier.

Yet it was not just their goods and chattels, or their own security that the men of the garrison hazarded while on duty here. A good many would have been accompanied by their wives and families. For both auxiliaries and legionary troops up to the rank of centurion it was officially forbidden to contract marriage with a woman, whether she was a Roman citizen or of peregrine status, while serving with the colours: the *ius connubii* (right to contract a legal marriage) was conferred, along with Roman citizenship for the auxiliary troops, only after they had retired (Watson 1969, 134–6). Naturally the men were reluctant to leave the rearing of a family until what might have been relatively advanced years, and most who wished to do so contracted irregular marriages with women native to the province in which they were serving. Up till about AD 140 the children of such marriages were both legitimised retrospectively and granted citizenship when their father became a citizen, but after that date only the children born to the union subsequent to retiral were accorded that honour. The motive behind this change was to encourage recruitment to the *auxilia* from the families of time-expired soldiers, and for a while the tradition of following father into the regiment had the effect of producing, as it were, a military caste. Monstrously, to more sensitive modern ears, the wife was not awarded the rights of citizenship, either before or after the change in regulations, and the matter was not rectified until Caracalla in AD 212 granted citizenship to all free people in the Empire (Watson 1969, 136–7).

There is little material evidence for the presence of the ordinary soldiers' wives and children and absolutely no way of telling how many followed their husbands to the northern frontier. Yet, at least one dedicated an altar while present on the Wall. Vibia Pacata, wife of centurion Flavius Verecundus of *legio VI Victrix* who was presumably commanding the garrison at Westerwood, made an offering to the *Silvanae* and *Quadriviae Caelestes* (the nymphs of the forest and the holy spirits of the crossroads) (pl.9.3); the combination of divinities suggests that her husband had seen previous service in Pannonia or Africa, and the personal names of Vibia Pacata herself are common enough in Africa too (Wright 1968). The purpose of the offering is uncertain, but as Silvanus himself was regarded as a harmful influence on women in child-

PLATE 9.3 *Altar from Westerwood dedicated by the wife of Flavius Verecundus, centurion of* legio VI Victrix.

birth, and the spirits of the crossroads also possessed a less auspicious aspect, it is just possible that Vibia was then in an interesting condition. The remains of extremely small leather shoes, particularly *calcei*, at Bar Hill (Robertson *et al.* 1975, 78–83) (pl.9.4), and to a lesser extent at Balmuildy and Castlecary, show more closely than any other form of testimony that young families were reared in the shadow of the Wall; the quantity of women's and children's shoes from Bar Hill makes it unlikely that all can be attributed to the families of officers living within the fort (*pace* Salway 1965, 160–1), and points strongly to the existence of a civilian settlement outside it. At Shirva, a little to the east of Auchendavy, there is the grimmer testimony of tombstones recording the former presence of civilians on the Wall: Verecunda, an unknown woman, probably a soldier's wife or daughter (RIB 2183); and a young man Salmanes buried by his father of the same name (RIB 2182). The latter was

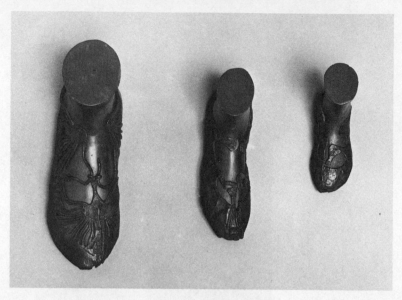

PLATE 9.4 *Range of leather shoes from Bar Hill.*

evidently a Syrian, which might hint at an association of some kind with the Syrian regiment of Hamii stationed at Bar Hill, the next fort to the east. Together with what has been interpreted as a baby's feeding bottle from Mumrills, this evidence conjures up a picture of domestic life that might seem at first somewhat incongruous amongst all the monuments of Rome's military achievements.

Unhappily, these northern civilian settlements, or *vici* – not to be confused with the defended annexes which provided additional storage and parking space of a strictly military kind – have been so little studied that their extent and development is virtually unknown (Salway 1965; Birley 1977). Little structural evidence has been forthcoming on the line of the Wall itself despite a number of excavations in recent years with that particular aim in mind. At Croy Hill few traces of buildings were recovered, but artefactual evidence pointed to the existence of quite a vigorous settlement on a plateau to the west of the fort, while on its opposite side systems of fields or pens have been noted, one of which contained a pottery kiln (Hanson 1979) (fig.9.5). Air-photography has revealed a possible parallel situation at Carriden where the fort is adjoined by a regular geometric system of fields and enclosures which appears to be aligned on a road leading into the east gate of the fort, thus strongly suggesting that the two elements are contemporary. By happy coincidence the site has also produced an altar dedicated to Jupiter Optimus Maximus by a body styling themselves the *vikani* or *vicus*-dwellers of the *castellum* Veluniate under the supervision of one Aelius Mansuetus (Rich-

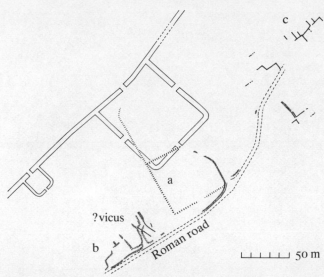

FIGURE 9.5 *Traces of a civilian settlement outside the fort at Croy Hill; a) pre-fort enclosure re-used in part; b) ditches for drainage of settlement; c) enclosures and field boundaries.*

mond and Steer 1957) (pl.9.2). While the precise context of the dedication is uncertain, it would appear that this was an official act showing the close relationship between the people of the settlement and the garrison of Carriden at the most important ceremony of the military year, the consecration of the unit to its Imperial task.

Aerial photography has also been responsible for the discovery of enclosures of a similar type to those above, exhibiting a similar relationship to a Roman road, to the south-east of the Antonine fort at Inveresk (pl.9.5). Recent excavation rather nearer to the fort has revealed remains of what was interpreted as some form of commercial activity, possibly a tavern (Thomas 1979), thus confirming to some extent the reports of early antiquaries who spoke of Roman structures of the most elaborate kind extending for hundreds of metres from the site of the known cavalry fort (Richmond and Hanson 1980, 287 and 298). At Cramond, however, ongoing excavations have revealed evidence of various industrial processes of probably military origin (Grew 1980, 354 *contra* Holmes 1979, 13–14), although this need not imply that none of the scattered evidence of extra-mural activity was civilian in nature, for an ordnance depot – if it is not too premature to apply that term – is even more likely to attract merchants and other civilians, in addition to wives and families, than a normal garrison.

The evidence already noted of more exotic foodstuffs and imported pottery at most fort sites indicates that quite long-distance transactions did

189

PLATE 9.5   *Field system associated with extramural settlement at Inveresk, from the air.*

indeed take place between the army and civilians, though at what level is uncertain. It has generally been assumed that contracts for much-used items like pottery were placed with civilian manufacturers by the army, which then distributed the goods to the troops, but a recent reconsideration makes this interpretation difficult to maintain (Breeze 1977). The great diversity of the pottery assemblage from any one site and the overall distribution in the north of certain closely identified wares suggests that pottery was purchased from civilian shops in the *vici* in much the same way as modern transactions in the High Street. Thus market forces as well as personal relationships can be seen at work in determining the establishment and subsequent growth of civilian settlements outside forts.

The great expense of overland transport already noted meant that, wherever possible, goods would have been transported by sea. The distribution of one of the most common coarse pottery wares found on the northern frontier suggests that it was shipped up the east coast, probably direct from the Thames estuary (Gillam 1973, 57). Either Cramond or Inveresk may have filled the role of harbour, for both seem to have developed extensive extra-

PLATE 9.6   *Tombstone of Nectovelius, a Brigantian serving at Mumrills.*

mural settlements, the latter of sufficient importance to attract the attention of the supreme financial administrator of the province, the Imperial procurator (Maxwell 1982c). The presence of such an eminent figure in the civil government of Britain at such a site may, however, reflect interest on the part of the Roman treasury in the economy of the rich and fertile heartland of the Votadini nearby (Macinnes 1982). Alternatively, it has recently been suggested that Camelon may have served as the main harbour for the Wall (Tatton-Brown 1980), but there is insufficient known at present about changes in sealevels to be certain that the site was readily accessible by sea in the Roman period. The existence of a harbour has also been postulated at the western end of the Wall at Old Kilpatrick (Miller 1928, 7–8) or Dumbarton (Macdonald 1934, 332), although the supporting structural evidence is unconvincing.

Finally we should note that not all the troops responsible for the construction and manning of the Wall were destined to depart on its evacuation. At Shirva near Auchendavy were found gravestones recording the deaths of one or possibly two soldiers of *legio II Augusta* (RIB 2179 and 2181, but cf. Davies 1976), while an uninscribed tombstone depicting three legionaries is known from the vicinity of the fort at Croy Hill. These legionaries may have been in garrison on the Wall, but it seems more likely that they were members of the legionary construction parties (see above p.153). Most forts would have had their own cemetery, situated in all probability beside the roads leading to and from the site, but apart from the cists discovered outside the fort at Camelon

(Breeze *et al.* 1976) and the unidentified cremation at Croy Hill (Hanson 1979, 20) none has been precisely located. The normal method of burial would have been cremation, although the rite observed at both Camelon burials was inhumation, and since the ashes would have been inserted in a plain jar or urn before deposition there is less likelihood of chance discovery. The more substantial tombstones are comparatively rare discoveries, since not all troops could afford to commemorate their deaths in this way. Apart from those mentioned, there are only two known: the memorial to the prefect of the Hamii at Bar Hill, C. Julius Marcellinus (RIB 2172) and the tombstone of Nectovelius, son of Vindex, a soldier of *cohors II Thracum* from Mumrills (RIB 2142) (pl.9.6). The latter is a suitable subject with whom to conclude this brief summary of life on the Antonine Wall. He was only twenty-nine years old when he died. How he came to die so young, whether by disease, as is most likely, or as a result of enemy action, we can never know. But he was a Brigantian by birth, a member of the confederacy of tribes in northern England who in pre-Roman times had probably been at daggers drawn with most of the tribes in southern Scotland, and more recently had apparently shown considerable animosity to the occupying army. And yet Nectovelius died in the service of one, protecting the other; a mute testimony to the alchemy by which Imperial Rome transmuted the fighting spirit of so many of its enemies.

X. SUCCESS OR FAILURE?

The question which forms the title of this chapter is practically unanswerable. Since, as we have seen (above p.59ff), it is impossible to identify with certainty the motives of Antoninus in ordering the abandonment of the Hadrianic line in AD 139, there is even less likelihood of assessing the degree to which these aims were ever realised, though if his own insecurity was a factor, Antoninus' lengthy and successful reign speaks for itself. A consideration of the success of the enterprise in local terms again relies upon an accurate assessment of its aims. It has been suggested (above p.164) that these were basically twofold: to repel such assaults as were made on the frontier from the north, and to foster the growth of a system of local government by which national spirit could be transmuted into the appearance of autonomy without in reality stepping beyond the bounds of subservience. The frontier zone had, in other words, to function as a safety-valve or regulator which absorbed the dynamic stresses of the northern territories and allowed the romanisation of the civilian zone of the province to proceed without check or hindrance, the latter being assured by strategically placed garrisons in the hinterland. All this was to be achieved without undue expenditure of men and materials, the definition of undue being relative to the resources available in the Empire at any given time, for it should not be forgotten that the fortunes of the province of Britain were closely allied to those of the Empire as a whole.

Yet, less than a quarter of a century after construction began, the Antonine Wall was finally abandoned. One could argue that the very shortness of its life tells its own tale: the Wall proved to be an expensive failure and was rapidly abandoned by Antoninus' successor. But a closer examination of the later history of Roman contact with Scotland does not allow the Antonine Wall to be written off quite so readily.

193

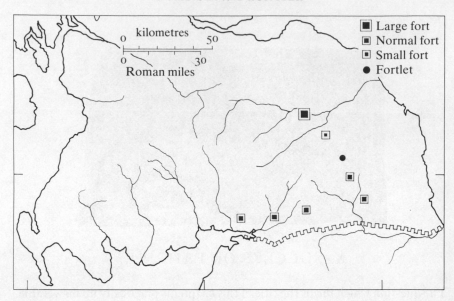

FIGURE 10.1 *Hadrian's Wall and its outpost forts* c. *AD 165.*

The decades following the evacuation of the Wall in *c.*AD 164 were far from peaceful for the imperial frontiers. As the Augustan History records, the echoes of war reverberated on three fronts, against Vologeses in Parthia, against the Chatti in Upper Germany and Raetia, and against the Britons, presumably on the northern frontier. The first action of Calpurnius Agricola, who was thereupon appointed governor of Britain, seems to have been to abandon the already reduced frontier installations north of Cheviot, with the exception of one or two outposts – Newstead and probably Cappuck on Dere Street – and revert to Hadrian's Wall as a main line of defence (fig.10.1). On the east, Risingham, probably High Rochester and possibly Chew Green provided a link with the outermost garrisons in the Tweed basin, while to the west, Bewcastle and Netherby and possibly Birrens resumed their role as out-posts on the northern fringes of Brigantia. This forward deployment of listening-posts thus presents a striking contrast with the state of affairs before the Antonine advance, when it would appear that it was the north-western end of Hadrian's Wall and the adjacent territories north of the Solway which represented the greatest source of anxiety to the Wall garrison. In the im-mediate post-Antonine phase the advance garrisons now extended furthest on the eastern flank, providing protection for the Votadini and an early-warning zone whose depth emulated and even exceeded that which had existed beyond the Antonine Wall shortly before. There were other ways in which the re-occupied Hadrianic frontier was influenced by its northern twin. A lateral road, facilitating communications between forts and other installations on the

Wall, was now built some way to the rear of the curtain, like the Military Way on the Antonine Wall; evidently this was one element of the northern Wall which had proved particularly effective, and its importance on the southern frontier is seen from the fact that in places it was allowed to override or run along the north mound of the Hadrianic *Vallum*. Spur roads were also provided connecting the new Military Way with the fortlets and turrets as well as forts. On the other hand, there seems to have been a large-scale abandonment of installations guarding the Cumberland coast on the left flank of the Wall, very few of the towers (Bellhouse 1954, 47–9) and not all of the milefortlets in that sector being brought back into commission (Bellhouse 1970, 19 and 28: cf. Potter 1977, 182). It would thus appear that the tribes inhabiting south-western Scotland across the Solway Firth were no longer reckoned to present as great a threat to the security of the Wall as had previously been thought. This evidence accords well with the partial dismantling some time before AD 164 of the fortlet system in the valleys of the Annan, Nith and Clyde; for that area too had probably been the scene of considerable inter-tribal bickering and unrest before the construction of the Antonine Wall (see above p.54f). Apart from these changes, however, the Hadrianic frontier reverted to what it had been before the Antonine advance took place. The gates were re-hung in the milecastle entrances, the forts were re-occupied, and the *Vallum* was brought back into service, its great ditch being cleaned out and the spoil deposited, significantly, on the south berm; at the same time the numerous crossings or causeways which had been provided to give easy access across the *Vallum* while Hadrian's Wall no longer served as the frontier, were now dug away. This action, particularly when taken together with the changes on the Cumberland coast, makes it clear that the Roman High Command were still seriously concerned about the security of the Wall-zone from the rear. Whatever the source of the military threat which became apparent in the late 160s, at the very least, therefore, it seems most unlikely that the tribes of south-western Scotland were in any way implicated, as they had possibly been in the later Hadrianic period. If it had achieved nothing else, this pacification of the peoples living north of the Solway would have justified much of the effort of establishing, even temporarily, the Antonine frontier. For it meant that henceforth the Tyne-Solway barrier was to be securely buttressed on the western flank by a considerable tract of friendly, or at least peaceful, territory, and, until the first descents by invaders from across the Irish Sea, the defenders of the Wall could turn their attention to the northern foe and, if necessary, the enemy within.

Building and repair on Hadrian's Wall and the hinterland forts continued through the governorship of Calpurnius Agricola, as may be seen from dedications at Corbridge, Carvoran, Chesterholm and Ribchester (RIB 1137, 1149, 1792, 1809, and 589), and the same work-programme was still proceeding, in all probability, after his departure in c.AD 166; not that this should occasion any surprise, for there was much to be done. Much of the turf Wall had still to be replaced in stone, and the existing stretches of the stone curtain were doubtless also seriously in need of repair and maintenance, having been largely neglected for at least two decades. That such reconstruction was not solely cosmetic may, however, be implied by the fragmentary historical record: another 'bellum Britannicum' was said to be impending around AD 170–2 (SHA Marcus XXII, 1), and 5500 Sarmatian cavalry – the equivalent of eleven quingenary alae – were despatched to the province in AD 175; this transfer represented the bulk of the large body of mounted troops furnished to Rome under the terms of a peace treaty with the rebellious Danubian Iazyges. It is possible that the troops were sent to Britain because it was the most isolated of provinces and suitably distant from their homeland, the move having little to do with Britain's military requirements. However, it is curious that they were not, in that case, transferred to Syria, which was equally remote and urgently in need of reinforcements, since it was the rebellion in that province which had compelled the emperor to come to terms with the Iazyges in the first place. On the balance of probability, Britain may be reckoned to have had a genuine need for additional cavalry, and it may be significant that the governor appointed at this time was Q. Antistius Adventus (RIB 1083), a man with a distinguished military record and a career in provincial administration that mirrored those of Platorius Nepos, Lollius Urbicus and Julius Verus (Birley 1981, 129–32), all of whom had been chosen for the governorship of Britain when the post seemed likely to demand exceptional skill and authority.

It is, unfortunately, impossible to identify with precision the cause of this anxiety. Although it has been suggested that unrest in Wales may be the explanation, and this could conceivably have been associated with destruction in such major urban centres as Wroxeter and Worcester (Frere 1978, 186), the evidence is far from convincing. Consequently, it may be wisest to accept the testimony afforded by the disposition of frontier forces which hints very strongly at a policy directed towards maintaining communication between the eastern end of Hadrian's Wall and the Tweed basin by way of Dere Street. The purpose of such deployment would have been at least twofold: to provide adequate surveillance of the Selgovae in Upper Tweeddale and to afford a modicum of protection to the Votadini. That the Selgovae were not, however, a particularly potent source of danger seems to be implied by the lack of equivalent precautions in the upper valleys of the Esk or Annan. It is therefore probable that, if any threat to the frontier or to allied peoples was then perceived, it came from Eastern Scotland beyond the lands of the Votadini. If this was the situation, the milliary ala which was then stationed at Newstead (Richmond 1950, 23–5), would have had a role to test its mettle. Its presence at the furthest limit of Roman territory was the equivalent of a small legionary base, and as emphatic a statement of imperial intent to dominate the land beyond the frontier as the adventurous policy of Severus almost half a century later. The extensive long-range patrolling which such a policy demanded, and which only a base like Newstead could provide, would doubtless have bene-fited from the friendly relations which had been fostered during the life of the Antonine Wall between the occupying army and the Votadinian tribesmen. The regular, recurrent visits of Roman patrols may have gone some way to-wards reassuring the local population in Lothian and the Merse, whose way of life, both economic and political, must have been considerably disturbed by the withdrawal of the Roman garrison.

Whether any station on the Antonine Wall was used, even if only tem-porarily, for the extension of such patrolling duties cannot be determined on the basis of the evidence available to us. The latest certainly dated coin from the Wall is a fairly well-worn bronze *as* of Marcus dating to AD 173–4 which was found at Mumrills (Robertson 1975a, 417); furthermore Professor Mann has suggested (1963) that the '*cives Italici et Norici*' of *legio VI Victrix* who dedicated an altar to Mercury at Castlecary (RIB 2148) (pl.7.1), may have been troops recently transferred to that legion from *legio II Italica*, in which case the combination of nationalities is unlikely to have existed outside the period AD 175–190. Nevertheless, the absence from the Wall of pottery, par-ticularly samian, significantly later than the Antonine period makes it im-possible at present to accept that any site was actually reconstructed for such a purpose, and we must therefore imagine that all the surveillance was executed by units operating out of the northernmost bases, Newstead or Birrens, or possibly on occasion moving out from the line of Hadrian's Wall itself. It is possibly in such a context that we should view the operations referred to by a legate of *legio VI Victrix* who set up an altar at Kirksteads at the western end of the Wall, giving thanks for '*res trans vallum prospere gestas*' (RIB 2034). Had this been a thank-offering for the successful outcome of major conflict, as has sometimes been suggested, we might have expected a more explicit refer-ence to the action, but, as the event is described as 'the fortunate outcome of action conducted beyond the Wall' and the date cannot be fixed more closely than the later second century AD, it may be more likely that a less dramatic tour of duty was in the dedicator's mind. As officer commanding the legion at York, the legate would have been the senior officer immediately responsible for the security of the Wall-zone and its approaches.

The outbreak of hostilities which had twice threatened during the reign of Marcus Aurelius could not, however, be delayed for ever. Cassius Dio tells us that, when Commodus was on the throne, 'the tribes in the island crossed the wall that separated them from the Roman garrisons. They did great damage, killing a certain general and the troops that he had with him' (LXXII, 8). There is much that is not clear in this brief account. To begin with, the precise date: although the context suggests that this occurred after the death of Marcus Aurelius, and that the subsequent despatch of Ulpius Marcellus to take control of the situation was the alarmed response of Commodus alone, an inscription from Benwell appears to indicate that Marcellus was already in Britain before Marcus' death (RIB 1329). Secondly Dio, or rather the Byzantine author upon whose summary of Dio we must rely at this point, does not specify the Wall crossed by the barbarian horde; we now assume that it was the refurbished Hadrianic frontier, and not the abandoned Antonine work that failed to stem the invasion, although in the context of Severus' campaigns the same author refers to a wall which can only be the Antonine barrier (see below p.203). Likewise the identity of the general slain in the assault must remain uncertain; the epitome of Dio uses the Greek word 'strategos' so that we cannot tell if the original reference was to the governor of the province, a legionary legate, or lesser rank in charge of either the Wall garrison or an *ad hoc* field-force (*contra* Birley 1981, 135–6).

Reverting to the matter of the date, one should note that if the events referred to took place in AD 180 and Ulpius Marcellus was already in office, Commodus' despatch being merely the issue of orders for punitive action to commence, the ensuing campaign would seem to have been unduly protracted, for the issue of coins commemorating a victory in Britain and the addition of the imperial title 'Britannicus' did not take place until AD 184 at the earliest (RIC Commodus 451–2, 459e). On the other hand, it has been argued that the Ulpius Marcellus mentioned in the Benwell inscription was a homonymous governor who held office under Caracalla (Birley 1981, 140–2); the matter does not seem to be susceptible of proof one way or the other, but the invention of a second Marcellus is not absolutely necessary (Jarrett 1978). Similarly, although it is difficult to believe that the Antonine Wall was then garrisoned, and did not therefore rate as a military obstacle, it should be remembered that invading tribesmen would not have needed to cross Hadrian's Wall to come to grips with Roman garrisons of considerable strength; it was to deal with dangers such as this that the outpost forts had been positioned in the way described above. However, it would seem that the outpost forts must have been by-passed, for, although little excavation has been undertaken in any of them in recent years, none has produced evidence of destruction which can be dated to this period. Along Hadrian's Wall, on the other hand, evidence of extensive burning commensurate with enemy action has been noted at two forts: Halton Chesters, where Dere Street crosses the line of the Wall, and Rudchester the next fort to the west (Gillam *et al.* 1973, 82). The only other site in the area to produce clear evidence of devastation is Corbridge, also on Dere Street, only two miles (3·2 km) to the south. Although previously assigned to the end of the second century, the famous Corbridge destruction deposit has now been convincingly redated to the 180s (Gillam 1974, 7–10). Thus the destruction on the frontier seems to have been concentrated at the point where Dere Street crosses the Hadrianic Wall; such a conclusion would combine with the implied evidence from the outpost forts, as well as the known distribution of coin hoards of Commodan date north of the Forth (Robertson 1978, 201–4), and the location of the third-century campaigns, to suggest that the trouble may have originated in the far north and have been channelled south along the Roman road towards Hadrian's Wall.

Of the orgy of destruction implied by Cassius Dio there is little evidence. Traces of destruction have been recorded from sites as far afield as Ravenglass in Cumberland and Bainbridge and Ilkley in Yorkshire (Potter 1979, 33–4; Hartley 1966b, 33 and 1960, 114). In the past this has all been attributed to a disaster in AD 197, but the direct dating evidence, that is the pottery, need not carry the occupation so late in any of the three examples quoted, and a context in the 180s might be more appropriate. But such actions are more likely to represent some minor conflagration amongst the local Brigantes, since the sites are all too remote from the major centres likely to have attracted marauding tribesmen from the north.

Nevertheless, whatever its origin, the danger was real enough to draw forth terrible retribution from the governor; thus the 'rout of a mighty host of barbarians' celebrated in an inscription of probable Commodan date from Carlisle (RIB 946), while not necessarily a reference to the campaigns of the ruthless Ulpius Marcellus, nevertheless conveys the spirit in which they were conceived and mounted. The victory which was eventually won by AD 184 did not, however, serve to restore the *status quo* on the frontier. The direct Roman grip on Dere Street was now considerably weakened with the abandonment of Newstead, Cappuck, and possibly even one of the outposts nearer to Hadrian's Wall at Risingham. To the south-west, Birrens was in all probability also given up at this time (Robertson 1975b, 284–6), the northernmost outliers of the frontier system now being Bewcastle, Netherby and High Rochester. However, the relationship with the northern tribes may have been underpinned by some form of treaty, for similar arrangements were certainly in existence by the end of the century (Dio LXXV, 5, 4). The marked reduction in the units detailed for advance surveillance duties was accompanied by changes in the garrisons and installations on the Wall itself; the latter included the abandonment of a number of turrets (Charlesworth 1977, 20–2; Breeze and Dobson 1976a, 130–1), probably those whose continuity of use was not absolutely essential to the maintenance of communications and forward observation. Milecastles, too, were adapted to meet the new situation. Although few were abandoned altogether, several underwent alterations which effectively blocked or restricted the flow of traffic through their north or south gates; this has been seen as no more than the removal of superfluous installations, and thus merely a streamlining or labour-saving exercise (Breeze and Dobson 1976, 130–1), but, if so, it is strange that the opportunity was not taken earlier, and accordingly military necessity should perhaps be acknowledged as at least a contributing factor. However, the activities of Marcellus, or indeed any Commodan governor, are but rarely attested in the epigraphic record from the forts on the Wall. Apart from the dedication in the temple to Antenociticus at Benwell, which must have been made before the start of his campaigns (above p.198). the only inscription to mention Marcellus is that which records the construction of an aqueduct at Chesters (RIB 1463). In fact, the lack of evidence for rebuilding of forts under Commodus has in the past weighed heavily against acceptance of a destruction on Hadrian's Wall at this time (Gillam and Mann 1970, 26–7). It should not be forgotten, however, that on his death the memory of Commodus was damned by senatorial decree, so that inscriptions bearing his name were likely to suffer destruction at the hands of zealous adherents of the new regime. Their notable absence from the Wall, and indeed from the Empire as a whole, is then less of a surprise. However, bearing in mind the comparatively large number of building inscriptions from the Wall and its immediate hinterland attributable to the early Severan governors (see below p.203f), a number of forts may have been allowed to fall into disrepair, or more probably not have required repair at this stage.

There is, unfortunately, even less evidence to tell us what the effects of the warfare were on the native population of the area between the two Walls. To what extent they were the victims of aggression by northern tribes or in what ways their relationship with the Roman army was altered by the new policies of Ulpius Marcellus, are questions which cannot be answered at the present time. It may have been on this occasion that some of the intrusive brochs and duns were built in the Tyne-Forth Province (see above p.63f), but even if it was, the circumstances of their construction remain unknown; whether they were the homes of victorious invaders or merely the result of speculative building by exotic elements capitalising on a local breakdown in the normal structure of society is not demonstrable. Two souterrains, or underground buildings, at Crichton and Newstead, incorporated Roman masonry in their fabric, quarried no doubt from adjacent Roman military installations, and a similar re-use of Roman sculptures and inscribed stones may have occurred at Shirva on the Antonine Wall. Yet, even in such cases of direct interference with Roman sites to build structures that may have derived from more northerly regions, it is impossible to determine how soon the pillaging occurred after the Roman withdrawal. One might expect that in such troubled times as the historical sources depict there would have been a resurgence in the fortification of native sites, but, if there was, few archaeological traces have been recognised. In the sequence of structures identified during excavations at Hownam Rings in Roxburghshire, for example, after the abandonment of the multivallate fort, presumably on the first entry of Roman troops into Scotland, settlement appears to have been of a non-defensive kind, with round stone-based houses sprawling over the interior and defences of the fort (C. M. Piggott 1950). Similar open settlements have been observed at many other sites in northern Northumberland and the south-east of Scotland, in each case succeeding a 'fortified' enclosure (Jobey 1974, 22) (fig. 1.4), and the same sequence occurred at Norman's Law in Fife overlooking the estuary of the Tay, suggesting that this manifestation was common throughout much of Scotland that fell within the active sphere of Roman influence. At the latter site, the summit of the hill is crowned by an oval univallate stone-walled fort of no great size, which post-dates the multivallate work and is presumed to be later than the open settlement (Feachem 1963, 125). There are a number of comparable sites in lowland Scotland, the majority of them occurring to the south of the Tay; known as 'defensive enclosures', and in many cases little larger than the most impressive members of the dun class, they appear to be the most likely candidates for identification as post-Roman fortifications (Feachem 1966, 82–5). With their superficial resemblance to the univallate forts of the Atlantic Province, it is not impossible that some may have been constructed in the immediately post-Antonine phase. On the other hand, it is difficult to imagine that the Roman army would have countenanced the construction of new fortified sites in the period before AD 185, and they may, in fact, belong to a considerably later epoch, like the so-called 'nuclear' forts of the Early Christian period (Alcock 1980, 74–80); one such fortification at Rubers Law in Roxburghshire incorporated dressed stones from a nearby Roman work, usually presumed to have been a signal-station. Although, in general, it is impossible to read the fluctuating fortunes of the frontier from the evidence of native habitation sites, it might be expected that the remarkable body of material recovered from the tribal capital of the Votadini at Traprain Law would cast at least a glimmer of light upon the situation. Unfortunately, the methodology of the early excavations and the nature of the published reports preclude a detailed assessment of the periods of occupation on the site. It has been suggested that Traprain was abandoned for a generation or more at some time around the end of the second century on the basis of a gap in the coin series and changes in the metalwork from the site (Feachem 1956b, 288). If true, this might be equated with the trouble of the 180s, as it has been previously with the postulated patterns in the 190s, but the absence of later second- and early third-century coins is not paralleled in the record of Roman pottery from the site, so that any gap in its occupation must remain unproven (Jobey 1976, 200).

The signs are that by AD 185 Ulpius Marcellus's policies had secured a temporary peace, and indeed the army in Britain had sufficient leisure to turn its attention to politics, indulging in mutinous rumblings to such good effect that the senior army officer in Rome, the Praetorian Prefect, Perennis, was removed. A period of dissension and unrest in both province and empire followed: after the fall of Perennis, P. Helvius Pertinax, a man of considerable experience, was appointed as governor of Britain, with the express purpose of restoring stability and confidence to the army of the frontier; in this he, too, failed, a second mutiny breaking out, which almost cost him his life. Barely six years later, in AD 192, the empire itself was in turmoil; on the last day of the year, Commodus was assassinated and civil war broke out.

Among the contenders for the throne was D. Clodius Albinus, governor of Britain, who watched his recent predecessor, Pertinax, attempt but fail to grasp the reins of power. By AD 196 Albinus had also seen the successor of Pertinax, Didius Julianus, and later the aspiring governor of Syria, fall before the relentless advance of L. Septimius Severus, governor of Pannonia. Although an attempt had already been made by Severus to placate him with the title of Caesar, Albinus now realised that it was only a matter of time before he, too, succumbed to open assault or the assassin's dagger, and he made his move. In the autumn of AD 196 he crossed to Gaul with as many troops as he could muster from the provincial garrison, but in February 197, after initial successes, he was defeated in battle at Lyons and subsequently committed suicide. The consequences for his former province have for long been a matter of debate.

We do not know the exact size of Albinus's army, the total of 150,000 given by the historian Dio being impossibly high (LXXV, 6.1). It might be reasonable to think that the strength of Severus' Danubian legions would have driven Albinus to pare the garrison of the frontier to the very bone to augment his more limited legionary resources. But that Albinus stripped the northern frontier of troops is inference not fact. Indeed, despite previous assertions, there is no evidence that the garrisons in the Wall forts after AD 197 were any different from those in occupation shortly before that date, as ought logically to be the case had they all been withdrawn for active, and unsuccessful, service in Gaul (Jarrett 1978, 291–2 *contra* Frere 1978, 195). On the contrary, the only evidence we have of the unit present at any Wall fort between AD 185 and 197, from Chesters (RIB 1463), indicates that it was the same garrison which continued unchanged into the third century and beyond.

It has been generally believed, and the view remains quite widely held (Frere 1978, 195–7), that the northern tribes grasped the opportunity, took advantage of the temporary depletion of the frontier garrison and poured into the province, leaving behind them a trail of destruction. Such a view can no longer be substantiated, even if there was some withdrawal of troops from the frontier. What evidence there was of destruction along the frontier, notably at Corbridge, is now dated some twenty years earlier, on the basis of a reassessment of the pottery (see above p.199). Signs of conflagration at forts in the hinterland need no longer be attributed to the situation in Albinus' governorship if dated by archaeological means alone (see above p.199); it may further be argued that rebuilding could either have been considerably delayed or spread over a number of years, as is indicated by epigraphic evidence from Bowes and Bainbridge (RIB 730, 740, 722 and Wright 1961, 192). The number of forts in the hinterland at which building is attested under the new governor Virius Lupus (RIB 637, 730, 1163) contrasts sharply with the absence of evidence of such rebuilding over a decade earlier after a historically attested disaster of major proportions; but this need not necessarily imply that an even greater catastrophe had occurred in AD 197. This is not to doubt, however, that there was considerable trouble on the frontier. Lupus apparently felt threatened by the prospect of an alliance between the Caledonii and the Maeatae and was obliged to purchase peace from the latter, receiving back prisoners in return (Dio LXXV, 5, 4). What exactly the Maeatae had been doing is unclear, but it seems likely to have been more than minor border skirmishing, while yet falling short of a major uprising. Indeed, had it been the latter, it would have been odd if Severus, who was in Gaul at this time, had not hastened over to deal with the problem himself. Even if the war in Parthia was considered pressing (Birley 1972, 184), the delay between the supposed 'disaster' in AD 197 and the Imperial expedition in 208 appears curiously long. Rather the evidence suggests that hostilities continued to escalate throughout the governorships of both Virius Lupus and his successor, Alfenus Senecio.

Dio's brief sentence noted above is our first clear reference to the source of Rome's problems in Britain since the much disputed passage of Pausanias. He goes on, in the context of Severus's campaigns, to locate the Maeatae 'close to the wall which divides the island in two and the Caledonians beyond them', indicating that both were large confederacies, the identities of all the other tribes being merged within them (Dio LXXVI, 12, 1). The Caledonii are familiar to us from the pages of Tacitus and may be assumed by this time to have incorporated most of the groups in the Highlands and beyond. The Maeatae are new to us, and somewhat more problematical. Dio's reference to the wall in describing their location ought to imply the more southerly frontier. However, all the other evidence points to the home of the Maeatae in Fife, Strathearn and Menteith (Maxwell 1975b, 45–6): place-name evidence, such as Dumyat and Myot Hill in Stirlingshire, the distribution of both late second- and early third-century coin hoards (Robertson 1978, 192–3), and the very location of Severus's campaigns as defined by the distribution of temporary camps (fig.10.2).

Native unrest certainly continued to be a problem on the northern frontier throughout the next decade; Severus even expressed irritation that the governor, probably L. Alfenus Senecio, was winning wars in Britain when he himself could not even deal with an infamous robber in Italy (Dio LXXVI,

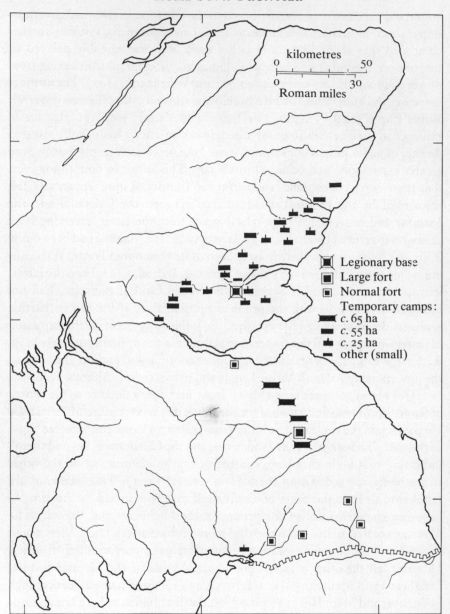

kilometres
0   50
0   30
Roman miles

☒ Legionary base
■ Large fort
▪ Normal fort
Temporary camps:
▬ c. 65 ha
▬ c. 55 ha
◆ c. 25 ha
▬ other (small)

FIGURE 10.2   *Forts and temporary camps of Severan date north of Hadrian's Wall.*

10, 6). Victories recorded on dedicatory inscriptions from Benwell on the Wall and Greetland in Yorkshire (RIB 1337 and 627) may commemorate military successes at this time, but there is no certainty that either is relevant to the situation under consideration (Breeze and Dobson 1976a, 133). Nor, it seems, were the British wars serious enough to deter successive governors from a relatively massive programme of structural refurbishing, which even encompassed one of the outpost forts, at Risingham, that site having apparently fallen into decay through neglect over a period of years (RIB 1234).

Eventually, it seems, the governor was obliged to call for more troops or an imperial expedition, because 'the barbarians had risen and were overrunning the country, carrying off booty and causing great destruction' (Herodian III, 14). Our alternative and generally more reliable source for this period, the historian Dio, makes no mention of such trouble; on the contrary he states that 'Severus went to war in Britain since his sons were adopting bad habits and the troops were being corrupted by idleness' (LXXVI, 11). While the disciplining of wayward sons is hardly acceptable as the primary motive for a major campaign, it might well have been a contributory factor in such a decision if a suitable occasion had arisen. In the case of the British campaigns of Severus, the simple motives of personal glory and territorial aggrandisement should not be discounted. Both are hinted at in the historians' accounts: Herodian states that Severus was a lover of glory who wanted to add a British victory to those he had already achieved elsewhere in the Empire and, to this end, he rejected the overtures of peace made by the British tribes on his arrival (III, 14); while Dio indicates that Severus intended to subjugate the whole of Britain (LXXVI, 13, 1). Continued rumblings on the northern frontier will eventually have provided the appropriate arena for an imperial campaign; but even the Romans preferred to wage a *justum bellum*, and Herodian simply reproduces the official justification for the *expeditio felicissima Britannica* (Birley 1972, 186–8).

Accordingly in AD 208 (RIC Severus 225a) Severus set off to take personal command of the war, accompanied by his two sons, Caracalla and Geta, and the empress Julia Domna, and attended by an army of reinforcements that included several legionary vexillations (CIL XIII 3496). By a combination of archaeological and literary evidence we are able to reconstruct Severus' campaigns in Scotland in more detail than any since the time of the Flavian conquest. The distribution of two major series of temporary camps, the 63-acre (25·5 ha) and the 130-acre (52·6 ha), which are generally accepted as marking the routes of Severan armies (St Joseph 1973, 230–33), confirm both the large size of the forces marshalled and the location of the main area of hostility in the lands of the Maeatae and Caledonii, as implied by Dio (LXXVI, 12, 1 and 15, 2) (fig.10.2).

The 63-acre (25·5 ha) group of camps is the earlier of the two (St Joseph 1970, 167–71; Hanson 1978b, 146–8) and presumably marks the progress of the first campaigns in AD 208 or 209. The camps provide an almost complete series indicating a march from the Forth to the North Esk and back, with outliers in Fife. Dio states that the location of the campaign was in Caledonia, but a brief foray into the territory of the Maeatae early in the campaign would have made good tactical sense. Indeed, since there are no clear traces of a line of march south of the Forth-Clyde isthmus, the troops may even have been transported by sea to some point on the isthmus at the beginning of the operation. Certainly the fleet was intimately involved in the campaigns: the fort at South Shields at the mouth of the Tyne was converted into a fortified storehouse containing at least eighteen stone-built granaries and has produced a number of lead seals bearing the heads of Severus and his two sons, derived from official materials in transit (Dore and Gillam 1979, 61–6); while there is epigraphic evidence of a combination of the fleets of Germania, Moesia, Pannonia and Britannia at about this time (CIL VI 1643). From Fife the march north involved a crossing of the Tay, probably at Carpow where a large polygonal enclosure beneath the Severan legionary base lies opposite a likely bridgehead camp at St Madoes (St Joseph 1973, 117–18). Additional support for such a venture has been adduced by reference to a unique coin or medallion of Caracalla issued in AD 209 (RIC Caracalla 441) which portrays a pontoon bridge and the legend TRAIECTUS (crossing). While caution in accepting the correlation has recently been advised (Robertson 1980, 137), such a plan is not inherently unlikely, for a similar use of a pontoon bridge across the lower Forth was planned by Edward I in 1303 during the Wars of Independence, with the object of crossing the river well below the lowest bridge and so turning the enemy's flank (Barrow 1976, 178). However, Dio implies that there was a considerable amount of marching about without ever bringing the enemy to battle, with large Roman losses sustained in ambushes in difficult terrain (LXXVI, 13, 1): the field of operations may therefore have extended more widely than is yet indicated by the distribution of camps. Nevertheless, Severus seems to have compelled the Caledonians to come to terms before returning to York (Dio LXXVI, 13, 3).

Ironically, since earlier overtures of peace had been rejected in favour of a successful campaign, Severus seems to have stirred up something of a hornet's nest. There is some confusion in the very brief historical accounts available as to the precise timing and sequence of events, but the Maeatae were joined in revolt by the Caledonians and a further campaign, probably headed by Caracalla alone, was mounted against them (Dio LXXVI, 15, 1–2; Herodian III, 5). This time a predominantly land-based campaign seems likely. Massive forces seem to have been assembled on Dere Street at Newstead, where the first of a series of immense temporary camps is attested, each member probably extending over an area of some 165 acres (66·8 ha). North of the Forth the size of the force seems to have been reduced slightly, a contingent possibly being detached to begin the construction of the base at Carpow, and a series of camps 130 acres (56·6 ha) in extent can be traced north from Ardoch as far as the Howe of the Mearns and possibly beyond (St Joseph 1977, 143–4;

PLATE 10.1 *Legionary vexillation-fortress at Carpow, Perthshire, from the air.*

Hanson 1978b, 145), following a route through Strathmore similar to that of the previous season, the sites of camps of the two series being situated in close proximity to each other at Innerpeffray and Scone, and actually overlapping at Ardoch.

Whether Severus intended a permanent re-occupation of Scotland has been much debated. The considerable reconstruction work undertaken earlier in his reign along Hadrian's Wall has led most scholars to reject this interpretation, for such time-consuming activity would have been made largely redundant by extensive re-building further north (Steer 1958, 94–7). However, it is conceivable that by the time the campaigns were mounted, Severus may have been compelled to reappraise the situation, for a number of permanent forts were built in Scotland at this time, which indicates that something beyond a punitive campaign was intended: a 25-acre (10 ha) vexillation fortress is known at Carpow (pl.10.1), occupied by elements from the legions *II Augusta* and *VI Victrix* (Leach and Wilkes 1978) and a fort of 4·8 acres (1·9 ha) at Cramond on the Forth (Rae and Rae 1974). In addition, a study of the samian ware from the fort of Newstead has led Hartley to suggest that there was a Severan presence somewhere in its vicinity (1972, 54). A case has also been made out at various times for a Severan occupation of the Antonine Wall (Jarrett and Mann 1970, 204), the shadowy third phase of reconstruction being interpreted as a preparation for the refurbishment of the northern Wall during the governorship of Senecio or a little later. Steer examined the data almost twenty years ago and concluded that the case for a third occupation of the Wall was not proven (1964, 29–38), but suggested that a start might have been made. A further critical assessment of the evidence, however, leaves little doubt that this period III is totally illusory. Discounting the evidence from bath-buildings, which are notoriously prone to alterations throughout their life-span and whose structural periods thus need bear no relation to periods of occupation within the fort, the only sites where three phases of internal buildings are postulated are Mumrills, Croy Hill, Cadder and Old Kilpatrick. At Croy Hill the earliest period consists of two post-holes, which Macdonald himself would not have distinguished from the succeeding phase had he not been specifically seeking a third period (1936, 50), and a stretch of gutter beneath the granary. At Mumrills only the *principia* demonstrates three structural periods; but the lean-to structure of post-hole construction along the west wall of the building, which distinguished the second phase, lacks convincing parallels, and the way that all the post-holes coincide exactly with period I suggests that they might more appropriately be interpreted as the remains of half-timbered construction in that first period. A precisely analogous construction method is known at Corbridge, also in an Antonine context (Richmond and Gillam 1950, 168). At Cadder the remains of the postulated first period are far too fragmentary to be convincing as the remnants of a complete stone building, and it would not be surprising if minor alterations were found to have taken place in the commandant's house more frequently than in other buildings, given the frequency with which commanders were changed (Birley 1953, 137–8). Only at Old Kilpatrick, where the third period was indicated by occasional traces of rough walling offset from the face of a secondary foundation in the *principia* (Miller 1928, 27 and pl.VI B), is it difficult to offer an alternative explanation within the limitations of the published data. It is just possible, moreover, bearing in mind the dedication to the Baetasii of putatively third-century date (pl.10.2) (see above p.157f), that this particular fort, situated as it is on the very bank of the Clyde, was re-used during the Severan campaigns because of its accessibility by sea; it must be noted, however, that the excavations there recovered no third-century artefacts.

It is not known precisely when construction began on any of the certain or presumed Severan sites in Scotland. At Carpow, however, the dedicatory slabs above the fortress gates do not seem to have been completed until after the death of Geta in February AD 212 (Wright 1966 and 1974), although there are

PLATE 10.2   *Putative third-century altar from Old Kilpatrick, dedicated by the* cohors I Baetasiorum.

hints of an earlier phase when the gateways were timber-built (Leach and Wilkes 1978, 51). The fresh unweathered state of the dedication slabs, however, indicates that they had not stood in position for any length of time, and confirms that Severus' policy, although maintained for a time, was given up sufficiently swiftly to merit the reproof of critical historians (Dio LXXVII, 1.1; Herodian III, 15, 4–7).

The skeletal disposition of Severan forts in Scotland, perhaps eked out by an as yet undiscovered example guarding the crossing of the Forth at or near Stirling, presents at first sight an alarmingly vulnerable appearance. Yet it was no more so than the dispositions made by Severus in Mesopotamia, a province created after his second Parthian War. This new province, like the outer *limes* in Britain, 'stood like a great arrow thrust forward from Syria, with one of the legions . . . standing at the very tip' (Mann 1974a, 524). The potential success of such a policy lay not so much in its return to positive, aggressive thinking, although there was much in that, as in its ability to rely on a secure base. It is clear from what we must take to be Severus' intended dispositions in north Britain, that there was as considerable confidence in the base represented by the southern lowlands of Scotland as the emperor had reposed in Syria. Unfortunately, his views were not shared by Caracalla; had it been otherwise, the later history of the Roman frontier and of Britain itself might have been significantly different. Even without these forward bases, the effect of the Severan campaigns was such as to bring peace to north Britain for close on a hundred years, that is until the Picts made their appearance on the political scene.

After the abandonment of Carpow and Cramond (and presumably Newstead) at some time around AD 215, the surveillance of the lands beyond the Hadrianic barrier appears to have been carried out by *'exploratores'* or reconnaissance units of various kinds (fig.10.3). They were based ultimately in outpost forts, like High Rochester and Risingham on Dere Street, or Bewcastle and Netherby (Castra Exploratorum) in the west. Inscriptions of just such an irregular unit (a *vexillatio*) of Raetian spearmen and the first cohort of Vardulli, which were found in the ruins of the abbey at Jedburgh (RIB 2117–2118; Macdonald 1923), have usually been taken to indicate the presence of small detachments guarding an installation at the crossing of the River Teviot. Both units were stationed in the early third century at outpost forts on Dere Street, and the Jedburgh inscriptions are thought to be a token of a considerably wider dispersal of small detachments in the area immediately north of Hadrian's Wall. However, it is no longer possible to see them as part of a system which afforded a wider means of surveillance, involving tribal assemblies meeting under Roman jurisdiction at traditional moots or *loca* (*pace* Steer 1958, 107–8). This theory stemmed largely from a misinterpretation of the *loca* list which appears in the Ravenna Cosmography. Previously thought to be an official roster of authorised tribal assemblies, the list now seems to be little more than a medley of 'unconsidered trifles' swept together by a textual collator more interested in neatness of presentation than factual significance (Rivet and Smith 1979, 212). Nevertheless, even without the organisation implied by the Ravenna *loca*, the provisions made by Caracalla or his provincial administrators served well enough to assure the frontier an apparently undisturbed age of tranquillity.

The relevance of this to the success or failure of the Antonine Wall is considerable, because it confirms that, with the slightest degree of supervision and protection, the peoples living between the two isthmuses were capable of forming a stable community that would have offered no serious threat to an army of occupation, be it on the Forth-Clyde or the Tyne-Solway line. Indeed, the evidence within the Tyne-Forth Province of non-defended, probably expanding native settlements (Jobey 1974), which continued to acquire Roman goods, if only on a very small scale, lends great support to this

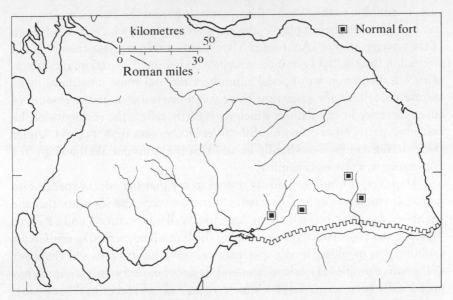

FIGURE 10.3 *Hadrian's Wall and its outpost forts after the withdrawal of Caracalla from Scotland.*

thesis. Yet there was one important proviso: the tribes living to the north of the Antonine Wall, the peoples of Caledonia, had to be prevented from combining in arms. It was to ensure this, above all, that the Antonine outpost forts and the Severan legionary vexillations were disposed respectively along the Ardoch-Strageath-Bertha axis, and on the south shore of the Tay estuary; the existence of the Gask Ridge '*limes*' in the late first century shows that this fundamental point had been grasped at an early stage. From what we have seen of the prehistoric evidence, it is clear that the above dispositions would also have capitalised on the cultural barrier between Brittonic and proto-Pictish peoples which appears to have run along the estuary of the Forth and curved northwards into eastern Perthshire. It is therefore not true to say that the Roman vacillation between the Antonine Wall and Hadrian's Wall is of merely antiquarian interest (Mann 1974a, 531). The Antonine *limes* as finally developed in the 140s was a realistic and potentially successful solution to Rome's frontier problems in north Britain. Why then did it not endure? The answer appears to lie in an unfortunate combination of events: the unexplained troubles in north Britain in the 150s and early 160s, combined with the accession of a new emperor, who was less influenced by the propaganda value of his most northerly frontier, and major problems elsewhere in the empire. In the East, the Parthians had seized Armenia and defeated two Roman armies; the Chatti threatened to descend on Raetia and Upper Germany, and before long there were few sectors of the imperial frontier that were not under pressure. In addition to this, Verus' forces returning from the Parthian campaign had brought with them a plague, the *pestis Antoniniana*, which ravaged much of the western empire (Ammianus Marcellinus XXIII, 7); its presence is not attested in Britain, but even if the province had escaped visitation, the effects of such a disruption on imperial administration and trade must have made themselves felt. At the same time there was a marked drop in the amount of silver currency in circulation, which may partly reflect the incidence of the epidemic, partly other economic difficulties (Robertson 1978, 194–6). Under these circumstances it can hardly be said that the Antonine Wall was given a fair chance to show its capability.

However, it would be equally untrue to say that the effort expended on its construction was entirely wasted. On the contrary, the signs are that the twenty-odd years during which the Antonine Wall was occupied, and a Roman presence was continuously maintained in the hinterland, served to reinforce a tradition that moulded, if only in a marginal way, the attitudes and character of the native peoples of lowland Scotland. It does not necessarily mean, as has occasionally been suggested (Richmond 1940, 114–16; Steer 1958, 124–30), that the Britons of Lothian, or Tweeddale, or Strathclyde became at any time client-kingdoms, bound by treaties to stand sentinel for Rome over the northern outlands (Mann 1974b). More probably the ties that existed, from the evacuation of the Antonine Wall to the reign of Valentinian I, took the form of a mutual dependence. The fortunes of Hadrian's Wall and the lowland tribes were inextricably entwined; when the Tyne-Solway frontier was menaced by the northern enemy, the security of the southern tribes was also under threat; when the Wall experienced peace, the southern tribes enjoyed prosperity. But the rise of the Pictish nation, the confederation of tribes north of the Forth, including the Caledonii (*Pan. Lat. Vet.* VI (VII) 7, 1–2), which becomes apparent in the Roman sources from the late third century, marked the beginning of the end for the Romans in Scotland. The success of the 'barbarian conspiracy' in AD 367, when the Picts, Saxons, Scots and Attacotti descended simultaneously on the province, brought the close relationship with the lowland tribes to a conclusion (Mann 1974b, 35–6). It may be that the natives in the lowlands chose neither to oppose the invasion nor warn the Roman frontier of its imminence, a function which they may previously have fulfilled in a semi-official capacity, possibly as the *areani* referred to by Ammianus Marcellinus (XXVIII, 3, 8; XXVII, 8, 1), seeing on this occasion that it was wiser to bend with the wind. Be that as it may, although punitive campaigns continued to be waged against the Picts for several decades (Hanson 1978b, 140–1), the Romans were no longer able to control the territory north of Hadrian's Wall; the final battle of the northernmost frontier had long since been lost.

Appendix 1. Emperors and Governors of Britain
from Augustus to Caracalla

Emperor and date of assuming title	Provincial Governor and date of tenure of office
JULIO CLAUDIAN Augustus 31 BC	
Tiberus AD 14	
Gaius (Caligula) 37	
Claudius 41	A Plautius 43–7
	P Ostorius Scapula 47–51/2
	A Didius Gallus 51/2–57/8
Nero 54	
	Q Veranius 57/8–58/9
	C Suetonius Paullinus 58/9–61
	P Petronius Turpilianus 61–3
	M Trebellius Maximus 63–9
Galba 68	M Vettius Bolanus 69–71
Otho 69	Q Petillius Cerealis 71–73/4
Vitellius 69	Sex Julius Frontinus 73/4–77/8
FLAVIAN Vespasian 69	Cn Julius Agricola 77/8–83/4
Titus 79	
Domitian 81	Sallustius Lucullus post 83/4
Nerva 96	P Metilius Nepos 97/8
Trajan 98	T Avidius Quietus 98–
	L Neratius Marcellus 103–
	M Appius Bradua

213

Hadrian 117

Q Pompeius Falco 119–22
A Platorius Nepos 122–24+
Sex Julius Severus 127/33
P Mummius Sisenna 135

Antoninus Pius 138

Q Lollius Urbicus 139–42
Cornelius Crispianus 142–5
Cn Papirius Aelianus 145–6+
Cn Julius Verus 158
—anus *c*.159–60

Marcus Aurelius 161
and Lucius Verus
M Aurelius alone 169
M Aurelius and
Commodus 176
Commodus alone 180

M Statius Priscus 161/2
Sex Calpurnius Agricola 163
Q Antistius Adventus 169/180

Ulpius Marcellus 184
P Helvius Pertinax 185/90

Pertinax 193
Didius Julianus 193
Pescennius Niger 193
Septimius Severus 193
Albinus *Caesar* 195
Caracalla *Caesar* 196
Caracalla *Augustus* 198

D Clodius Albinus 192–7

Virius Lupus 197
M Antius Crescens
(acting legate?)
C Valerius Pudens 205
L Alfenus Senecio 205/7

Geta *Augustus* 209
Caracalla and Geta 211
Caracalla alone 212

APPENDIX 2. THE ROMAN NAMES OF THE FORTS
ON THE ANTONINE WALL

In contrast to the evidence available for Hadrian's Wall, there is only one literary source, the Ravenna Cosmography, which provides a list of names supposedly representing sites along the line of the Antonine Wall. The Cosmography is an early eighth century AD compilation of place-names, which lists separately rivers, islands and habitations.

The British section of the Cosmography is surprisingly full, even for the north. In their study of it, Richmond and Crawford were content to accept most of the text at face value (1949), but a recent re-assessment has revealed that, over and above the errors that one would expect from any document which had been copied and re-copied over the centuries, the original compiler was guilty of considerable carelessness (Rivet and Smith 1979, 187). There is little or no distinction between the types of settlement, whether fort, town or mere posting-station, for all are subsumed under the title '*civitates*'. Furthermore, close study makes it clear that there is often confusion between the three main elements, with, for example, rivers listed as towns, or *vice versa*.

The nature of the compiler's introductory remarks and the sort of errors which occur make it certain that he derived much of his information directly from maps (Rivet and Smith 1979, 191). One of the main original source-maps for Britain would seem to have been quite detailed, possibly dating from the fourth century AD, since London is referred to by its late title of Augusta. Since by then Scotland had long ceased to be part of the Roman empire, the inclusion of many sites north of Hadrian's Wall in the lists would be surprising unless an earlier source was also being employed. The close correspondence between the Cosmography and the mid-second century *Geography* of Ptolemy implies the use of a common source, probably a military map.

The Cosmography lists ten settlement names which have generally been accepted as referring to forts along the Antonine Wall (Table A). If the source in this instance was a Severan map based upon a Flavian original, as Rivet and Smith argue (1979, 193–6), one might be excused for assuming that no specifically Antonine sites would be represented. Indeed, Rivet and Smith seem quite reluctant to make any such correlations. However, the compiler of the Cosmography is quite specific about the geographical features of the Forth-Clyde isthmus and states that the sites are in a straight line connected by a road.

TABLE A   *Sites across the Forth-Clyde isthmus listed in the Ravenna Cosmography and their possible identification*

Ravenna Cosmography	Richmond and Crawford (1949) Suggested identification	Rivet and Smith (1979) Suggested identification	Suggested original Latin form
Velunia	Balmuildy	Carriden	Velunia
Volitanio	? Cadder	tribe	Votadini (Ptolemy)
Pexa	fort	tribe	Pecti/Picti
Begesse	Bar Hill	—	—
Colanica	fort	Camelon	Colania (Ptolemy)
Medio Nemeton	fort	Arthur's O'on	Medio Nemetum
Subdobiadon	fort	—	—
Litana	? Inveravon	Ardoch	Alauna (Ptolemy)
Cibra	fort	Barochan Hill	Coria (Ptolemy)
Credigone	Carriden	tribe	Creones (Ptolemy)

Although the same description could possibly have applied to the Agricolan frontier (see chapter 2), the identification of the first named site, Velunia, as an Antonine Wall fort was confirmed in 1956 by the discovery at Carriden of an altar bearing the name Veluniate (Richmond and Steer 1957). Unless it is assumed that the fort was also occupied under Agricola, which was not indicated by trial excavation at the site (St Joseph 1949, 167–9), there seems no reason why other Antonine Wall forts should not be represented in the Ravenna lists. But this does not mean that the rest of the list can be read off from east to west. Apart from the obvious problem of only ten names for at least 16 forts, Rivet and Smith suggest on palaeographic grounds that possibly three of the entries are tribal names, though only one derivation (Credigone from Creones) is entirely convincing. For similar reasons, they equate three others with place-names in Ptolemy's *Geography*, though once again not all three derivations are equally convincing. Moreover, their identification of Arthur's O'on with Medio Nemeton (middle grove or sanctuary) has little more to commend it than Piggott's suggestion of the native ritual- and burial-monument at Cairnpapple Hill (1948, 118). While it is unlikely that the latter would have featured on Roman maps, it seems no less improbable that the former, a victory monument, would have acquired a Celtic name. Rather, one should seek a centrally situated native ritual site with Roman connections. Feachem suggested either Croy or Bar Hill, on the grounds that both forts were built over native sites, preferring the latter because of its famous well (1969). The interpretation of the pre-fort enclosures at these sites as native in origin has been disproved by recent excavation (see above p.120), but other signs of pre-Roman occupation were evident at Croy Hill (Hanson 1979). Moreover, the presence of natural springs on the hilltop at the latter site and the discovery of a dedication to the Nymphs (RIB 2160) might point to the existence of a ritual site which would fit the requirements of Medio Nemeton. In the absence of even circumstantial evidence from other sites, however, any additional attempts at site identification would be foolhardy. Only chance discovery is likely to bring further enlightenment.

BIBLIOGRAPHY

Adcock, F. E. (1940) *The Roman Art of War under the Republic*. Cambridge (Mass.).

Alcock, L. (1980) 'Populi bestiales Pictorum feroci animo': a survey of Pictish settlement archaeology, in Hanson and Keppie 1980, 61-96.

Baatz, D. (1973) *Kastell Hesselbach (Limesforschungen 12)*. Berlin.

Barber, R. N. L. (1971) A Roman altar from Old Kilpatrick, Dunbartonshire, *Glasgow Archaeol. J. 2*, 117-19.

Barrow, G. W. S. (1976) *Robert the Bruce and the Community of the Realm of Scotland*. Edinburgh.

Bellhouse, R. L. (1954) Roman sites on the Cumberland Coast, 1954, *Trans. Cumberland Westmorland Antiq. Archaeol. Soc. 54*, 28-55.

Bellhouse, R. L. (1970) Roman Sites on the Cumberland Coast 1968-1969, *Trans. Cumberland Westmorland Antiq. Archaeol. Soc. 70*, 9-47.

Birley, A. R. (1972) Virius Lupus. *Archaeol. Aeliana 50* (4th series), 179-89.

Birley, A. R. (1974) Roman frontiers and Roman frontier policy, *Trans. Architect. Archaeol. Soc. Durham Northumberland 3*, 13-25.

Birley, A. R. (1979) *The People of Roman Britain*. London.

Birley, A. R. (1981) *The Fasti of Roman Britain*. Oxford.

Birley, E. (1953) *Roman Britain and the Roman army*. Kendal.

Birley, E. (1956) Hadrianic frontier policy, in *Carnuntina, Vorträge beim internationalen Kongress der Altertumsforscher Carnuntum 1955*, 25-33. Cologne.

Birley, E. (1961) *Research on Hadrian's Wall*. Kendal.

Birley, E. and I. A. Richmond (1939) The Roman fort at Carzield, *Trans. Dumfriess. Galloway Natur. Hist. Archaeol. Soc. 22*, 156-63.

Birley, R. E. (1977) *Vindolanda: a Roman Frontier Post on Hadrian's Wall*. London.

Bowman, A. K. (1974) Roman military records from Vindolanda, *Britannia 5*, 360-73.

Branigan, K. (1980a) *Rome and the Brigantes: the impact of Rome on northern England*. Sheffield.

BIBLIOGRAPHY

Branigan, K. (1980b) Villas in the north: change in the rural landscape?, in Branigan 1980a, 18-27.

Breeze, D. J. (1974) The Roman fortlet at Barburgh Mill, Dumfriesshire, *Britannia 5*, 130-62.

Breeze, D. J. (1975) The abandonment of the Antonine Wall: its date and implications, *Scottish Archaeol. Forum 7*, 67-80.

Breeze, D. J. (1977a) Review of Robertson 1975b, *Britannia 8*, 451-60.

Breeze, D. J. (1977b) The fort at Bearsden and the supply of pottery to the Roman army, in *Roman Pottery Studies in Britain and Beyond* (eds. J. Dore and K. Greene), 133-46. Oxford.

Breeze, D. J. (1979a) *Roman Scotland: some recent excavations*. Edinburgh.

Breeze, D. J. (1979b) The Roman fort on the Antonine Wall at Bearsden, in Breeze 1979a, 21-5.

Breeze, D. J. (1980a) Agricola the builder, *Scottish Archaeol. Forum 12*, 14-24.

Breeze, D. J. (1980b) Roman Scotland during the reign of Antoninus Pius, in Hanson and Keppie 1980, 45-60.

Breeze, D. J., J. Close-Brooks and J. N. G. Ritchie (1976) Soldiers' burials at Camelon, Stirlingshire, 1922 and 1975, *Britannia 7*, 73-95.

Breeze, D. J. and B. Dobson (1969) Fort types on Hadrian's Wall, *Archaeol. Aeliana 47* (4th series), 15-32.

Breeze, D. J. and B. Dobson (1972) Hadrian's Wall: some problems, *Britannia 3*, 182-208.

Breeze, D. J. and B. Dobson (1976a) *Hadrian's Wall*. London.

Breeze, D. J. and B. Dobson (1976b) A view of Roman Scotland in 1975, *Glasgow Archaeol. J. 4*, 124-43.

Brewis, P. (1927) The Roman Wall at Denton Bank, Great Hill and Heddon on the Wall. *Archaeol. Aeliana 4* (4th series), 109-21.

Bruce, J. C. (1851) *The Roman Wall*. London.

Bruce, J. C. (1978) *Handbook to the Roman Wall* (13th edn) (ed. C. M. Daniels). Newcastle-upon-Tyne.

Buchanan, M., D. Christison and J. Anderson (1905) Report on the Society's Excavation of Rough Castle on the Antonine Vallum, *Proc. Soc. Antiq. Scotland 39*, 442-99.

Bulmer, W. (1969) The provisioning of Roman forts: a reappraisal of ration storage. *Archaeol. Aeliana 47* (4th series) 7-13.

Burley, E. (1956) Metalwork from Traprain Law, *Proc. Soc. Antiq. Scotland 89*, 118-226.

Charlesworth, D. (1971) The defences of Isurium Brigantium, in *Soldier and Civilian in Roman Yorkshire* (ed. R. M. Butler), 155-64. Leicester.

Charlesworth, D. (1977) Turrets on Hadrian's Wall, in *Ancient Monuments and their interpretation: essays presented to A. J. Taylor* (eds. M. R. Apted, R. Gildyard-Beer and A. D. Saunders), 13-26. London.

Charlesworth, D. (1978) Roman Carlisle, *Archaeol. J. 135*, 115-37.

Charlesworth, D. (1980) The south gate of a Flavian fort at Carlisle, in Hanson and Keppie 1980, 201-10.

Cheesman, G. L. (1914) *The Auxilia of the Roman Imperial Army*. Oxford.

Christison, D. and M. Buchanan (1901) Account of the excavation of the Roman station of Camelon near Falkirk, Stirlingshire, *Proc. Soc. Antiq. Scotland 35*, 329-417.

Christison, D. and M. Buchanan (1903) Excavation of Castlecary fort, *Proc. Soc. Antiq. Scotland 37*, 271-346.

Christison, D., J. H. Cunningham, J. Anderson and T. Ross (1898) Account of the excavation of the Roman station at Ardoch, Perthshire, undertaken by the Society of Antiquaries of Scotland in 1896-97, *Proc. Soc. Antiq. Scotland 32*, 399-435.

Cichorius, C. (1900) *Die Reliefs der Trajansäule*. Berlin.

Clarke, J. (1933) *The Roman Fort at Cadder*. Glasgow.

Clarke, J. (1950) Excavations at Milton (Tassiesholm) in season 1950, *Trans. Dumfriess. Galloway Natur. Hist. Antiq. Soc. 28*, 199-221.

Clarke, J. (1952a) Milton (Tassiesholm), in Miller 1952, 104-10.

Clarke, J. (1952b) Durisdeer, in Miller 1952, 124-6.

Close-Brooks, J. (1981) The bridgeness Distance Slab, *Proc. Soc. Antiq. Scotland 111*, forthcoming.

Collingwood, R. G. and J. N. L. Myres (1937) *Roman Britain and the English Settlements*. Oxford.

Collis, J. (1973) Burials with weapons in Iron Age Britain, *Germania 51*, 121-33.

Coppock, J. T. (1976) *An agricultural atlas of Scotland*. Edinburgh.

Cunliffe, B. (1971) Some aspects of hill-forts and their cultural environment, in *The Iron Age and its Hill-forts* (eds. M. Jesson and D. Hill), 53-69. Southampton.

Cunliffe, B. (1978) *Iron Age Communities in Britain*. London.

Daniels, C. M. (1970) Problems of the Roman northern frontier, *Scottish Archaeol. Forum 2*, 91-101.

Daniels, C. M. and G. D. B. Jones (1969) The Roman camps on Llandrindod Common, *Archaeol. Cambrensis 118*, 124-33.

Davidson, J. M. (1952) The bridge over the Kelvin at Summerston, in Miller 1952, 88-94.

Davies, R. W. (1968) The training grounds of the Roman cavalry, *Archaeol. J. 125*, 73-100.

Davies, R. W. (1969) Joining the Roman Army, *Bonner Jahrbücher 169*, 208-32.

Davies, R. W. (1970) The Roman military medical service, *Saalburg Jahrbuch 27*, 84-104.

Davies, R. W. (1971) The Roman military diet, *Britannia 2*, 122-42.

Davies, R. W. (1974) The daily life of the Roman soldier under the Principate, in *Aufstieg und Niedergang der Römischen Welt II 1* (ed. H. Temporini), 299-338. Berlin.

Davies, R. W. (1976) A lost inscription from Auchendavy, *Glasgow Archaeol. J. 4*, 103-7.

Dickson, J. M., C. A. Dickson and D. J. Breeze (1979) Flour or bread in a Roman military ditch at Bearsden, *Antiquity 53*, 47-51.

Dore, J. N. and J. P. Gillam (1979) *The Roman fort at South Shields: excavations 1875-1975*. Newcastle-upon-Tyne.

Feachem, R. W. (1956a) Six Roman camps near the Antonine Wall, *Proc. Soc. Antiq. Scotland 89*, 329-39.

Feachem, R. W. (1956b) The fortifications on Traprain Law, *Proc. Soc. Antiq. Scotland 89*, 284-9.

Feachem, R. W. (1963) *A Guide to Prehistoric Scotland*. London.

Feachem, R. W. (1966) The hill-forts of northern Britain, in Rivet 1966, 59-88.

BIBLIOGRAPHY

Feachem, R. W. (1969) Medionemeton on the *limes* of Antoninus Pius, Scotland, in *Hommages à Marcel Renard III* (ed. J. Bibouw), 210-16. Brussels.

Ferguson, R. S. (1893) On a massive timber platform of early date uncovered at Carlisle and on sundry other relics connected therewith, *Trans. Cumberland Westmorland Antiq. Archaeol. Soc. 12*, 344-64.

Fitz, J. (ed.) (1978) *Limes: Akten des XI Internationalen Limeskongresses.* Budapest.

Frere, S. S. (1967) *Britannia: a history of Roman Britain.* London.

Frere, S. S. (1978) *Britannia: a history of Roman Britain* (2nd edn). London.

Frere, S. S. (1979) The Roman fort at Strageath, in Breeze 1979a, 37-41.

Frere, S. S. (1980) Hyginus and the first cohort, *Britannia 11*, 51-60.

G.A.S. (1899) *The Antonine Wall Report.* Glasgow.

Gibb, A. (1901) New measurement of the Vallum of Antoninus Pius, *Scottish Antiquary 16*, 20-9.

Gillam, J. P. (1953) Calpurnius Agricola and the northern frontier, *Trans. Archit. Archaeol. Soc. Durham Northumberland 10*, 359-75.

Gillam, J. P. (1958) Roman and native, AD 122-97, in Richmond 1958, 60-90.

Gillam, J. P. (1973) Sources of pottery on northern military sites, in *Current Research in Romano-British Course Pottery* (ed. A. Detsicas), 55-62. London.

Gillam, J. P. (1974) The frontier after Hadrian – a history of the problem. *Archaeol. Aeliana 2* (5th series), 1-12.

Gillam, J. P. (1975) Possible changes in plan in the course of the construction of the Antonine Wall, *Scottish Archaeol. Forum 7*, 51-6.

Gillam, J. P. (1977) The Roman forts at Corbridge. *Archaeol. Aeliana 5* (5th series), 47-74.

Gillam, J. P., R. M. Harrison and T. G. Newman (1973) Interim report on excavations of the Roman fort of Rudchester 1972. *Archaeol. Aeliana 1* (5th series), 81-6.

Gillam, J. P. and J. C. Mann (1970) The northern British frontier from Antoninus Pius to Caracalla. *Archaeol. Aeliana 48* (4th series), 1-44.

Goodburn, R. (1978) Roman Britain in 1977: sites explored, *Britannia 9*, 404-72.

Goodburn, R. (1979) Roman Britain in 1978: sites explored, *Britannia 10*, 267-338.

Grew, F. (1980) Roman Britain in 1979: sites explored, *Britannia 11*, 346-402.

Guido, M. (1974) A Scottish crannog redated, *Antiquity 48*, 54-6.

Hanson, W. S. (1978a) The organisation of Roman military timber supply, *Britannia 9*, 293-305.

Hanson, W. S. (1978b) Roman campaigns north of the Forth-Clyde isthmus: the evidence of the temporary camps, *Proc. Soc. Antiq. Scotland 109*, 140-50.

Hanson, W. S. (1979) Croy Hill, in Breeze 1979a, 19-20.

Hanson, W. S. (1980a) The first Roman occupation of Scotland, in Hanson and Keppie 1980, 15-44.

Hanson, W. S. (1980b) Agricola on the Forth-Clyde isthmus, *Scottish Archaeol. Forum 12*, 55-68.

Hanson, W. S. (1982) Roman military timber buildings: construction and reconstruction, in *Woodworking Techniques before AD 1500* (ed. S. McGrail), 169-86. Oxford.

Hanson, W. S., C. M. Daniels, J. N. Dore and J. P. Gillam (1979) The Agricolan supply base at Red House, Corbridge. *Archaeol. Aeliana 7* (5th series), 1-97.

Hanson, W. S. and L. J. F. Keppie (eds) (1980) *Roman Frontier Studies 1979 : papers presented to the Twelfth International Congress of Roman Frontier Studies.* Oxford.

Hanson, W. S. and L. Macinnes (1980) Forests, forts and fields: a discussion, *Scottish Archaeol. Forum 12*, 98-113.

Hanson, W. S. and G. S. Maxwell (1980) An Agricolan *praesidium* on the Forth-Clyde isthmus (Mollins, Strathclyde), *Britannia 11*, 43-9.

Hanson, W. S. and G. S. Maxwell (1984) Minor enclosures on the Antonine Wall at Wilderness Plantation, *Britannia* forthcoming.

Hartley, B. R. (1960) The Roman fort at Bainbridge, *Proc. Leeds Philosoph. Lit. Soc. 9.3*, 107-32.

Hartley, B. R. (1966a) Some problems of the Roman military occupation of the north of England, *Northern History 1*, 7-20.

Hartley, B. R. (1966b) The Roman fort at Ilkley, excavations of 1962, *Proc. Leeds Philosoph. Lit. Soc. 12.2*, 23-72.

Hartley, B. R. (1971) Roman York and the Northern military command, in *Soldier and Civilian in Roman Yorkshire* (ed. R. M. Butler), 55-69. Leicester.

Hartley, B. R. (1972) The Roman occupation of Scotland: the evidence of samian ware, *Britannia 3*, 1-55.

Hartley, B. R. (1980) The Brigantes and the Roman army, in Branigan 1980a, 2-7.

Hassall, M. W. C. and R. S. O. Tomlin (1977) Roman Britain in 1976: inscriptions, *Britannia 8*, 426-50.

Haupt, D. and H. G. Horn (eds) (1977) *Studien zu den Militärgrenzen Roms II : Vorträge des 10 Internationalen Limeskongresses.* Cologne.

Haverfield, F. (1904) On Julius Verus, a Roman governor of Britain, *Proc. Soc. Antiq. Scotland 38*, 454-59.

Hill, P. (1979) *Broxmouth Hillfort Excavations 1977-78 : an Interim Report.* Edinburgh.

Hind, J. G. F. (1977) The 'Genounian' part of Britain, *Britannia 8*, 229-48.

Hobley, B. (1971) An experimental reconstruction of a Roman military turf rampart, in *Roman Frontier Studies 1967 : the proceedings of the 7th International Congress held at Tel Aviv* (ed. S. Appleburn) 21-33. Tel Aviv.

Hobley, B. (1974) A Neronian – Vespasianic fort at 'The Lunt' Baginton, England, in *Roman Frontier Studies 1969* (eds E. Birley, B. Dobson and M. G. Jarrett), 70-83. Cardiff.

Holder, P. A. (1980) *The Auxilia from Augustus to Trajan.* Oxford.

Holmes, N. M. (1979) Excavations at Cramond, Edinburgh 1975-78, in Breeze 1979a, 11-14.

Hooley, J. and D. J. Breeze (1968) The building of Hadrian's Wall: a reconsideration. *Archaeol. Aeliana 46* (4th series), 97-114.

Hunnysett, R. (1980) The milecastles of Hadrian's Wall – an alternative identification. *Archaeol. Aeliana 8* (5th series), 95-107.

Jackson, K. S. (1963) *The oldest Irish Tradition : a window on the Iron Age.* Cambridge.

Jarrett, M. G. (1965) Roman officers at Maryport, *Trans. Cumberland Westmorland Antiq. Archaeol. Soc. 65*, 115-32.

Jarrett, M. G. (1978) The case of the redundant official, *Britannia 9*, 289-92.

Jarrett, M. G. and J. C. Mann (1970) Britain from Agricola to Gallienus, *Bonner Jahrbücher 170*, 178-210.

Jewell, P. A. (ed.) (1963) *The experimental earthwork on Overton Down*. London.

Jobey, G. (1966) Homesteads and settlements of the frontier area, in *Rural Settlement in Roman Britain* (ed. A. C. Thomas), 1-14. London.

Jobey, G. (1974) Notes on some population problems in the area between the two Roman Walls. *Archaeol. Aeliana 2* (5th series), 17-26.

Jobey, G. (1976) Traprain Law: a summary, in *Hillforts. Later Prehistoric Earthworks in Britain* (ed. D. W. Harding), 192-204. London.

Jobey, G. (1978a) Unenclosed platforms and settlements of the later second millennium BC in northern Britain, *Scottish Archaeol. Forum 10*, 12-26.

Jobey, G. (1978b) Burnswark Hill, *Trans. Dumfriess. Galloway Natur. Hist. Antiq. Soc. 53*, 57-104.

Jones, G. D. B. (1976) The western extension of Hadrian's Wall: Bowness to Cardurnock, *Britannia 7*, 236-43.

Jones, G. D. B. (1979) Invasion and response in Roman Britain, in *Invasion and Response: the case of Roman Britain* (eds B. C. Burnham and H. B. Johnson), 57-79. Oxford.

Jones, M. J. (1975) *Roman fort defences to AD 117*. Oxford.

Jorns, W. and W. Meier-Arendt (1967) Das Kleinkastell Degerfeld in Butzbach, *Saalburg Jahrbuch 24*, 12-32.

Kendrick, J. (1982) Excavations at Douglasmuir, 1979-81, in *Later Prehistoric Settlement in South-East Scotland* (ed. D. W. Harding), 136-40. Edinburgh.

Keppie, L. J. F. (1974) The building of the Antonine Wall: archaeological and epigraphic evidence, *Proc. Soc. Antiq. Scotland 105*, 151-65.

Keppie, L. J. F. (1975) The Distance Slabs from the Antonine Wall: some problems, *Scottish Archaeol. Forum 7*, 57-66.

Keppie, L. J. F. (1976) Some rescue excavations on the line of the Antonine Wall 1973-6, *Proc. Soc. Antiq. Scotland 107*, 61-80.

Keppie, L. J. F. (1978a) A Roman altar from Kilsyth, *Glasgow Archaeol. J. 5*, 19-24.

Keppie, L. J. F. (1978b) Excavation of Roman sites at Dullatur and Westerwood, 1974-6, *Glasgow Archaeol. J. 5*, 9-11.

Keppie, L. J. F. (1979) *Roman Distance Slabs from the Antonine Wall: a brief guide*. Glasgow.

Keppie, L. J. F. (1980a) Milefortlets on the Antonine Wall?, in Hanson and Keppie 1980, 107-12.

Keppie, L. J. F. (1980b) The Roman forts on Castlehill, Bearsden, *Glasgow Archaeol. J. 7*, 80-4.

Keppie, L. J. F. (1980c) Mons Graupius: the search for a battlefield, *Scottish Archaeol. Forum 12*, 79-88.

Keppie, L. J. F. and J. J. Walker (1981) Fortlets on the Antonine Wall at Seabegs Wood, Kinneil and Cleddans, *Britannia 13*, 143-62.

Kewley, J. (1973) Inscribed capitals on Roman altars from North Britain, *Archaeol. Aeliana 1* (5th series), 129-31.

Laver, P. G. (1927) The excavation of a tumulus at Lexden, Colchester, *Archaeologia 76*, 241-54.

Leach, J. D. and J. J. Wilkes (1978) The Roman military base at Carpow, Perthshire, Scotland: summary of recent investigations (1964-70, 1975), in Fitz 1978, 47-62.

Lenoir, M. (1977) Lager mit clavicula. *Mélanges de l'École Française de Rome: Antiquité 89*, 697-722.

Luttwak, E. N. (1976) *The Grand Strategy of the Roman Empire*. Baltimore.

McCord, N. and G. Jobey (1971) Air reconnaissance in Northumberland and Durham – 11. *Archaeol. Aeliana 49* (4th series), 119-30.

McCord, N. and J. Tait (1978) Excavations at Kerse, East Polmont, Stirlingshire, July 1963, *Proc. Soc. Antiq. Scotland 109*, 368-72.

Macdonald, G. (1921) The building of the Antonine Wall: a fresh study of the inscriptions, *J. Roman Studies 11*, 1-24.

Macdonald, G. (1923) A Roman inscription found at Jedburgh, and some Roman sculptures recently presented to the National Museum, *Proc. Soc. Antiq. Scotland 57*, 173-80.

Macdonald, G. (1932) Notes on the Roman forts at Old Kilpatrick and Croy Hill, *Proc. Soc. Antiq. Scotland 66*, 219-76.

Macdonald, G. (1933) Notes on the Roman forts at Rough Castle and Wester-wood, with a postscript. *Proc. Soc. Antiq. Scotland 67*, 243-96.

Macdonald, G. (1934) *The Roman Wall in Scotland*. Oxford.

Macdonald, G. (1936) A further note on the Roman fort at Croy Hill, *Proc. Soc. Antiq. Scotland 71*, 32-71.

Macdonald, G. and A. O. Curle (1929) The Roman fort at Mumrills, near Falkirk, *Proc. Soc. Antiq. Scotland 63*, 396-575.

Macdonald, G. and A. Park (1906) The Roman forts on the Bar Hill, *Proc. Soc. Antiq. Scotland 40*, 403-56.

Macinnes, L. (1982) Settlement and economy: East Lothian and the Tyne-Forth Province, in *Between and Beyond the Walls* (eds C. Burgess and R. Miket). Edinburgh, forthcoming.

MacIvor, I., M. C. Thomas and D. J. Breeze (1980) Excavations on the Antonine Wall fort of Rough Castle, Stirlingshire, 1957-61, *Proc. Soc. Antiq. Scotland 110*, 230-85.

MacKie, E. W. (1975) The brochs of Scotland, in *Recent Developments in Rural Archaeology* (ed. P. J. Fowler), 79-92. London.

MacKie, E. W. (1976) The virtified forts of Scotland, in *Hillforts: Later Pre-historic Earthworks in Britain and Ireland* (ed. D. W. Harding), 205-35. London.

MacKie, E. W. (1979) Excavations at Leckie, Stirlingshire, in Breeze, 1979a, 52-5.

Mackie, J. D. (1978) *A history of Scotland*. London.

Main, L. (1979) Excavations at the Fairy Knowe, Buchlyvie, Stirlingshire, in Breeze 1979a, 47-51.

Maitland, W. (1757) *History and Antiquities of Scotland*. London.

Mann, J. C. (1963) The raising of new legions during the Principate, *Hermes 91*, 483-9.

Mann, J. C. (1974a) The frontiers of the Principate, in *Aufstieg und Niedergang der Römischen Welt II 1* (ed H. Temporini), 508-33. Berlin.

Mann, J. C. (1974b) The northern frontier after AD 369, *Glasgow Archaeol. J. 3*, 34-42.

Manning, W. H. (1972) Ironwork hoards in Iron Age and Roman Britain, *Britannia 3*, 224-50.

Bibliography

Manning, W. H. (1975) Economic influences on land use in the military areas of the Highland Zone during the Roman period, in *The Effect of Man on the Landscape : the Highland Zone* (eds J. G. Evans, S. Limbrey and H. Cleere), 112-16. London.

Marsden, E. W. (1969) *Greek and Roman artillery : historical development.* Oxford.

Maxfield, V. A. (1979) Camelon 'south camp' excavation 1975-9, in Breeze 1979a, 28-32.

Maxwell, G. S. (1969) Duns and forts – a note on some Iron Age monuments in the Atlantic Province, *Scottish Archaeol. Forum 1*, 41-52.

Maxwell, G. S. (1972) Excavations at the Roman fort of Crawford, *Proc. Soc. Antiq. Scotland 104*, 147-200.

Maxwell, G. S. (1974) The building of the Antonine Wall, in *Actes du IXe Congrès International d'Études sur les Frontières Romaines* (ed. D. M. Pippidi), 327-32. Bucharest.

Maxwell, G. S. (1975a) Excavation in the Roman fort of Bothwellhaugh 1967-8, *Britannia 6*, 20-35.

Maxwell, G. S. (1975b) *Casus belli :* native pressure and Roman policy, *Scottish Archaeol. Forum 7*, 31-49.

Maxwell, G. S. (1976) A Roman timber tower at Beattock Summit, *Britannia 7*, 33-8.

Maxwell, G. S. (1977) A linear defence-system in south-western Scotland, in Haupt and Horn 1977, 23-30.

Maxwell, G. S. (1978) Air photography and the work of the Royal Commission, *Aerial Archaeol. 2*, 37-44.

Maxwell, G. S. (1980) Agricola's campaigns: the evidence of the temporary camps, *Scottish Archaeol. Forum 12*, 25-54.

Maxwell, G. S. (1982a) Cropmark categories observed in recent aerial reconnaissance in Scotland, *Scottish Archaeol. Rev. 2*, forthcoming.

Maxwell, G. S. (1982b) Recent aerial survey in Scotland, in *The Impact of Aerial reconnaissance on Archaeology* (ed. G. S. Maxwell). London, forthcoming.

Maxwell, G. S. (1982c) Two inscribed Roman stones from Scotland, *Proc. Soc. Antiq. Scotland*, forthcoming.

Meyer, H. D. (1961) *Die Aussenpolitik des Augustus und die augusteische Dichtung.* Cologne.

Miller, S. N. (1922) *The Roman fort at Balmuildy.* Glasgow.

Miller, S. N. (1928) *The Roman fort at Old Kilpatrick.* Glasgow.

Miller, S. N. (ed.) (1952) *The Roman occupation of south-western Scotland.* Glasgow.

Newall, F. (1976) The Roman signal fortlet at Outerwards, Ayrshire, *Glasgow Archaeol. J. 4*, 111-23.

Parker, H. M. D. (1928) *The Roman Legions.* Oxford.

Pauli, L. (1973) Ein latènezeitliches Steinrelief aus Bormio am Stilfser Joch, *Germania 51*, 85-120.

Piggott, C. M. (1950) The excavation at Hownam Rings, Roxburghshire 1948, *Proc. Soc. Antiq. Scotland 82*, 193-224.

Piggott, S. (1948) Excavations at Cairnpapple Hill, West Lothian, 1947-48, *Proc. Soc. Antiq. Scotland 82*, 68-123.

Piggott, S. (1950) Swords and Scabbards of the British Early Iron Age, *Proc. Prehist. Soc. 16*, 1-28.

Piggott, S. (1951) Excavations in the broch and hillfort of Torwoodlee, Selkirk-shire, 1950, *Proc. Soc. Antiq. Scotland 85*, 92-117.

Piggott, S. (1953) Three metal-work hoards of the Roman period in Scotland, *Proc. Soc. Antiq. Scotland 87*, 1-50.

Piggott, S. (1959) The carnyx in Early Iron Age Britain, *Antiq. J. 39*, 19-32.

Piggott, S. (1966) A scheme for the Scottish Iron Age, in Rivet 1966, 1-16.

Potter, T. W. (1977) The Biglands milefortlet and the Cumberland Coast defences, *Britannia 8*, 149-83.

Potter, T. W. (1979) *Romans in north-west England*, Kendal.

Powell, T. G. E. (1980) *The Celts* (2nd edn). London.

Proudfoot, E. V. W. (1978) Camelon native site, *Proc. Soc. Antiq. Scotland 109*, 113-28.

Rae, A. and V. (1974) The Roman fort at Cramond, Edinburgh: excavations 1954-66, *Britannia 5*, 163-224.

RCAHMS (1929) *An Inventory of the Monuments and Constructions in the Counties of Midlothian and West Lothian*. Edinburgh.

RCAHMS (1956) *Roxburghshire: an Inventory of the Ancient and Historical Monuments*. Edinburgh.

RCAHMS (1963) *Stirlingshire: an Inventory of the Ancient and Historical Monuments*. Edinburgh.

RCAHMS (1978) *Lanarkshire: an Inventory of the Prehistoric and Roman Monuments*. Edinburgh.

Rea, J. T. (1951) *How to estimate: being the analysis of building prices*. London.

Reed, N. H. (1971) The fifth year of Agricola's campaigns, *Britannia 2*, 143-8.

Richmond, I. A. (1940) The Romans in Redesdale, in *A History of Northumber-land*, vol. 15 (ed M. H. Dodds), 63-154. Newcastle-upon-Tyne.

Richmond, I. A. (1950) Excavations at the Roman fort of Newstead, 1947, *Proc. Soc. Antiq. Scotland 84*, 1-37.

Richmond, I. A. (1951) Exploratory trenching at the Roman fort at Cappuck, Roxburghshire, in 1949, *Proc. Soc. Antiq. Scotland 85*, 138-45.

Richmond, I. A. (ed.) (1958) *Roman and Native in North Britain*. Edinburgh.

Richmond, I. A. and O. G. S. Crawford (1949) The British Section of the Ravenna Cosmography, *Archaeologia 93*, 1-50.

Richmond, I. A. and J. P. Gillam (1950) Excavation on the Roman Site at Corbridge 1946-49. *Archaeol. Aeliana 28* (4th series), 152-201.

Richmond, I. A. and W. S. Hanson (1980) A Roman fort at Inveresk, Midlothian, *Proc. Soc. Antiq. Scotland 110*, 286-304.

Richmond, I. A. and G. S. Keeney (1937) The Roman works at Chew Green, Coquetdale. *Archaeol. Aeliana 14* (4th series), 129-50.

Richmond, I. A. and K. A. Steer (1957) Castellum Veluniate and civilians on a Roman frontier, *Proc. Soc. Antiq. Scotland 90*, 1-6.

Ritchie, J. N. G. (1969) Shields in North Britain in the Iron Age, *Scottish Archaeol. Forum 1*, 31-40.

Rivet, A. L. F. (ed.) (1966) *The Iron Age in Northern Britain*. Edinburgh.

Rivet, A. L. F. (1977) Ptolemy's Geography and the Flavian invasion of Scotland, in Haupt and Horn 1977, 45-64.

Rivet, A. L. F. and C. Smith (1979) *The Place-names of Roman Britain*. London.

Robertson, A. S. (1957a) *An Antonine Fort: Golden Hill, Duntocher*. Edinburgh.

Robertson, A. S. (1957b) A hoard of Roman silver coins from Briglands, Rumbling Bridge, Kinross-shire, *Proc. Soc. Antiq. Scotland 90*, 241-6.

Robertson, A. S. (1962) Excavations at Raeburnfoot, Eskdalemuir, *Trans. Dumfriess. Galloway Natur. Hist. Antiq. Soc. 39*, 24-49.

Robertson, A. S. (1964a) Miscellanea Romano-Caledonica, *Proc. Soc. Antiq. Scotland 97*, 180-201.

Robertson, A. S. (1964b) *The Roman fort at Castledykes*. Edinburgh.

Robertson, A. S. (1969) Recent work on the Antonine Wall, *Glasgow Archaeol. J. 1*, 37-42.

Robertson, A. S. (1973) *The Antonine Wall: a handbook to the Roman Wall between Forth and Clyde and a guide to its surviving remains* (2nd edn). Glasgow.

Robertson, A. S. (1974a) Roman 'Signal Stations' on the Gask Ridge, *Trans. Perthshire Soc. Natur. Sci. Special Issue*, 14-29.

Robertson, A. S. (1974b) Romano-British coin hoards; their numismatic, archaeological and historical significance, in *Coins and the Archaeologist* (eds J. Casey and R. Reece), 12-36. Oxford.

Robertson, A. S. (1975a) The Romans in North-Britain: the coin evidence, in *Aufstieg und Niedergang der Römischen Welt II.3* (ed. H. Temporini), 364-428. Berlin.

Robertson, A. S. (1975b) *Birrens (Blatobulgium)*. Edinburgh.

Robertson, A. S. (1978) The circulation of Roman coins in North Britain: the evidence of hoards and site-finds from Scotland, in *Scripta Nummaria Romana* (eds R. A. G. Carson and C. Kraay), 186-216. London.

Robertson, A. S. (1979) *The Antonine Wall: a handbook to the Roman Wall between Forth and Clyde and a guide to its surviving remains* (3rd edn). Glasgow.

Robertson, A. S. (1980) The Bridges on Severan coins of AD 208 and 209, in Hanson and Keppie 1980, 131-40.

Robertson, A. S., M. Scott and L. J. F. Keppie (1975) *Bar Hill: a Roman Fort and its Finds*. Oxford.

Robinson, H. R. (1975) *The Armour of Imperial Rome*. London.

Rüger, C. B. (1980) Research on the *Limes* of Germania Inferior (German part), 1974-79, in Hanson and Keppie 1980, 495-500.

Rusu, M. (1969) Das Keltische Fürstengrab von Ciumeşti in Rumänien. *Bericht der Römisch-Germanischen Kommission 50*, 267-300.

St Joseph, J. K. S. (1949) The Roman forts at Carriden and Brownhart Law, *Proc. Soc. Antiq. Scotland 83*, 167-74.

St Joseph, J. K. S. (1951) Air reconnaissance of north Britain, *J. Roman Stud. 41*, 52-65.

St Joseph, J. K. S. (1955) Air reconnaissance in Britain, 1951-54, *J. Roman Stud. 45*, 82-91.

St Joseph, J. K. S. (1965) Air reconnaissance in Britain, 1961-64, *J. Roman Stud. 55*, 74-89.

St Joseph, J. K. S. (1969) Air reconnaissance in Britain, 1965-68, *J. Roman Stud. 59*, 104-28.

St Joseph, J. K. S. (1970) The camps at Ardoch, Stracathro and Ythan Wells: recent excavations, *Britannia 1*, 163-78.

St Joseph, J. K. S. (1973) Air reconnaissance in Roman Britain, 1969-72, *J. Roman Stud. 63*, 214-46.

St Joseph, J. K. S. (1977) Air reconnaissance in Roman Britain, 1973-76, *J. Roman Stud. 67*, 125-61.

St Joseph, J. K. S. (1978) The camp at Durno and Mons Graupius, *Britannia 9*, 271-88.

Salway, P. (1965) *The Frontier People of Roman Britain*. Cambridge.

Schaaf, U. (1974) Keltische Eisenhelme aus vorrömischer Zeit, *Jahrbuch des Römisch-Germanischen Zentralmuseums 21*, 149-204.

Schönberger, H. (1969) The Roman frontier in Germany: an archaeological survey, *J. Roman Stud. 59*, 144-97.

Shotter, D. C. A. (1976) Coin evidence and the northern frontier in the second century AD, *Proc. Soc. Antiq. Scotland 107*, 81-91.

Shotter, D. C. A. (1978) Roman coins from Carlisle, *Trans. Cumberland Westmorland Antiq. Archaeol. Soc. 78*, 201-4.

Shotter, D. C. A. (1979) The evidence of coin-loss and the Roman occupation of North West England, in *The Changing Past* (ed. N. J. Higham), 1-13. Manchester.

Sibbald, R. (1707) *Historical Inquiries*. Edinburgh.

Simpson, F. G. and K. S. Hodgson (1947) The coastal milefortlet at Cardurnock, *Trans. Cumberland Westmorland Antiq. Archaeol. Soc. 47*, 78-127.

Simpson, F. G. and I. A. Richmond (1935) Randylands milecastle 54, *Trans. Cumberland Westmorland Antiq. Archaeol. Soc. 35*, 236-44.

Simpson, F. G. and I. A. Richmond (1936) The Roman fort on the Stanegate and other remains at Old Church, Brampton, *Trans. Cumberland Westmorland Antiq. Archaeol. Soc. 36*, 172-91.

Simpson, F. G., I. A. Richmond and J. McIntyre (1934) Garthside Turrets 54a, *Trans. Cumberland Westmorland Antiq. Archaeol. Soc. 34*, 138-44.

Simpson, F. G., I. A. Richmond and J. K. S. St Joseph (1935) The turf-wall milecastle at High House, *Trans. Cumberland Westmorland Antiq. Archaeol. Soc. 35*, 220-9.

Stead, I. M. (1979) *The Arras Culture*. London.

Steer, K. A. (1949) The Roman fort at Whitemoss, Renfrewshire (Bishopton), *Proc. Soc. Antiq. Scotland 83*, 28-32.

Steer, K. A. (1957) The nature and purpose of the expansions on the Antonine Wall, *Proc. Soc. Antiq. Scotland 90*, 161-9.

Steer, K. A. (1958) The Severan re-organisation, in Richmond 1958, 91-111.

Steer, K. A. (1961) Excavations at Mumrills fort 1958-60, *Proc. Soc. Antiq. Scotland 94*, 86-132.

Steer, K. A. (1964) John Horsley and the Antonine Wall. *Archaeol. Aeliana 42* (4th series), 1-39.

Steer, K. A. and E. A. Cormack (1969) A new Roman distance-slab from the Antonine Wall, *Proc. Soc. Antiq. Scotland 101*, 122-6.

Steer, K. A. and R. W. Feachem (1962) The excavations at Lyne, Peeblesshire, 1959-63, *Proc. Soc. Antiq. Scotland 95*, 208-18.

Stevens, C. E. (1966) *The Building of Hadrian's Wall*. Kendal.

Stevenson, R. B. K. (1966) Metalwork and some other objects in Scotland and their cultural affinities, in Rivet 1966, 17-44.

Bibliography

Tatton Brown, T. W. T. (1980) Camelon, Arthur's O'on, and the main supply base for the Antonine Wall, *Britannia 11*, 340-3.

Taylor, M. V. (1949) Roman Britain in 1948, *J. Roman Stud. 39*, 96-115.

Taylor, M. V. (1952) Roman Britain in 1951: sites explored, *J. Roman Stud. 42*, 86-109.

Thomas, G. (1979) Inveresk *Vicus* excavations 1976-77, in Breeze 1979a, 8-10.

Todd, M. (1980) *Roman Britain (55 BC – AD 400)*. Brighton.

Toynbee, J. M. C. (1924) 'Britannia' on Roman coins of the second century AD, *J. Roman Stud. 14*, 142-57.

Wacher, J. S. (1974) *The Towns of Roman Britain*. London.

Wainwright, F. T. (1963) *The souterrains of southern Pictland*. London.

Ward-Perkins, J. B. (1939) Iron Age metal horse bits of the British Isles, *Proc. Prehist. Soc. 5*, 173-92.

Watkins, T. (1980a) The excavation of an Iron Age open settlement at Dalladies Kincardineshire, *Proc. Soc. Antiq. Scotland 110*, 122-64.

Watkins, T. (1980b) Excavation of a settlement and souterrain at Newmill, near Bankfoot, Perthshire, *Proc. Soc. Antiq. Scotland 110*, 165-205.

Watson, G. R. (1969) *The Roman Soldier*. London.

Webster, G. (1978) *The Roman Imperial Army of the first and second centuries AD* (2nd edn). London.

Webster, G. (1980) A note on new discoveries at Viroconium (Wroxeter) which may have bearing on Hadrian's frontier policy in Britain, in Hanson and Keppie 1980, 291-6.

Wells, C. M. (1972) *The German Policy of Augustus*. Oxford.

Wells, C. M. (1978) Where did they put the horses? Cavalry stables in the early empire, in Fitz 1978, 659-65.

Wilkes, J. J. (1974) The Antonine Wall fortlet at Wilderness Plantation, *Glasgow Archaeol. J. 3*, 51-65.

Wilson, D. R. (1972) Roman Britain in 1971: sites explored, *Britannia 3*, 298-351.

Wilson, D. R. (1975) Roman Britain in 1974: sites explored, *Britannia 6*, 220-85.

Wright, R. P. (1959) Roman Britain in 1958: inscriptions, *J. Roman Stud. 49*, 135-9.

Wright, R. P. (1961) Roman Britain in 1960: inscriptions, *J. Roman Stud. 51*, 191-8.

Wright, R. P. (1964) Roman Britain in 1963: inscriptions, *J. Roman Stud. 54*, 177-85.

Wright, R. P. (1965) Roman Britain in 1964: inscriptions, *J. Roman Stud. 55*, 220-8.

Wright, R. P. (1966) An Imperial inscription from the Roman fortress at Carpow, Perthshire, *Proc. Soc. Antiq. Scotland 97*, 202-5.

Wright, R. P. (1968) A Roman altar from Westerwood on the Antonine Wall, *Proc. Soc. Antiq. Scotland 100*, 192-3.

Wright, R. P. (1974) Carpow and Caracalla, *Britannia 5*, 289-92.

Wright, R. P. and M. W. C. Hassall (1973) Roman Britain in 1972: inscriptions, *Britannia 4*, 324-45.

INDEX

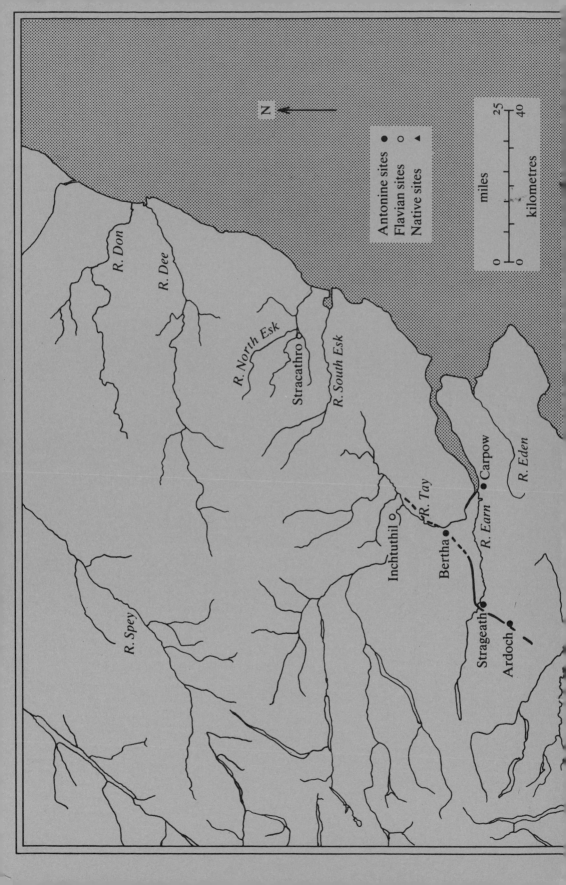

N

Antonine sites ●
Flavian sites ○
Native sites ▲

miles
0   25
0   40
kilometres

R. Don
R. Dee
R. North Esk
Stracathro ○
R. South Esk
R. Tay
Inchtuthil ○
Bertha ●
Carpow ●
R. Earn
R. Eden
Strageath ●
Ardoch ●
R. Spey